Cambridge Studies in Social Anthropology

General Editor: Jack Goody

61

FROM BLESSING TO VIOLENCE

For other titles in this series, turn to page 211.

From blessing to violence

History and ideology in the circumcision ritual
of the Merina of Madagascar

MAURICE BLOCH

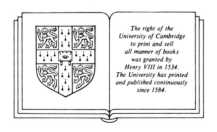

The right of the
University of Cambridge
to print and sell
all manner of books
was granted by
Henry VIII in 1534.
The University has printed
and published continuously
since 1584.

CAMBRIDGE UNIVERSITY PRESS
Cambridge
London   New York   New Rochelle
Melbourne   Sydney

Published by the Press Syndicate of the University of Cambridge
The Pitt Building, Trumpington Street, Cambridge CB2 1RP
32 East 57th Street, New York, NY 10022, USA
10 Stamford Road, Oakleigh, Melbourne 3166, Australia

First published 1986

Printed in the United States of America

Library of Congress Cataloging in Publication Data
Bloch, Maurice.
From blessing to violence.
(Cambridge studies in social anthropology; 61)
Bibliography: p.
Includes index.
1. Hovas – Rites and ceremonies.   2. Circumcision.
3. Hovas – History.   I. Title.   II. Series: Cambridge
studies in social anthropology; no. 61.
DT469.M277H683   1986   306.6   85–11325
ISBN 0 521 30639 6 hard covers
ISBN 0 521 31404 6 paperback

To
SIR RAYMOND FIRTH
in thanks for asking questions that I am still trying to answer

Contents

vii

Preface

This book has been almost fifteen years in the making because, when I started to produce a study that combined anthropological research and primary historical research, I did not realise the sheer practical difficulties of the enterprise. It is an attempt to combine knowledge of the intimate interconnections of all the aspects of life and the subjective empathy, which are the main values of participant observation, with the historical perspective, which is necessary to face up genuinely to the sociological questions and wider theoretical issues the material presents.

Perhaps it was the historical side that was most time-consuming for someone little used to dealing with archives. It was because of the help of several professionals that I got anywhere at all. I feel greatly indebted to the following historians, who have drawn my attention to potential sources and have commented on my use of this material: S. Ayache, G. Berg, S. Ellis, M. Esoavelomandroso, F. Raison-Jourde.

The anthropological field-work also required help of another kind. First of all it was only possible because of the willingness and even encouragement of the peoples whose lives I was able to share in the villages of Madagascar where the research was carried out. I learned a lot from them, notably about their customs and society, but also about myself and my society and the issues of life, death and moral commitment, which what they said and did forced me to reconsider. This research was made possible by financial help I received from various funding bodies. My research from 1964 to 1966 was principally funded by the Nuffield Foundation, and my field-work in 1971 was funded by the Social Science Research Council. I also received help of various kinds from the Universities of Madagascar and Cambridge and the London School of Economics.

The combination of anthropology and history has also posed practical problems in the preparation of the manuscript. It has been my intention to present a book that is of interest to a reasonably wide readership because it contributes to issues of general interest in the social sciences. In order to do this, I have had to omit much detail.

On the historical side I have not been able to deal with all of the very large number of references to the circumcision ceremony in the published literature. To have done so would have been out of place here because the majority of these references add nothing to what we know from the sources I have discussed, as they are almost entirely derivative. It would have been, however, more satisfactory to have reproduced the texts I discuss in full, but this would have made the book inordinately long. I hope to discuss some of these bibliographic problems elsewhere. On the anthropological side, I feel that some details of the rituals I witnessed are still missing. This is partly due to the incompleteness of my notes and, once again, to the problems of presentation in a short book. For example, the lack of transcription and detailed discussion of the music of the ritual is an obvious gap.

Two books are insufficiently acknowledged in the text. This is because I became acquainted with their contents after the part of the book to which they are relevant had been completed. The first is the little-known thesis by J. Foltz (1965), which is remarkably perceptive, especially bearing in mind that it is not backed by firsthand knowledge of the ritual. The other is a two-volume study by L. Molet (1979) that is a veritable encyclopedia of the literature on the Merina. It is an invaluable source, and I was glad to find that Molet's interpretations are often almost identical with mine.

Finally, I must acknowledge the great help I have received in preparing the book and in developing and forming the argument. Because this book has been so long in the making, I have presented parts of it to many academic seminars and have benefited from so many comments and criticisms that it is impossible for me to acknowledge them all. I must, however, particularly thank the University of Madagascar at Antananarivo and at Toliary; the Universities of Stockholm and Göteborg in Sweden; the National Museum of Ethnology, Suita, Japan; and the CEDRASEMI and the Ecole des Hautes Etudes, France, for the opportunities they have given me to present my arguments. Certain individuals have also made valuable suggestions and comments, especially T. Gibson, D. Lan, A. Papataxciarkis, S. Tanabe and C. Toren. Three people in particular have given me such help that without them this book would not have been possible in its present form: J. Parry and S. Roberts commented not only on one draft in great detail but even on different drafts of certain chapters and made major suggestions. This was also true of C. Toren, whose editorial work on the manuscript infinitely improved it.

1

The social determination of ritual

Social science originates in the radical idea that society and culture are natural, not God-given, phenomena and, therefore, are governed by general laws of an earthly character. Many thinkers and writers directly and indirectly related to the mainstream of social science have refused this starting point, but the attempt has always failed to change this basic premise, because the denial of the natural basis of culture and society negates the essential prerequisite for the idea of social science. Social science is therefore a materialist study in that it assumes that social phenomena are, in the end, to be explained as natural phenomena and it studies the factors creating society and culture. This is not to say that non-human material phenomena such as the properties of plants, animals and the soil and of man as a non-social being are what determine the ideas of human being. Such a view of materialism is a simple misunderstanding, making it patently false, since the influence of ideas on history is clear all around us. Rather, materialism sees that ideas also are, in the end, products of a complex yet natural process taking place in history.

All social science, therefore, attempts to explain the way the mechanisms of production and reproduction continuously produce social and cultural phenomena. Many social scientists would shy away from such a bold and bald statement of their position, partly because they may not want to be reminded of the impious basis of their endeavour, but also for two better reasons. The first is theoretical: They want to avoid the impression that they have already found what they are looking for. The second reason has two sides, one factual the other ethical. Explaining other peoples' beliefs and feelings can look like a refusal to accept the personal value of the emotions of joy and sorrow, even of illumination, of the participants in the practices analysed, and this is especially so in the field of religion. This is a particular danger in a study such as this, which detects in religious practices the expression of domination and militarist violence. Yet not to recognise the power and value of much of what is done for the participants is simply to introduce factual inaccuracy. When such an omission is used to distance ourselves from the people whose lives we have briefly shared in fieldwork and, as a result, a way in which we deny the continuity between them and

1

us, it becomes morally objectionable. Only a few anthropologists, such as V. Turner, have had the courage to make clear the continuity between their personal beliefs and those of the people they were studying (Turner 1962). But the recognition of this continuity, which I have tried to make clear in this book by using language that recalls our own culture, need not, in the end, make us feel, as Turner sometimes implies, that the phenomena are beyond explanation or criticism. Quite the contrary, it is precisely because of this continuity that we cannot see these phenomena as though they concerned another species, as the easy condemnations of ethnocentrism often invite us so to do. This attitude is not only repulsive but also counter-productive, as it makes us forget where we are heading and so lose any clear guiding purpose.

This book is an attempt to understand the factors determining a social phenomenon, a religious ritual, in a given historical period. It does not pretend, for reasons to be explained in the last chapter, to account for the phenomenon totally. It is, therefore, both a theoretical book, in that it proposes general conclusions, and also a book about specific events in specific places at specific times. This hybrid nature has been characteristic of anthropology since the time of Malinowski and Radcliffe-Brown and has, I believe, been one of its strengths, enabling it to avoid the empty platitudes 'pure' theory often means and the pointless particularity of some recent studies.

The main body of this book consists of an analysis of a particularly rich ritual practised by the Merina of Madagascar: that surrounding the circumcision of young boys. I saw this ritual performed eight times during a period of field-work between 1964 and 1966 and once during field-work in 1971. I also have indirect information about many other performances. The first substantive part of this book (Chapters 4–6) examines how symbolic analysis can explain the meaning of these performances in their social and cultural context and what connections can be established, causal or otherwise, with phenomena other than the ritual itself, using the various approaches available.

Chapter 7 deals with the history of the ritual, which, with difficulty, can be traced back almost two hundred years. These two centuries were particularly eventful for Madagascar in general and the Merina in particular, as they span a period when a large state developed, when the population was converted to Christianity, when colonisation by Europeans came and went, and when one of the most bloody anticolonial revolts in Africa south of the Sahara took place. Finally, Chapter 8 puts the historical and symbolic approaches together in order to explain what happens to such a ritual over time.

Generally, this study gives an example of how religion is involved in the rise of states, colonial rule and 'disestablishment', and, more generally still, how it is related to power, authority and violence. What changes and does not change in the ritual in some circumstances is one of the main concerns here, and this will be looked at in as much detail as possible, and perhaps beyond the endurance of the non-specialist reader, who might be advised to skip Chapters 4 and 7.

Such detail is, however, necessary if we want to move towards an understanding of how this kind of ritual is historically determined, since, in the end, causal propositions in the social sciences can be tested only historically.

As a preliminary, it is worthwhile reviewing briefly how the problem of the social determination of ritual has been approached or avoided in anthropology, to show why this study has taken the approach it has. The topics raised here in a preliminary way will be discussed again in greater depth in Chapter 8.

Perhaps the first writer to stress ritual in his analysis of society and to attribute a key role to it was the unorthodox theologian W. R. Robertson-Smith. Not only were his theories illuminating in themselves, but his influence on subsequent writers can hardly be overestimated. His theory of ritual offers us perhaps one of the clearest statements of the determination of ritual by other factors – in this case, clan organisation, which, it is implied, is the organising principle of the rather hazy society he is writing about.

He begins by insisting on the primacy of ritual over belief as the core of religion. His arguments for this are varied. First, he argues that in a preliterate society there is simply no forum where beliefs can be expressed or discussed outside the context of ritual. Second, he maintains that what matters to the participants, in themselves and others, is acting and participating rather than speculating. Consequently, one is not concerned in a primitive society with what other people think about the supernatural; one is only concerned about their proper participation. Third, and perhaps most interestingly in the light of what this study reveals, Robertson-Smith suggests that rituals are much more stable historically than beliefs (Robertson-Smith 1899, pp. 23–31).

Then Robertson-Smith turns to a consideration of the relationship between social groupings and ritual. In particular, he looks at sacrifice. Sacrifices, for him, are partly devices for restoring errant members of the community to the group, but principally they serve to reaffirm the solidarity of the group in a communal meal. The content of sacrifice is seen by Robertson-Smith as directly determined by the requirement of incorporation and reincorporation. It is partly because according to Robertson-Smith commensality has for all human beings the psychological meaning and effect of solidarity that sacrifices take the form of a meal, but also because, for him, this communal meal originally consisted in the eating of the totem of the clan. This totem was believed to share the same mystical substance as the clan members, and its communal ingestion entailed transformation of the participants into the same substance. Robertson-Smith's work retains much interest for us today, and the themes he dealt with will recur throughout this study. His discussion of the primacy and historical stability of ritual fits well the particular case discussed in this book, although I should be wary of accepting this view for all cases, especially for societies of a much less hierarchic character than the Merina that seem to manifest a real taste for metaphysical speculation (Lévi-Strauss 1964, 1966, 1968, 1971; Endicott 1979).

What is particularly striking in Robertson-Smith is the central proposition that ritual is determined by social organisation. His book is perhaps the simplest statement of the determination of ritual by non-ritual elements in the literature until we come to the writings of certain members of the American cultural-ecology school (Rappaport 1979). This makes Robertson-Smith's theory a useful starting point for examining the problems that arise from such a position.

There is no doubt that Robertson-Smith was mistaken about the nature of clans and sacrifices, both among the ancient Semites and in other parts of the world, as E. E. Evans-Pritchard (1965, pp. 51–3) pointed out with emphatic contempt, but this kind of theory has been re-echoed again and again, often with much better evidence (for example, in Radcliffe-Brown 1952).

The first point to note about this type of argument is that it hinges on a set of correspondences that are taken to be causal relationships. In Robertson-Smith's theory, the elements seen as corresponding are clans, ritual congregation and the emotions of commensality. The clans cause the ritual for the purposes of solidarity, and this maintains the clans. The argument is therefore teleological in that the effect of the commensal ritual, solidarity, is made to be its cause, implying a conscious or unconscious motivation on the part of the originators of the ritual – a motivation that would have to have been based on the same kind of knowledge of determination as that of Robertson-Smith himself. That is to say, the purpose of the initiators would have to have been based on knowledge of the effects of commensality, and if those who continue the ritual do not state this any more, it is because they have forgotten the wise intent of their ancestors, because they carry on the institution merely from habit, or because they conceal the real purpose of the ritual from others and perhaps from themselves as well by some strange process of the unconscious. This type of explanation, which has often been labelled functionalist, is both undemonstrated and totally unlikely. It has been incisively criticised again and again (Needham 1962; Jarvie 1965; Spiro 1965).

Even if we accepted that rituals such as sacrifices do maintain the unity of clans, or other social groups, we should still be a long way from understanding how they are formed. The question would arise whether the unity-maintaining function of the ritual accounted for *all* aspects of the ritual; otherwise the connection might be simply partial or even trivial. For example, there is a correspondence between the smaller unit of political administration in Britain and the congregation of Anglican churches at the parish level; but, clearly, to explain the Anglican religion in terms of the needs of this administrative unit would be preposterous. Robertson-Smith goes farther than many of his successors in accounting for details of the rituals he is dealing with in terms of the need for solidarity; for example, he explains sacrifice, the communal meal, the choice of sacrificial animal, but even he fails to account in sociological terms for the presupposition that underlies all this: the notion of totemism, which, unlike his predecessors, he just takes as given. By doing this, he leaves us with the problem that we are not even given the basic requirement for a theory of causation, a clear

4

statement that one type of phenomenon accounts in part or in whole for another. We are left simply with congruence; causation is only imputed.

The problem arises again when a somewhat different type of determination is proposed for a ritual in the work of R. Rappaport in his adventurous book *Pigs for the Ancestors* (1967). He argues that ritual should be seen as an adaptive mechanism of the human species in a given ecological balance. Rappaport seems to be arguing in his book, or at least in a subsequent article (Rappaport 1977), that a complex ritual of a New Guinea people is explained by its effect on the ecological balance, in particular by reducing the pig population when it reaches a critical threshold. The ritual then sets off a negative feedback, restoring the ecological balance. But, having given an explanation of this type, Rappaport finds that it raises a whole range of further questions. In particular, why, if the deleterious effects of the rising pig population are clear to the people – and Rappaport implies that they are (1967, pp. 158–9) – should the message have to be given in ritual form at all? His answer is that ritual makes the message imperative and beyond discussion because of its sacred character and that it is the only way in which such important actions can be enforced in uncentralised societies.

Rappaport, like a number of other functionalists, does not imply an original founder for the ritual, rather he replaces this mythical figure with natural selection that explains the continuance of this particular ritual. The form of the argument is, therefore, that culture, like genetic mutations, produces a large number of random forms and that the useful ones persist while the harmful ones disappear. In slightly less courageous form this argument is quite common in anthropology when it dissolves into merely noting the simultaneous occurrence of two phenomena – the weak functionalism of Jarvie (1965). Congruence, however, either is trivial or implies in a disguised form, as it usually does, the kind of argument clearly stated by Rappaport.

The problems in this sort of interpretation are many and have been discussed often (Friedman 1974, Rappaport 1977), but overall they are the same ones raised by Robertson-Smith's study. Stressing the effect of the ritual on the pig population and other ecological balances may be just a trivial observation. Since this ritual, like so many others, involves killing animals (in this case pigs), it inevitably affects the pig population. Passing from this observation of effect to the specification of cause is quite impossible. It would require Rappaport to show that somehow populations with the type of ritual he analyses outlive populations without it. It would lead to the implication that the ritual is like an instinct, something beyond conscious motivation. (Otherwise the notion of natural selection could not apply.) It would require an explanation of why the Tsembaga were unable to dispose of pigs in ways other than through this particular ritual. All this cannot be done.[1] In other words, the appearance of the demonstration of determination of the ritual is achieved in this explanation, as in that of Robertson-Smith, by confounding effect and cause. The same criticism could be directed at many other writers who have tried to explain rituals as the products of a simple determining process – Radcliffe-Brown, Freud, Gluckman, to cite only a few.

Another type of explanation of the determination of ritual by social phenomena is to be found in the work of a number of Marxist writers. Generally they draw on the notion of ideology. Ideology for them is a device whereby a ruling class imposes its ideas, values and image of reality on those whom it dominates. Few Marxist writers have have discussed ritual, but those who do, such as M. Godelier, see ritual as part of ideology and as determined by this purpose (Godelier 1973, Chapter 5), or more generally for maintaining order. Here again, however, we find the same problems as those discussed in relation to the writings of Robertson-Smith and Rappaport. A bizarre scenario seems to be implied for the origins of ideology, or of rituals that create and perpetuate ideology. It would involve ideology's being created as a plot by cynical rulers who deliberately invent subtle and totally convincing mystifying devices for the domination of others, or invoking, as Rappaport does, a theory of natural selection that explains persistence. Above all it makes the significance and power of religion for participants quite beyond comprehension. Although these writers tend to ignore the rather absurd notions implicit in their theory of ideology, the implications are nevertheless there. Otherwise one would have to make the totally un-Marxist supposition that ideology was created by other than human agency. Also present is the old problem that the demonstration of the alleged fact that ideological apparatuses such as rituals perform the functions of ideology does not mean that these functions are the cause of their being as they are.

Robertson-Smith, Rappaport and Godelier therefore all run into exactly the same difficulties. Their theories either imply a form of intentional action that is quite unlike anything we know and that they do not document, or, if they do not, their observations become nothing more than the noting of congruences that have nothing necessarily causal in character. Perhaps the weakness of such an approach can best be shown by pointing out that the opposite conclusions can be reached from similar data with equal plausibility. This is precisely the position of two other writers on ritual, N. Fustel de Coulange and Emile Durkheim, who were able to use Robertson-Smith's conclusions for their totally different theories. For them, in a variety of ways, it was the ritual, the emotions and the concepts embodied in it, that creates the social units with which they are congruent.

Fustel de Coulange's argument is that the concept of ancestor worship was to shape all Roman history and create the notion of the ancient city and its laws on the model of the original patriarchal family or minimal lineage (Fustel de Coulange, 1868). His work is, however, rather ambiguous as a general theory of determination, because he also shows how this concept of the city was undermined, and later defeated, by other types of groupings, not religious or ritual in origin, but corresponding to status groups or classes. A much more complex picture therefore emerges than the declared idealist posture of the author leads us to expect. None the less, the fact remains that precisely the opposite point of view to that of Robertson Smith can be deduced from similar data with as much, or as little, plausibility.

Many of the views of Fustel de Coulange were taken over in Durkheim's work, particularly in his book *The Elementary Forms of the Religious Life* (Durkheim, 1912). Unlike Fustel de Coulange, Durkheim sees religion and ritual as ultimately determined by material conditions, especially demography. In so far as he sees a relationship between rituals and such social categories as clans, however, it is the former that determine the latter. Durkheim sees ritual as the device by which the categories of understanding organising our perception of nature and of society are created and given their categorical, hence inevitable, and compulsive nature. In other words, the theories of Durkheim and Fustel de Coulange are mirror opposites of those of such writers as Robertson-Smith, Rappaport and Godelier, because a connection between ritual and social organisation does not itself constitute a demonstration of causation. It appears to be a demonstration of causation because all the writers hypothesise an unknown historical period when the one element directly and in a flash created the other. Of course, if such historical events had taken place the matter would be settled. However, none of the people concerned give any evidence of this historical moment, and as soon as we try to imagine it, it becomes preposterous. Determination cannot be demonstrated by hypothetical history, only by real history.

In spite of the apparent differences among these writers they all have one thing in common: Their treatment is highly reductionist. This is another familiar criticism of functionalist theories but it remains none the less valid. The problem is that any theory that explains rituals in terms of their socially regulative functions pays attention to only a few aspects of very rich and complex phenomena. There is no way that such functions can account for the complexity of what we find, as will be shown, yet again, with the example that forms the subject matter of this book.

The reason for this reductionism is actually no different from the reason for the failure to demonstrate causation in functionalist theories. It is the false notion of history that such theories imply. In these theories the social need for solidarity, or domination, or ecological balance, created the ritual. The moment when this occurred in envisaged as a very simple one: Before, there was nothing significant; afterwards, there was the ritual. A ritual created so simply can therefore only be accounted for by the simple function it is required to perform. Of course rituals are much more complex, but since the theory implies such simple punctual historical creation, the theoretician must just ignore what is in front of him or her and only note what fits. As will be argued more fully throughout this book, it is only when one looks at *real history* in all its complexity, a history that has no starting point, that we can understand the possibility of an intricate process of determination producing a phenomenon as complex as the ritual we shall examine.

7

From blessing to violence

The realisation of the reductionism inherent in functionalist analysis led in anthropology to a different approach to ritual. This reaction is exemplified in the writings of theorists such as Horton, but is already implied in the work of Radin and the later works of Evans-Pritchard and even earlier writers (Evans-Pritchard 1956). Their approaches vary significantly, as will be discussed in Chapter 8, but for the sake of brevity here they can be grouped together under the label of intellectualists and symbolists. Basically such authors see religion as an explanation of the world and man in fairly traditional theological terms. They see religion as a speculation on nature and an intellectual accommodation of the beyond. They are very critical of functionalism, as they recognise it as a device for ignoring the content of ritual. They refer to Robertson-Smith's view on the unimportance of belief as proof of this.

Certainly the reaction they represent has shown that there is much more to be seen in rituals than has previously been supposed. This is also true of other writers who take a somewhat similar attitude, with different stylistic modes of presentation, using various diagrammatical or logical devices for presenting their data. These would include Biedelman, Maybury-Lewis and Willis. The close analysis of the content of ritual that this antifunctionalist approach produced has clearly been a major advance and I have attempted to follow the examples they offer in Chapters 4 and 5. The whole approach has, however, raised problems as fundamental as those of functionalism. Perhaps the first and most fundamental of these difficulties was Robertson-Smith's starting question. Why, if rituals are to be seen as intellectual speculation, do they take the form of ritual? Why is participation so important? Why do rituals have power? Finally, how and why do they come about? As soon as we begin to attempt an answer we seem to be thrown back to the functionalist questions and at the same time to their methods.

In order to avoid reductionism, the intellectualists have made of rituals something that they clearly are not: a discourse on the nature of man in the universe. Indeed, as has been shown by G. Lewis (1980) this misrepresentation leads to totally unwarranted additions in that the intellectualists complement what they can observe with other deductions in order to produce the kind of scheme that in the anthropological literature is referred to as cosmology. The antifunctionalists therefore fall into another form of reductionism that may well be even more dangerous.

Thus the problem of intellectualist and symbolic approaches is very similar to that of functionalist ones: The former theories assume that rituals are as they are in order to fulfil a single function, that of explanation. This view also implies a pseudo-history, a just-so story of an absolute beginning, when a thinker, unbound by society or the necessities of life or for that matter any previous intellectual preconceptions, worked out the whole thing. This is totally ludicrous and contradicts everything we know of real human beings in history, with the possible exception of certain philosophers who have never been attributed with initiating rituals of the type discussed here. Of course most of the writers who adopt

8

such a position would deny any such strange scenario, but again, as for the functionalists, unless they believe that the schemes they construct fell ready-made from heaven, they cannot escape the implication.

Not only does the substitution of false history for real history lead to the adoption of untenable theories of causation, it also leads as it did for the functionalists to reductionism. With such a simple imputed cause nearly all the aspects that make the ritual a ritual and not a Platonic dialogue have to be ignored. Here, indeed, these authors rejoin some of the Marxist writers who see in ideology an 'alternative theory' of the world to the true one. What they both miss is that the image so created is of a different kind to non-ritual knowledge because of the way it is created phenomenologically and historically. Again, we find that it is only if we return to the reality of the historical process that the complexity and the many facets of rituals can begin to be accounted for. The functionalist, the intellectualist and the symbolist positions that have dominated anthropology will be shown, therefore, to be equally, and for very similar reasons, unsatisfactory.

It may appear that we are, therefore, doomed in the study of ritual to be endlessly bouncing between two walls – a functionalist wall, which implies a process of formation that is clearly wrong and that leads us to ignore most of what can be observed, and an intellectualist or symbolist wall, which fails in any way to explain or place rituals in their social context, and as a result leads us to misrepresent our data by making us pretend that it is a different type of activity than it patently is, that is, by making it look as though it were a theological treatise.

However, the picture in anthropology is not quite so bleak. There have been some writers who have attempted to combine the sociological with the symbolic approaches. Foremost amongst these has been V. Turner. It is impossible to do justice to Turner's very subtle theory here, and in any case perhaps its greatest strength lies in the fruitful method of analysis of particular cases it implies. However, what he proposes is that we should note the symbolic side of ritual, together with its emotional and its sociological aspects. What he fails to do is to bring these together convincingly, except by suggesting that the ambiguity and complexity of symbolism make it suitable for social manipulation. Although this point is undoubtedly valid, it does not explain how the social brings about the symbolic, and Turner denies strongly that this will ever be possible.

The reason is that the social considered by Turner is the very short term, for example a segmentation dispute, a struggle between two different potential leaders. On a short time-scale it is quite clear that the social does not bring about the symbolic, and to suggest that it does, as is done in functionalist theories, is, as Turner clearly sees, wrong. This does not mean, however, that the establishment of a causative link between the history of the social formation and the ritual cannot be attempted. It is simply that the connection cannot be understood either synchronically, or in the very short term. Indeed, this book will show that for the Merina circumcision ritual, two hundred years are quite insufficient for doing more than beginning to understand the nature of determination. The reason is not far to seek. People act in terms of what they know and what they know is the product of their historically constructed culture. They may transform and change this culture but they do not do it from a zero starting base. Because of this the study of determination must be not a study of initial creation, but of the principles of transformation.

It is this problem that forms the approach used in this book. The circumcision ceremony will be considered not only as a symbolic system but also as a symbolic system being created in history, as far as it is possible to do so, because this process of creation occurs on a much longer time-scale than anthropologists have usually been willing to consider. This point is implied in most of the work of Lévi-Strauss but never demonstrated by him, simply because he has never done a genuinely historical study. It is attempted here, although, as must inevitably be the case, the historical determination of the ritual through time can be only partially examined. The reason is simple: The processes of formation the ritual must have imply a much longer time-scale than the two hundred years examined here. Because only two hundred years will have been examined, only a part of the ritual can be accounted for. This should not surprise us. After all, we know that there are much larger continuities in culture than are covered by two centuries. Indeed, the idea of culture areas, which is accepted implicitly or explicitly by most anthropologists, inevitably implies this.

Of course these considerations apply to any cultural phenomenon but the general problem becomes somewhat modified when we turn to ritual. The reason for this lies in the very character of ritual as a special kind of activity. One of the criticisms of the intellectualist position is, as we saw, that it presents rituals as though they were an intellectual treatise: as cosmologies. A number of writers have pointed out how misleading this is. Foremost amongst the anthropologists are Bateson (1958) and Turner (1967), who have emphasised in different ways the emotive and sensuous aspects of ritual. More recently Sperber (1974) has shown how totally wrong it is to approach ritual and symbolism as though the task in hand was a matter of decoding and translation. More practically a number of anthropologists (Bloch 1974, Rappaport 1979, Tambiah 1979, Lewis 1980, Ahern 1981) have tried to isolate the particular nature of the communication used in ritual to understand what relation the symbolic content of the ritual has to other types of communication. In spite of a number of disagreements and varying emphasis all these writers agree that what characterises ritual is that it lies somewhere between an action and a statement. Because of this any representation of the 'argument' of a ritual as such is misleading. But because ritual does have elements that are like statements, because it does retain some propositional force, the opposite attitude, which would deny any validity to an analysis of content of ritual would also be misleading. We are, therefore, faced with a genuine difficulty, which originates in part from the literary and narrative techniques anthropologists must use if they are to be readable. When representing the nature of

10

ritual, they can neither analyse rituals as though they were propositions nor totally ignore their propositional character. The solution adopted here follows the lead of several of the writers already mentioned: It first analyses the ritual symbolically as though it were a proposition and then heavily qualifies this presentation, in part by examining its historical destiny.

This is merely to recognise the special and difficult nature of rituals and explains why the study of ritual has offered such a challenge and has figured ever more prominently in anthropology. On the whole, the problem has been faced by ever refining the formal analysis of ritual with help from communication theory, psychology, philosophy, even literature and literary criticism. I have no doubt of the value of these approaches and I feel we have genuinely advanced in our understanding of ritual. However, I also have a feeling that these studies, including my own, represent attempts to grasp what, in the end, it is impossible to grasp: what rituals mean to the participants and the onlookers. This type of search for meaning, although not pointless, has no end.

There is, however, another way of doing the same thing that for a moment at least bypasses the difficulty, and that is to look at what happens to rituals in the course of history. Quite simply, if rituals are a special kind of phenomena, it follows that they will be manifested in history in a special way. If this is so, it is also reasonable to assume that the special way rituals are manifested in history will reveal what kind of phenomena they are. The advantage of this approach is that, unlike other attempts at getting at the nature of ritual through seeing what it means for the participants, it uses as its basis much more easily graspable phenomena: the way rituals are affected by events.

There is, however, yet a further advantage in this approach: It enables us to bring together the functional and the intellectual sides of the study of ritual in that it enables us to follow the interplay between the two aspects without reducing one to the other. The aim of this book is therefore to show that the meaning and nature of a ritual can be understood in the process of its historical formation and that by this means the recurring problems of the study of ritual can be overcome. But some attempt will be made beyond this to reconsider the question of ideology in general and to see how some of the conclusions reached concerning ritual can illuminate the more fundamental questions raised by this controversial concept. It seems to me that it is only by combining the knowledge of what the experience of ideology is, something that anthropologists with the experience of field-work behind them are able to do, and the knowledge of history that we can advance our understanding in this area.

2

Background politico-religious history of the Merina, 1770–1970

To trace the development of ideology in central Madagascar during the nineteenth and twentieth centuries a specific case has been chosen, that of the circumcision ritual, because it is only in the light of a really clear and detailed case that vague discussions on ideology can be genuinely put to the test. This narrow focus, however, is the source of a difficulty. It would be totally misleading to imagine that by looking closely at this one ritual, however important it may be, it is possible to understand the nature and processes of Merina history. It is first necessary to outline the general background in order to show the significance of the ritual and its transformation. This chapter sets out to do this and briefly covers the history of central Madagascar, paying particular attention to religion. Similarly, the next chapter provides the background for social organisation and symbolism. Neither chapter represents genuinely original work, but the approach is different from that of most other writers on these topics in relation to Madagascar.

Madagascar has always been considered an anthropological oddity, due to the fact that although geographically it is close to Africa the language spoken throughout the island clearly belongs to the Austronesian group spoken in Southeast Asia; more particularly Malagasy is linked to the languages spoken in western Indonesia. These surprising facts are also reflected in the biological and cultural affinity of the people. Although there is much controversy over the relative importance of the African and Indonesian element in the population, there is general agreement that we find the two merged together throughout the island. In some parts one side of this dual inheritance is more important; in other regions it is the other side that seems to dominate. For example, all commentators agree that among the Merina, the people with whom this book is concerned, the Southeast Asian element is particularly strongly marked. This seems to be confirmed by comparative ethnography, and I would also stress that the systems of social organisation and culture that seem to correspond most closely to the Merina are those traditionally found in the general area of the southern Celebes and Borneo. In spite of these similarities, all Malagasy cultures, and Merina culture in particular, remain very different from the systems to which they are genetically re-

12

lated, probably largely due to the fact that they involve a unique combination of Africa and Asia.

Imerina, the land of the Merina, is situated in the centre of Madagascar on a mountainous plateau whose altitude gives it a Mediterranean type of climate strongly marked by the alternation of a dry, cold and a wet, hot season. The most important form of agriculture is, and has been since our earliest records, irrigated rice agriculture. This is carried out on terraces on or near valley bottoms, which are separated from one another by large expanses of relatively poor hillside. In a few places larger areas are drained for a different type of wet rice cultivation and depend on high dikes; these large-scale works are often associated with larger political and administrative centres.

Apart from wet rice cultivation the Merina have also always carried out various types of shifting cultivation on the hillsides, where they plant such crops as sweet potatoes, maize, manioc, and various types of beans, and more recently a number of cash crops such as ground-nuts. The Merina also have permanent garden sites, where they grow a wide variety of crops including fruit, bananas, taro, green vegetables. Most people have some livestock, from chickens to cattle, although it appears they were more abundant in the past.

The Merina have been recognised as good craftsmen since our earliest records. Certain skills such as spinning, weaving and basket making are more or less universal, others are restricted to specialists. These include most forms of metal work and more complicated carpentry and stone working.

Overall the Merina are best described by the general label of peasants, if not too much theoretical weight or precision is attached to the term. They have been the most prominent group in Madagascar since at least the end of the eighteenth century, and they are the best-known Malagasy people outside it, because from that period until the end of the nineteenth century they were the dominant political power in the island and as such were the people with whom the threatening colonial powers of Britain and France were most concerned.

There are indirect indications from earlier European sources of technological sophistication on the part of the Merina well antedating the first written account in 1777 (Mayeur 1913); and it is also plain that some sort of centralised political formations existed before that date (Délivré 1974, pp. 11–13). This is made clear in the abundant oral traditions that began to be written down in the earlier parts of the nineteenth century but refer to earlier periods. We therefore know that the state that grew up at the end of the eighteenth century in Imerina and principally concerns this book was partly similar to that which had existed before although in many other respects, such as size, permanence, technological and administrative development, it was quite different (Bloch 1977a).

In contrast to this little-known earlier period, Merina history is well documented from the end of the eighteenth century onwards, although it remains far from thoroughly studied. The beginning of Merina expansion is usually seen as occurring during the period of ascendancy of the famous Merina King Andrianampoinimerina, whose reign lasted from probably 1780 to 1810 (Délivré 1974). This period corresponds with the increased development of the export of slaves from Madagascar toward Réunion, Mauritius and beyond. The slaves seem to have been in part exchanged for weapons (Filliot 1974), which were to be a key element in the expansion of the Merina state. Ellis, one of the earliest commentators on the Merina, had no doubt of this: 'During the reign of Impoina [Andrianampoinimerina], Imerina and the interior of the country generally became an extensive mart for slaves. They consisted principally of the prisoners taken in war, who were exchanged to the slave dealers for arms and ammunition, by which further conquests might be made, and additional supplies for the slave market produced' (Ellis 1838, vol. 2, p. 127). A somewhat similar view was held by the Merina historian Raombana, who gave vent to his hostility towards the king by describing him as a slave trader (Raombana 1980, pp. 244–6) but at the same time attributing his success to this type of activity.

The dramatic development of a large-scale Merina state under Andrianampoinimerina is not simply to be explained by his slave trading. Other factors, such as the agricultural and trading reforms that he instituted, must also be taken into account. Equally important was the fact that his reign was marked by the organisation of various governmental and military institutions, which gave the nascent state a solid foundation. This administrative structure was in part realised by using, renovating and reorganising a variety of traditional institutions such as the great royal oratorical assemblies, 'Kabary'; the establishment of legal structures in the form of courts, and commercial structures in the form of markets; the use of traditional forms of taxation and corvées on an unprecedented scale. It is clear, however, that the very scale of the kingdom under Andrianampoinimerina meant that new administrative techniques had to be found to supplement and organise the older institutions.

From the start of Andrianampoinimerina's reign, approximately 1780, the Merina state began to develop some form of bureaucracy and a standing army. The capital of the kingdom was moved from the old village of Ambohimanga to the village of Antananarivo (a previous capital), which turned into a sizeable town. The transformation was dramatic, and in order to make it permanent Andrianampoinimerina and to an even greater extent Radama, his son, started to look for administrative and military expertise from outside.

The administrative expertise that Andrianampoinimerina sought was at first mainly in the field of writing (Bloch 1968a). As a result he naturally turned to the Antaimoro people of Madagascar, who had retained a form of Arabic script, used principally for astrological purposes. Andrianampoinimerina invited several Antaimoro astrologers to his court and employed them as secretaries and record keepers. It is also clear that these Antaimoros taught writing and perhaps astrology to a number of Merina. Thus Radama, Andrianampoinimerina's heir, knew how to write in Antaimoro/Arabic script (Munthe, 1982). Although the Merina seemed to have used writing almost exclusively for secular purposes it is probable that the contact with the Antaimoros, which the development of the state encouraged, also led to various religious innovations, which may account for various Islamic elements in subsequent Merina religion, although there are a number of other ways by which these elements could have been introduced.

Apart from this influence it does not seem as if the reign of Andrianampoini-merina was one of great religious innovation. As in the political field, the period appears to be marked by strengthening rather than the replacing of earlier institutions. Of particular importance here is the strengthening of the religious aspects of kingship that certainly took place during this reign. One aspect was the development of royal rituals, and this book as a whole is concerned with the development of one such ritual. The second was the development and growth of royal 'medicines', or *sampy*. These involved various cults of different origin, which were brought to the capital together with their officials to swell the ranks of the court and emphasise the supra-natural character of the king. These medicines have recently been the subject of a number of historical studies, but their social and religious significance remains somewhat obscure (Domenichini 1971, Berg 1979, Raison-Jourde 1983).

The political and military success of Andrianampoinimerina meant that he began to expand his kingdom beyond the traditional boundaries of Imerina. First of all, because the traffic in slaves was of crucial importance to him since it supplied him with the weapons he needed, he tried successfully to extend his influence towards the east coast, where a growing trade was in the hands of foreign traders and local princes linked with the Mascarene Islands (Mauritius and Réunion). One result of this push to the east was that, as the Merina took control of the slave trade ever nearer its source, they became involved, although indirectly, with European culture and powers. This contact became much more significant when, as a result of the Napoleonic wars, Reúnion temporarily, and Mauritius permanently, became British. It is this contact that characterises the period immediately following the reign of Andrianampoinimerina: the reign of his son Radama I from 1810 to 1828.

The British in Mauritius, under their governor Sir Robert Farquhar, pursued a much more determined policy towards Madagascar, partly because they realised the importance of the trade in slaves, rice and cattle for their new colony, and partly because they saw in their developing connection with the Merina the possibility of increasing their political influence in and possible control of Madagascar. This was a difficult matter because up to the time of the British conquest of Mauritius, and for some time afterwards, the basis of the indirect link between the Mascarenes and the Merina had been the exchange of slaves for arms, and the British were coming under strong domestic pressure against the slave trade.

The policy of Farquhar seems to have been based on a number of principles. The first was to increase aid and trade with the Merina, to maintain and increase their military domination in Madagascar and their dependence on Britain. This involved the continued supply of weapons and an offer to train the Merina army,

15

a task carried out largely by a West Indian sergeant called Brady. At the same time the British convinced Radama to send two children, who were his close relatives, to be educated in Mauritius. It was the beginning of a series of such educational transfers, which were later to be extremely significant politically, as many of the British-educated Merina gained tremendous influence in Madagascar in the subsequent half-century (Ayache 1976, pp. 25–7).

The second step involved the establishment of a major treaty in 1817, which despite many vicissitudes, survived throughout the whole of Radama's reign. The treaty was many-sided, but its best-known aspect was the agreement by both sides to strive towards the abolition of the trade in Malagasy slaves outside Madagascar. In return Radama was assured of a continuing supply of the goods that had previously been obtained through the slave trade, the most important being an annual supply of weapons and ammunitions.

The advantages of this treaty for Radama were many. It not only ensured a continuing supply of military and technological aid for both administrative and industrial purposes but also gave him a monopoly of these European goods and services inside Madagascar. This was because under the terms of the treaty the British navy had to patrol Madagascar to stop the overseas slave trade; thus it simultaneously blocked the traditional means by which rivals of Radama could have obtained Western goods and services.

For the British the treaty was both a response to humanitarian pressure in Britain and a way whereby Farquhar believed he could make Radama more dependent on Britain. This was very important, partly because of expansionist plans, and partly because the British government was keen to ensure the essential supply of rice and cattle for Mauritius in order to feed its booming population. The need for slaves on the island was much less for a British colony than it had been under the French, because from the time of the British take-over an ever greater number of Indian indentured labourers were brought to Mauritius and proved a cheaper source of labour than slaves. What these labourers needed was food; as Mauritius could not meet their needs in this respect, Madagascar was the only practical place where it could be obtained.

Perhaps the most important result of the treaty, however, was peripheral to its stated intention. It was the coming of missionaries from the London Missionary Society. A group of missionaries had been sent from North Wales to Madagascar in 1817 but had got no further than Mauritius and the coast of Madagascar, the reason being that the 1817 treaty was not properly activated until 1820. After that time the missionaries were given a conditional welcome by Radama. The missionaries who came were Welsh Congregationalists, whose faith and moving self-denial must win the admiration and wonder of the most hostile observer. Radama was most unenthusiastic about the religious aims of the missionaries and only allowed them some latitude in this direction in return for those services that he did want: the supplying of administrative and technological skills, the most important of which was efficient literacy (Raison-Jourde 1977b).

Politico-religious history of the Merina

As we have noted, Andrianampoinimerina had already attracted to his kingdom Malagasy who could write in Arabic script, partly because of their astrological skills, but also because their writing skills could be used for administration. During Radama's reign Roman script was also used and Radama had obtained the services of a Mauritian Creole secretary, Robin. This proved insufficient, and in any case Radama, as a result of his foreign policy, became specially interested in literacy in English.

Radama therefore welcomed the missionaries as a kind of replacement for the Arabic writing astrologers. He particularly encouraged them to open schools for the growing administrative class and later the missionaries were even allowed to set up a printing press. Radama's need for writing expertise accounts for the early success of the missionaries at court. They became an essential element in the operation of the Merina state.

Apart from teaching reading and writing and introducing printing the missionaries were also encouraged by Radama to supply other technological experts and the first missionaries were soon followed by a number of extremely impressive and able 'missionary artisans' who little by little transformed a whole range of Merina techniques during Radama's reign.

In many ways the relation of Radama and the missionaries was based on continual bargaining. In exchange for the right to Christianise, the missionaries had to supply the king with various types of technical expertise. This is made quite clear in the first official letter from Radama to the London Missionary Society, a letter written with the help of David Jones, one of the first missionaries in Madagascar, who was already acting as the king's adviser. The letter is as follows:

> I request you to send me . . . as many missionaries as you may deem proper, together with their families, if they desire it; provided [underlining in the original] you send skilful artisans to make my people workmen, as well as good Christians. [Ellis 1838, vol. 2, p. 275]

Accompanying this letter to England were eight Malagasy youths, six of whom were to be taught by the missionaries and were ultimately to become important politicians on their return. There were also two others 'who were sent to some of the establishments of government, to learn the art of making gunpowder etc.' (Ellis 1838, vol. 2, p. 275). The letter and the destination of the young people demonstrates well Radama's interests with the London Missionary Society.

The close but difficult relations between Radama, the British and the missionaries revealed in this letter and other similar documents continued until the death of the king in 1828. This was a period of extraordinary expansion and consolidation for the Merina state, although not one of total stability. One of the problems was the growing influence of the British and the following reign, that of the Queen Ranavalona I, was marked by an attempt on the part of the Merina to free themselves from the tightening foreign grip on their island that the king's political and military ambitions had partly engendered.

From blessing to violence

The coming to power of a queen always marks in Imerina the assumption of control of the state by non-royal groups who because of their lowly descent cannot become monarchs themselves. Instead, the non-royal groups solve the problem by putting a royal woman on the throne and then marrying her to one of their number.

It is clear, however, that the change following Radama's death and the coronation of Ranavalona I was much less sudden than it has often been represented. Gradually relations between the Merina and the European powers worsened. France, and especially the restored French colony of Réunion, had always been opposed to the Anglo-Merina treaty. Réunion, unlike Mauritius, could not so easily substitute indentured labour for slave labour. Many of the plantation owners in Réunion, who in any case had close links with the traders long established on the east coast of Madagascar, succeeded in encouraging the French navy to try to enforce shadowy French claims to the east coast, leading to forays that were disastrous for the Merina.

The details of the political history of the reign of Ranavalona cannot be told here, and indeed they are only now beginning to emerge clearly. The main features, however, are outside and internal opposition matched by great success in the establishment, organisation and subjugation of the unwieldy empire left by the queen's predecessors, as well as a deliberate attempt to distance the kingdom from the foreign powers who were trying to control the Merina. All these general features are reflected in the religious history of this period, which forms the necessary background for the understanding of the circumcision ceremony.

The attacks of the French made the missionary artisans all the more valuable and as a result the missionaries grew bolder. Previously they had been almost totally subservient to the Merina. Radama had exercised extraordinarily tight control over them; he was able to do this partly because they were dependent on his good will and partly because they were not strongly backed by the British Government, either in London or in Mauritius. The missionaries were Nonconformists, often of Welsh descent, and were considered with a certain distaste by the British authorities. They were acceptable in so far as they maintained good relations between Britain and Radama, and that was all; they would not have been supported if they had offended the king in any way. Radama had ensured that the schools that they had set up had rapidly become preliminaries to military or administrative service. Under Ranavalona I, however, the missionaries, feeling more confident, took a new and significant step: They began to baptise Malagasies and to organise Christian congregations.

The reaction of the Merina, against a background of ever more open and clear imperialist designs from Britain and France, was inevitably hostile. The action of the missionaries was seen as political in two ways. The first was, as Ranavalona herself repeatedly made clear, that Christianity involved a repudiation of the ancestral customs of the country, established by previous monarchs who were

18

her ancestors. The queen's legitimacy depended entirely on her relation to her predecessors, who had given the kingdom to her. Furthermore, she was in some sense the ancestor of her subjects, their great parent, the head of the descent group the Merina represented themselves to be. She was queen because she was the descendant of the royal ancestors, who were in a mystical sense the ancestors of all the Merina. To deny her mystical power was to repudiate not only her but also the ancestors, the quintessence of good and blessings. This was how her power was represented in her person and this was demonstrated in all the state rituals. She was the custodian of a holy trust. In such a system, as anthropologists often stress, there is no conceptual separation of kinship, economics, politics and religion. Christianity was therefore treason, a denial of the representation of the state as one descent group. In Ranavalona's words it was 'the substitution of the respect of her ancestors, Andrianampoinimerina and Radama, for the respect of the ancestor of the whites: Jesus Christ'. She saw the introduction of a new religion as a political act, and there is no doubt that she was right. If the missionaries imagined that in a state such as the Merina state religion could be separated from politics, they were making the mistake of using an inappropriate imported model of society. It is, however, quite possible that they were to a certain extent conscious of the implication of what they were doing.

The second aspect of Christianity that disturbed Ranavalona's government was less metaphysical. It was that Christianity involved assemblies, associations and societies (Ellis 1838, vol. 2, p. 493) that were beyond governmental controls and as such were potentially seditious. The possibility of assemblies not concerned with kinship or royal rituals was a totally alien phenomenon, and at no time did the Merina monarchs allow associations that were not set up under royal or familial (i.e., ancestral) authority: They allowed Christianity to flourish only when it was under their control. The development of uncontrolled associations was, in any case, particularly threatening during the earlier part of the reign of Ranavalona because of the continuing and rising social unrest that marked Merina society at that time and because of the continual internal subversion in the interest of various foreign powers.

The unrest was due, in part, to the increasing exactions that the growing Merina state required, if it was to be administered and armed. The Merina were, after all, only a small group of people ruling over a gigantic area without any very advanced administrative means. The reign of Ranavalona, especially, involved continual fighting all over the island and the people were hard pressed, mainly by military service. It is clear that during the reign of Ranavalona the semi-autonomous nature of church organisation made it a focus for opposition to the ever increasing exactions of the state, an important factor in the growth of Christianity in this period.

If we look at the nature of the membership of the growing Christian churches in Imerina under Ranavalona, it seems to reveal that Christianity appealed principally to two different social groups. On the one hand, there was a popular anti-government, anti-military service group, containing many women. On the other, there was a palace faction, trying secretly to overthrow the government and put itself in its place, which used Christianity as its rallying point (Gow 1979; Ellis 1858).

Christianity became under Ranavalona not only an internal threat but also a form of treason. During most of her reign, relations with the predatory British and French became worse as the Malagasy government tried to resist commercial or armed aggression. The Merina government under Ranavalona was under continual threat both internally and externally and defended itself as best it could, keeping contact with Europeans at a minimum. The Christians were inevitably under suspicion of collaborating with the enemy. Shortly after Ranavalona's reign began, all the missionaries were expelled and the government tried to make up for the loss of the 'missionary artisans' by employing Europeans, such as the Frenchman Laborde, who had no ties with either his government or the missions but who, none the less, had technical skills (Deschamps 1972, p. 165).

As a result of the threat they were seen to pose, the Christians under Ranavalona became a persecuted but growing minority, cut off from the foreign influences that had introduced the religion to the island in the first place. In such circumstances Merina Christianity developed an independent character both in its theology and its social implications and struck deep, if somewhat unexpected roots, made sacred by persecution and martyrs. It is both ironic and revealing that Christianity became truly established during the very period when missionaries were excluded from Madagascar.

If the political history of the reign of Ranavalona had a direct significance for the growth and development of Christianity this was equally so for what Christianity came to be seen as opposed to: Merina religion. It is not too much to say that it was Christianity that created 'Merina religion' as an entity in itself, distinct from other aspects of society. This is expressed extraordinarily forcefully by the reported speeches of Ranavalona herself. For the first time Merina ancestral custom was seen as something to be valued against the threat of something else: Christianity and European encroachment.

The Merina had previously not distinguished between their politics and religion, because their culture, like all others of this type, did not separate these aspects. As a result, they did not believe in the genuineness of the alleged distinction between them made by the missionaries for their system. Indeed, the dubious activity of several of the missionaries made such a distinction particularly unconvincing. But the effect of the attack presented by Christianity on the Merina state meant, ironically, that the Merina were forced by the dialectic of the situation to talk of 'their religion' and 'their custom' as though they were distinct entities. This was partly for internal consumption, so that something could be contrasted and valued against the foreign import. It was also partly for foreign consumption, in order to convince outsiders that the Merina were not lacking in religion, and in order to impress with the splendour and coherence of their cults.

The political situation did not only affect how religious activity came to be seen as a whole. The content of this religion, at least in so far as it concerned the state, changed too. This was not only as a reaction to Christianity but also as a result of the establishment of the Merina state as a large-scale bureaucratic and military institution.

The religious innovations were principally of two sorts. The first concerned the so-called palladia, the *sampy* and the medicines derived from them, the *ody*. The *sampy* appear to have been basically of two kinds, either fashionable cults imported from outside to strengthen the king by their virtue, or semi-independent localised cults of rather indeterminate 'medicines' (Vig 1969). *Sampy* had always been associated with royalty, and *sampy* keepers from time to time helped various rulers. From the time of Andrianampoinimerina and especially under Ranavalona the royal *sampy* cult seem to have increased in importance and become internally organised to form some kind of priesthood of rather low status. At the same time, local *sampy* with their keepers were gathered at the palace after the area had been taken over by the Merina, thereby making military conquest the same thing as religious conquest. These local *sampy* added to the royal *sampy* created a highly complex system that has been recently analysed by several historians (Domenichini 1971, Berg 1979, Raison-Jourde 1983).

The other facet of the development of a state religion under Ranavalona was the growth of various state rituals into ever grander and more complex occasions. This manifested itself in the yearly ritual of the royal bath but especially in the circumcision ritual, the subject of this book.

The reign of Ranavalona, in so far as it concerned Merina religion, therefore saw the elaboration and development of all aspects of state religion. The trend was already clear in the time of Andrianampoinimerina, but under Ranavalona the process increased in both speed and extent, in a totally new way.

The development of 'Merina religion' and the unsuccessful persecution of Christians paralleled the isolationism of the Merina in the face of European attempts at domination, whether economic or political. The only factor working in favour of the Merina during that period was the intermittent rivalry of Britain and France, which gave this national policy some degree of success. From 1854 on, however, the overall attitude of the Malagasy government to the outside began to change, in part because growing pressure from Britain and France and the temporary understanding between the two imperial powers made it clear to the Merina that they could no longer afford to ignore the possibility of a joint attack. As a result Ranavalona cautiously opened various doors to the outside world so that by the end of her reign the policy of isolationism had been largely abandoned. This change reflected a period when internally, too, her own power was weakened, principally in relation to her various 'prime ministers', a series of related politicans who managed to control the kingdom more or less directly through their influence and wealth. They had been in evidence throughout her reign, but at some periods it looks as though the queen herself was largely in control, although this was not the case for the second half of her reign.

The most obvious manifestations of Ranavalona's weakness and of Anglo-French intrigues were the various attempts to influence Ranavalona's appointed heir, the future Radama II. These took extraordinary forms, involving among many others the famous Austrian traveller and adventurer Ida Pfeiffer, whose journey was well analysed recently by F. Esoavelomandroso (1981), and such colourful characters as French priests masquerading as piano teachers. These activities on the part of Europeans did in the end lead to a lessening of the persecution of Christians, but they had no visible effect on the development of Merina religion, as far as can be judged from our sources. Indeed the demonstration that Radama II was Ranavalona's chosen heir took place at one of the largest and most innovatory royal rituals ever seen: the prince's circumcision. This will be discussed in detail in Chapter 7.

Radama II finally did come to the throne in 1861, but instead of the installation of the Europeans' favourite leading to a lessening of tension the stage was set for one of the most extraordinary episodes in Merina history. The reader needs to turn to the recent descriptions by F. Raison-Jourde (1977a)[1] to get some idea of its flavour. For our purpose here it is sufficient to note that this short reign was a period when all controls over internal and external influences seem to have been removed, resulting in a vague modernistic chaos and attempts by foreign powers to take what advantage they could. Radama II tried to ignore the political and economic realities that had constrained his predecessors and were to constrain his successors and as a result his reign was a brief and odd interlude without lasting significance. This state of affairs seems to have brought about two very different conservative nationalist reactions.

The first was a kind of popular millenarian movement called the *Ramanenjana,* which occurred in 1863. This movement was violently anti-European and was motivated by a mystical belief in the 'return' of Ranavalona I and the reassertion of 'traditional religion' under her second kingdom. The notion of 'Merina religion' had by then become clearly formulated. We saw how it had begun to take shape as a result of Ranavalona's self-conscious rejection of Christianity, which had led her to value an alternative. By the time of Radama II's reign the reversal of this process meant the rejection of previous 'Merina' practices and led to their final conceptual formation as an entity with a rationale of its own – in other words, as something like an independent religion in opposition to foreign Christianity (Raison-Jourde 1976), a comparison that made both alternatives seem to be the same kind of thing. The outward manifestation of this simultaneous realisation of the existence of such an entity and its loss through undisciplined innovations by the king was a movement described by the commentators of the time as 'dancing mania'. Individuals became possessed by unnamed spirits, which made them dance until exhausted. The possession was catching and was passed on from person to person. The dancers could not bear to see anything European and especially anything in any way connected with Christianity. They often asserted that Ranavalona was still alive and that she would come back and drive out all things foreign. This kind of possession has been and is still fairly common in Imerina. What was exceptional about the *Ramanenjana* was the scale of the epidemic, and its clearly overt political content. The movement culminated in a huge march on the capital by people from the countryside who believed themselves to be carrying on their heads and shoulders the luggage of the returning Ranavalona, mystically present in their midst; on arrival she would reassert her reign. The chaos that this movement caused formed the background to Radama II's murder.

The irony of this situation is that we get the strong impression that the forces that had once fed Christianity under Ranavalona were the same as, or similar to, those at the source of the anti-Christian *Ramanenjana,* which brought to an end the reign of Radama II. The reason for this was simply that when Ranavalona's government represented itself as 'traditionalist' the opposition was Christian, whereas when under Radama II the government proclaimed itself pro-European the opposition became traditionalist and indeed pro-Ranavalona. This, however, is less strange when we remember the character of Christianity under Ranavalona. It had always been a Malagasy movement, not a European movement. It could even be represented as a 'traditional' movement, going back to the more pro-Christian time of Radama I's reign. In any case the root cause of opposition remained the same. The expansion of the Merina kingdom led and continued to lead to ever greater exploitation and opposition and there was always a fund of discontent to coin a variety of forms.

In terms of the development of Merina religion this period is important in many ways. First, it increased the self-conscious character of traditional Merina religion, making it an 'alternative' to Christianity. Second, it brought about a division in the previously total unity of traditional religion and politics. Radama II himself was either a sceptic or a metaphysical experimenter. He was interested in all the religions he could find out anything about and he was greatly amused by sectarian disputes within Christianity. He even took an interest in atheist and radical ideas from Europe. His view of 'traditional' Merina religion was equally contemptuous, and he refused to take part in the great state rituals developed by Ranavalona or to countenance the *sampy* cults. Merina religion, however, continued, to an extent, under his reign but without the participation of the court; it became a matter for common people. This made religion for the first, and last, time in pre-colonial times an institution separate from the Merina royalty.

If the *Ramanenjana* was one popular reaction to the Europeanisation of the kingdom under Radama II, the other reaction was less picturesque but historically more significant. Radama had been put on the throne by the powerful major-domos of the latter part of Ranavalona's reign, the 'prime ministers.' During the melodramatic events of the reign these people and the group they represented faded into the background for a while. But when it became clear that phenomena like the *Ramanenjana* were threatening the very basis of royal authority, they initiated their own traditionalist revival, although in this case the initiative was firmly in the hands of government. When Radama II refused to cooperate, they murdered him in 1863.

From the time of Radama II's death until the coming of the French, one or another prime minister controlled the country. This was done indirectly by the device of putting a woman from the royal family on the throne as queen, and by the prime minister's 'marrying' her.

The rule of the prime ministers was also characterised by a renewed attempt to put into practice Ranavalona's old policy, and to control the ramshackle empire of the Merina through the traditional means of corvée labour and military power. The problem of the relation with the European powers was, however, still unresolved. The end of the reign of Ranavalona and the reign of Radama II demonstrated that the British and the French could not be kept at arm's length and that they were determined to enforce their growing control in Madagascar. The Merina state was all the time becoming more and more dependent on the administrative, industrial and military technology from abroad, the original reason that had caused Radama I to invite the British in the first place. Once it became clear that it was no longer possible to keep the Europeans out, the 'prime minister' revived the alternative strategy, that of playing off the British and the French against one another. This proved possible only to a limited extent, and ultimately the whole policy collapsed, when the British and the French allied and made a deal that gave the French Madagascar in return for a British free hand in Zanzibar. The deal led to the French invasion, but long before it the British and the French, as well as other foreigners, had been increasingly encroaching on Merina sovereignty, thus making the last years of independence a humiliating experience.

The death of Radama II therefore caused a reappearance of the political situation that had been faced by Ranavalona towards the end of her reign, and this was also true in religious matters, which as always were closely linked with the political situation. The state religion again became 'traditional Merina religion' and the Christians yet again formed an organised threat to both the religious and the political aspects of the kingdom. The Christians, however, were much more powerful after the death of Radama II than they had ever been under Ranavalona because by then they were far more numerous. This was in part an indirect result of the continuing bureaucratisation of the state, which grew both because of the way bureaucracy feeds off itself and because state matters became more and more concerned with complexities of administration and foreign relations. One form of Christianity in Madagascar had, from the first, been closely linked with administration because of its role in education and the spreading of literacy. This link was renewed after the death of Ranavalona and the missionaries established a very large number of excellent schools. However, there was a new element:

24

Politico-religious history of the Merina

The period was marked by the coming of far greater numbers of missionaries than had been the case before and also by the establishment of Christian churches in the remoter parts of Imerina. This meant that the administration of the church itself grew dramatically and quickly rivalled that of the state in scale and efficiency. Christianity appeared to the authorities, therefore, as an indispensable aspect of national organisation, which could only be excluded from civil administration at the cost of renewed chaos.

In 1869 a solution was found to the threat posed by the institutional existence of Christianity – and it was a radical solution. The solution was to make Christianity the state religion by means of the public conversion of the queen and the prime minister. In this way the organisation of the church came directly under the control of the state and could be used by the state for its own purposes. As a result, on the religious front Christianity of the Protestant Congregationalist variety grew rapidly. Instead of being persecuted it became encouraged in no uncertain way by the civil authorities and grew between 1869 and 1895 to become the framework of the administrative structure of the state. The missionary schools became part of a wider organisation providing compulsory civil and military training for the future administrators and soldiers of the Merina empire. The missionaries became, more or less willingly, technical administrators, advisers and almost partners in the Merina state. At the same time the 'traditional' opposition to Christianity was largely, if only temporarily, disarmed; as the state religion, it was no longer easily represented as a dangerously foreign influence or as an attempt to undermine the legitimacy of the ruler, as had been the case under Ranavalona. It was only later that the Merina began to realise that the conversion was not simply a matter of the Merina state using Christianity as it had used other cults, but that it really meant the beginning of a process by which the Merina ruling classes were abandoning their subjects by aligning themselves, and finding a place, in a totally new proto-colonial order. The 'traditionalist' argument regained currency, but by then it was too late.

Making Christianity the state religion had of course religious implications as well as political ones. The most important of these was that Merina Protestant Christianity became a compromise, and that the contrast between Christianity and pre-Christian religion was not emphasised officially by the government as it had been previously, but was actually played down. This was true not only inside Madagascar but also outside. The Protestant missionaries who had gained such prominence as a result of the royal conversion made themselves the spokesmen of the Malagasy and of their 'civilisation' to the outside world and especially to the British public. This was in part due to the fact that as the missionaries achieved such success from their association with the Merina rulers, they also became ever more fearful of the implications of possible colonisation, even by their own countries, because such colonisation would lead to a loss of the direct influence that they exercised through their partnership with the Merina state.

The rather ambiguous nature of Merina Christianity after 1868 is reflected in

25

the way the missionaries dealt with non-Christian practices and beliefs. In the case of certain elements of pre-Christian religion, such as the *sampy* and the *ody* 'medicines', they were implacable in their opposition. The role of the *sampy* has been well discussed by Berg among others (Berg, 1979). They consisted of symbolic objects representing an imprecise supernatural entity and were guarded by various ritual specialists. These *sampy* were in turn the source of the power of medicines and charms of a more personal nature: the *ody*, which gained their protective power by being placed in contact with the *sampy*. The role of *sampy* and their associated *ody* was principally as instrumental supernatural powers that could be used for various ends, and their instrumental nature explains well one of their characteristic features. They were permanently 'on trial' and therefore permanently changing – coming into and going out of favour. If they proved their worth, they were kept; if not, they were got rid of, often burnt. This is most likely why the Merina, probably unconsciously, directed the attention of the missionaries to them, because *sampy* and *ody* were elements of their religion that were 'in question'. The missionaries for their part clearly wanted to change religious beliefs, but they had found themselves in something of a quandary in Imerina. From the first European missionaries continually complained about the vagueness of Merina beliefs in supernatural beings, whether gods or ancestors. They felt unsure what they were attacking. The *sampy* seemed to be the only obvious target, and they identified them as the 'enemy' fairly early, clinching the process by describing them as 'idols', a term that was particularly charged with unfavourable overtones for fundamentalist Protestants, always on their guard against not only the idolatry of pagans but also that of Rome. The *sampy* cult was thus defined, by a process of mutual accommodation, as the battlefield between the traditionalists and the missionaries and when the latter won in 1869 the *sampy* of the court at any rate, and any others easily available, were duly burnt.

The *sampy,* however, represented only a small aspect of Merina religio-magical life, and focussing on the *sampy* meant that, by and large, other aspects were left alone by both the missionaries and the Christian state. These other aspects involved beliefs that in many ways appeared so fundamental to the Merina that they could not be in question, whereas the missionaries for their part felt, probably for that very reason, that they were best left alone. This is easily explained when we remember that the missionaries were largely dependent on the Malagasy during the period of the Christian state. They could not, as they did elsewhere, turn for support to their native countries for this would have involved inviting these countries to Madagascar, and thereby destroying the basis of their influence. They therefore left well enough alone and hardly commented on a whole range of beliefs that in many ways seem more fundamental than ideas about the *sampy*. Beliefs of this kind concerned the significance of the tomb and the ancestors in them, the idea of ancestral blessing, the notion of witchcraft, which is intimately linked with ideas about the tomb (Bloch 1971a), and certain beliefs about kinship and incest.

As a result Christianisation for the Merina meant adding to beliefs and practices. Only in a few areas was this a matter of replacing old beliefs and practices by new ones. It would also be necessary to look carefully at which parts of the Christian religion offered by the missionaries were taken up and which ignored to understand fully the significance of the wholesale conversions that took place following the queen's adoption of Christianity. This would require a detailed study, but a few points are fairly clear. For example, many commentators have remarked on the prominence of the Old Testament in folk Malagasy Protestant theology and the lack of emphasis on New Testament themes such as the passion.

The period from 1868 to 1895 was, therefore, in the religious field, dominated by state Protestantism, and what challenge there was came mainly from the growing influence of Roman Catholic missionaries, who inevitably became a focus for much the same forces as had centred on Protestantism under Ranavalona, and 'traditionalism' under Radama II. These Catholic missionaries had begun to arrive in significant numbers after Ranavalona's death. It is often said that as far as Imerina was concerned their influence was limited to the slave population. There is some truth in this, in that the total merging of state and church during the latter half of the nineteenth century meant that church membership came to be equated with citizenship. As a result the government authorities were very reluctant to allow slaves to become members of the state church, as this more or less implied their freedom. This, however, is only part of the story. In a belated effort to keep a balance between France and Britain, the Merina government, in spite of its official Protestantism, never totally turned its back on Catholicism because it believed, not altogether accurately, that the French were backing the Catholics and the British were backing the Protestants. Quite apart from this there were also a certain number of free Merina, who for various reasons favoured Catholicism even after the queen's conversion. Often this was a means of expressing some sort of very limited dissent.

If a kind of religious *modus vivendi* was achieved during this period, this was less so in the political field. Internally the problems of administration and of growing opposition continued unabated. Externally, however, the greatest threat remained the imperialist designs of Britain and France, which increased throughout the period until the French invasion of 1896 and were only tempered partly by the opposition in France to colonial wars (Boiteau 1958, pp. 182–7) and partly by the rivalry between Britain and France. This rivalry, however, greatly diminished after the French defeat of 1871 and especially after the treaty of 1890, when Britain and France agreed on mutual spheres of influence, leaving Madagascar to France. From then on Madagascar was left at the mercy of the sordid intimidation of France, egged on by Réunionais commercial interests.

Such external pressure led to further internal difficulties because the commercial and military bullying by France led to ever greater exaction by the Merina government, anxious, alternately, to appease the foreign powers by granting them concessions or to attempt some sort of military resistance, which required increased taxation and military service. Furthermore, the evident weakness of the Merina government and its accommodation of foreign interests made it fall under suspicion of collaboration from the nascent nationalist movement, a factor which aroused yet further disaffection. These internal weaknesses led to the relatively easy fall of Madagascar in 1895 to the French. At first the French attempted a protectorate but this was rapidly followed by a complete direct colonial government under the governorship of Gallieni.

The effect on religion of the fall of Madagascar is complex and needs to be seen against the background of growing humiliation and oppression that accompanied it. On becoming the state religion, the Protestant Church had transformed itself into a government administration, used especially for the recruiting of forced labour and military service. In the process, the corruption and brutality of state officials became totally indistinguishable from the corruption of the church. This meant that Protestantism during the Christian period became something completely different from the religion of protest that it had been under Ranavalona. In addition, the period up to the French conquest was marked by the attempt on the part of the missionaries, aided by the government, to kill off the remnant of the independent Merina Christian tradition that had grown up during the time of persecution. As a result, organisational independence of the native Christian churches was largely suppressed by the government and their theological independence was extinguished by the European missionaries, who became more and more hostile and suspicious of their Malagasy colleagues (Gow 1979, pp. 150–227). In this suppression the missionaries were supported to a large extent by the Merina government, ever fearful of possible forms of revolt.

The reaction to such a situation was twofold. On the one hand, the anti-Christian 'traditional' Merina religion that had been forming throughout the nineteenth century reasserted itself, especially when the French were at the gates (S. Ellis 1985, pp. 68–73), with the old *ody* and *sampy* coming to the fore, probably precisely because they had been so dramatically singled out by the Christians as their 'enemy'. On the other hand, there developed within the Protestant Church itself an anti-European and anti-state religious movement, which seems to have been a continuation of the independent and popular form of Christianity that had existed under Ranavalona. That such a tendency did not simply lead to a revival of the traditionalist religion is no doubt in part due to the genuineness of the Christian beliefs of many Merina who, although opposed to foreign domination and corrupt government, could not for all that abandon their beliefs. The other reason seems to be connected with the growing influence of the Catholics.

As we saw, from the reign of Radama II Catholic missionaries, mainly Jesuits, had increased their influence in Madagascar and, although opposed by the government, they were protected by the French. As a result, they had become something of an antigovernment party and had obtained a certain amount of support both at the court and in the countryside. This Catholic party was in the main pro-French and Jesuit missionaries often acted as agents and spies for the French (Boiteau 1958, p. 193). Thus as the foreign threat to Madagascar became more and more focussed on the French, resentment against the defeatist element in Imerina became focussed on the Catholics. The corollary of this situation was that it became possible to combine Protestantism and genuine nationalism. This probably saved Protestant Christianity, as it meant that it was able to be subsequently seen by some people as something different from the tool of the corrupt royal administration that it became during the days of the Christian state. An example of this type of attitude is illustrated by the famous Protestant pastor Andrianory, who preached to the Merina troops awaiting the final French attack and encouraged them to destroy *all* white 'rats' (Gow 1979, p. 219). The link between anticolonialism and Protestantism was subsequently to have great significance during the colonial period.

The main politico-religious event immediately after the French conquest was a major revolt against the colonial invaders that began in 1896, usually called the *mena lamba*. It was led by traditionalist anti-Christian elements (S. Ellis 1985). At first the *mena lamba* was a loose confederacy of different revolts caused by spontaneous disgust at the weakness of Merina reaction to the French. After a while the rebels achieved a greater degree of internal organisation and for quite a time constituted a major challenge to the French, and became a much tougher opponent than the Merina government had ever been. The *mena lamba* were strongly anti-Protestant because they saw the conversion of the Merina monarchs and the Christianisation of the state as one cause of its weakness before the invaders. They attacked and killed missionaries and burned churches. The French reaction was uncertain until the coming of Gallieni, who carried out a highly effective policy of repression. He assumed, wrongly, that several court officials, the Protestant churches and the rebels were all in alliance, an assumption that led, among other things, to the execution of several leading Merina Protestants. Little by little this repressive policy inevitably brought about the very association Gallieni had imagined: The anti-Christian *mena lamba,* the anti-European Protestants and the remnants of the Merina administration were drawn together in an uncomfortable alliance in opposition to the French and the Catholics. The latter were to make good use of the situation after the defeat of the *mena lamba* at the hands of the French.

This regrouping completed in a new way the apparently easy compromise between pre-Christian Merina religion and Protestantism that had begun at the time of the conversion of the queen. Then the reason for compromise had been that Christianity had been introduced as a kind of complement to state religion. As we have seen, although they were the bringers of a new faith, the missionaries were there on tolerance of the Malagasy rulers and could not antagonise them by attacking certain fundamental beliefs. After the *mena lamba* Protestantism and the pre-Christian elements were further united in that they came to represent nationalist opposition to the French and the Catholics (S. Ellis 1985).

The pattern created by the *mena lamba* rebellion and the French response to it became the dominant framework in Merina religion until independence from France in 1960. During this period the alignments stayed roughly the same and many of the revolts of that period seem to be re-enactments of the *mena lamba*.

Around the time of the First World War the beginnings of a nationalist movement called the VVS[2] began to form. This movement was brutally put down before it had gained much significance. None the less in its occurrence it further sealed the alliance of Protestantism and anti-colonialism that had largely been encouraged by the French response to the *mena lamba*. Many of the leaders of the VVS were Protestant pastors. The Protestant Church, however ambiguous its relationship had been to the Merina state in the past, was all that was left of it. The Protestants represented one of the few genuinely independent institutions at that time that could act relatively openly. There were also a few Catholic priests involved in the VVS and this reveals what was to become even more evident later, that even if the Catholic Church had at the time of the conquest been a direct tool of the French, this became less so with time. In particular there arose within the Catholic Church a growing division between Malagasy and foreign, mainly French, clergy. This did not, however, lead to the Catholic Church's ever taking a leading part in the nationalist movements, because, unlike the Protestant Church, it remained totally dominated by French clergy.

The next major event in the history of Madagascar to concern us here was the revolt of 1947. The effect of World War II on Madagascar was complex and led among other things to a demonstration of the weakness of the French in Madagascar. They had gone over to Vichy and were then subsequently easily defeated by the British. The British then handed over the government to the Free French under de Gaulle. Free French colonial policy during the war was remarkably progressive. This was in part because of American pressure, since the United States chose to represent itself during this period as anticolonial. It was also partly due to an attempt to gain the support of the colonial people for their side. As a result the French promised many of their colonies, including Madagascar and Indochina, a great degree of independence. But as soon as the war had been won and a Gaullist government was in control in Paris, they went back on their promises. In Indochina this led to the beginning of the Vietnam War, and on Madagascar it had a similar result, which, however, was less clear cut in origin and less successful in outcome.

Much work still remains to be done on this rebellion, which led to the death of probably eighty thousand people, but we do possess a very valuable study by J. Tronchon (1974). Tronchon makes clear that the rebellion was a complex accumulation of different types of movements with ambiguous encouragement

Politico-religious history of the Merina

from various politicians. From the religious point of view the 1947 rebellion combined uncomfortably the traditionalist anti-European, anti-Christian movement with a pro-Protestant movement, and at no time was the religious element the most significant. The ambiguity of the position is well reflected in the letters of someone calling himself the commander-in-chief of the rebels, who ended: 'Down with Rome! Down with freemasons![3] Down with Protestantism, Down with Anglicanism, Down with Adventism, Long Live Rakelimalaza![4] Long Live Madagascar!' (Tronchon 1974, p. 354). In contrast, the oath administered by the rebels combined Protestantism and ancestral religion in a clear unity because it was taken both on the Bible and on earth from ancestral tombs (Tronchon 1974, p. 351).

An equally revealing fact is that the rebellion of 1947 took place at what would have been the traditional time for the ritual of the royal bath. The royal bath was probably the central moment in the royal religion of the Merina until the conversion of the queen. The ritual was continued by the Merina rulers after the queen's conversion, although it became somewhat Christianised (Sibree 1900). The timing of the rebellion was therefore a clear reference to pre-colonial independence. The traditional date for the royal bath had also been the occasion of the *mena lamba* rebellions and so the choice of that day for the beginning of fighting linked the revolt of 1947 both to the independent past and to the first attempt at liberation by the Malagasy.

If the 1947 revolt was not a particularly religious affair at first, the association of Protestantism with nationalism was strengthened, as it had been after the *mena lamba,* by the actions of the colonial government. From the beginning of nationalist activity, but especially from 1940 onwards, the French tried to exacerbate tensions between the Merina and the coastal peoples of Madagascar by employing a 'divide and rule' policy. They therefore chose to identify the revolt of 1947 with the Merina, although all the evidence was against this (Tronchon 1974, p. 164 and passim). Furthermore, the Merina were identified with Protestantism, partly because the Protestant clergy were mainly Merina and partly for the sake of colonialist propaganda, which resulted in an attempt to represent the revolt of 1947 as Merina- and Protestant-inspired. This totally inaccurate version of events was actually partly successful in convincing a number of Malagasy because it indirectly touched on a different, but growing, social division between the largely urban and professional middle class and the poorer, largely rural, peasantry and proletariat.

The colonial period had begun with the political defeat of the Merina, but leading Merina individuals had gained some lasting advantage from their past association with royal administration and Protestantism. Most important was the high level of education achieved in the royal Protestant schools, which served the defeated rulers in good stead in the colony. Important urban Merina also managed to retain considerable wealth after the French invasion. Many Merina, therefore, were soon remarkably successful under French administration, gaining

31

administrative positions and taking advantage of educational opportunities both in Madagascar and in France. This led to the formation of a rich professional middle class, mainly in Tananarive, who also had close links with rich landowners and merchants in other parts of the island. Because of the nature of Merina kinship these people became the social focus of their descent groups, many members of which gained educational and administrative advantage from the prominence of their kinsmen (Bloch 1980). This meant that a substantial number of Merina of free descent in the colonial period either belonged to a bourgeois class or were sufficiently closely associated with it to identify their interest with the interests of that class. At the same time there were many Merina who were not associated with this successful element; this was so for many descendants of free men and for the majority of the descendants of slaves (Bloch 1980). These poor people realised their class situation and to a certain degree realised their common interest with the non-Merina peoples of Madagascar, who with a few notable exceptions, had similarly become poorer and more humiliated during the colonial period. The class structure of Madagascar during the colonial period did not therefore correspond with the division between Merina and non-Merina or with the division between Protestant and non-Protestant, but the situation did have a loose correlation with the division between Protestants and non-Protestants in that Protestantism had been associated with high status in the Merina kingdom and this initial advantage had been transformed and expanded in the new situation. As a result, French colonial propaganda aimed at dividing the population along religious and ethnic lines struck chords that were to become significant later.

The situation so created remained basically unchanged until legal independence from France in 1960 and, indeed, continued during the period up to 1972. From the time of independence to the overthrow of Tsiranana Madagascar was not legally a colony any more, but the old system was maintained as President Tsiranana had been placed by the French at the head of the new independent state. Tsiranana, although originally a Malagasy Nationalist, had been used by the French during the period following the 1947 revolt as a tool of their divisive policy of opposing the coastal peoples to the Merina, who were, as we have seen, represented by the colonial powers as having been the only anti-French element in the population. The extensive financial, political and military backing that the French gave Tsiranana ensured that following the brutal suppression of all nationalist parties after 1947 he and his party were ultimately established as a subject government in Tananarive. These were the people to whom the French nominally handed over power after independence.

The rather phoney independence obtained by Tsiranana gave him a relative popularity for a time even in Imerina, but soon he was faced by growing opposition. Politically the main opposition was centred on a party called the AKFM, which came to be associated with successful Merina and with Protestants. This association was again the product of the propaganda put out by Tsiranana and the French, but it none the less gained credence and brought about what it pretended to describe. In this way the merging of Protestantism and nationalism continued (Raison-Jourde 1983, p. 54).

During Tsiranana's government, however, opposition of another kind was also growing. This came from the poorer classes of Merina society. During the colonial period and Tsiranana's government the poorer people and the bourgeois anti-French nationalists were thrown together, in part by their common interests, in part by the deliberate policy of the French to bunch them together. Towards the end of the 1960s, however, these two partners became more and more antagonistic to each other in the Merina countryside. Although the Tsiranana government was in conflict with the Merina bourgeoisie, they prospered under it. As a result the class conflict between the urban bourgeoisie and the peasants heightened. This was one element which led to the fall of Tsiranana in 1972. The situation also had religious significance (Raison-Jourde 1983, p. 60). It led to a renewal of anti-Christian feeling in the countryside as Protestants, and to a certain extent Catholics, became more associated with rich traders, lawyers and doctors who exploited their rural compatriots whenever they could, and expressed their contempt for them at every turn. In the areas where I did field-work in the early 1960s the churches were leading social institutions and Christian rhetoric dominated much of life. By 1971 this had largely changed. Churches were badly attended, and a new pride in pre-Christian customs, such as the circumcision ceremony, was everywhere to be found.

The reason was that the opposition to the central government had once again taken on an anti-Christian element. This was a fairly complex matter. Most of the people still considered themselves Christian and there were many individuals deeply committed to their religion. On the other hand there was a feeling that central institutions would always fall into the hands of a ruling class of some sort and there was a general opposition to all that this might represent. This feeling in the Merina countryside was only one side of Madagascar-wide unrest, which soon erupted in a revolution that toppled Tsiranana and ultimately led to a different type of government. This book, however, is only concerned with the period up to 1971.

3
Background to Merina social organisation and religion

The historical processes outlined in the preceding chapter have meant that present-day Merina society is extremely diversified. Many Merina live in towns, especially in the capital, Antananarivo; many live abroad in France and Réunion; but many still live in the countryside of Imerina or beyond, often in new lands they have colonised during this century.

The way of life of the Merina and their class affiliations are as varied as the places where they live. There are rich Merina businessmen and professionals and poor urban slum dwellers; there are wealthy merchants and small-scale agriculturalists. What links these people together is their reference to a common historical past, as well as their kinship system, which ensures that some of the ancient groupings are reproduced.

Fundamental aspects of Merina social organisation

The social division coming from the past that is probably still most relevant to them is that between the descendants of freemen and those of slaves. The descendants of freemen do not usually intermarry with the descendants of slaves. This has great significance in that since richer Merina are mainly of free descent, so the marriage barrier reproduces in terms of wealth the difference in precolonial status.

The distinction between slaves and freemen also has importance for kinship. The descendants of slaves tend to form a relatively undifferentiated group. They intermarry freely and kinship ties among them form the typical undifferentiated web of bilateral societies. They have no notion of descent groups. The descendants of freemen, on the other hand, still attach great importance to a vague descent principle, which regulates marriage and forms the basis of social divisions. This fact is closely linked to the continuing importance of rituals such as the circumcision ceremony. It is therefore necessary to describe the basic features of Merina kinship here, although they have been discussed more fully elsewhere (Bloch 1971a, Bloch 1981, Razafindratovo 1971, Vogel 1976).

The basic unit of rural Merina social organisation for the descendants of free-

34

men for most of the period under examination was the grouping I have called the deme (Bloch 1971a, pp. 41–50). Even though the deme is today no longer a grouping of crucial importance many aspects of society and belief that continue to be central can be understood only in relation to what it was.

The deme was a group of people symbolically associated in perpetuity with a specific territory. This territory, its ancestral lands, was focussed on one or a number of irrigated rice valleys. At one level the deme can be said to have owned this land in common, because only members of the deme could be legitimate individual owners, and also because there was a rather vague notion that, although individual rights were the economically significant ones, these were temporary and shifting, as opposed to the eternal mystical identification of the deme as an undifferentiated group and the land as an undivided unity. The deme, therefore, had a territorial aspect and a descent aspect, and it would be totally misleading to try to separate the two, because for the Merina they were, and are, two sides of the same thing.

Thus today the members of the deme are seen as the children of previous deme members, who themselves were children of deme members, back to the founders of the deme, usually shadowy figures from an unspecified time. But the members of the deme are also the heirs to rights to the land of the ancestors since that land is the clearest manifestation of the trust passed on by the ancestors to their descendants. This total equation between descent and ancestral locality is sealed by the central symbol of Merina life, the communal tomb.

Merina tombs must be on the ancestral land of the deme and there is no stronger obligation on deme members than to ensure that the bodies of co-deme dead relatives are buried in these tombs in the ancestral locations. The tombs stand for the permanent unity of people and land; they place the ancestors in the land. It is significant that the Merina do not distinguish between the dead body and the ancestor. For them putting the corpse in the tomb makes the deme land, quite literally, the land of the ancestors. The permanence of this association is marked by the construction of the tombs themselves, semi-subterranean stone structures made to last for ever. The tombs are the focus of the notion of Merina descent and what gives it meaning. The main theme the tombs illustrate is the maintenance of the group through time, the maintenance of the association of people with land. This requires the continual regrouping of the dead members of the deme in the tombs, the solidarity of the living deme members through their attachment to the tombs and to their ancestral lands and the continual regrouping of rights to the land itself, so that it will not be dispersed.

The fear of dispersal and loss of the resources of the deme is a major concern for the Merina; it is linked to an aspect of Merina kinship not discussed so far. Merina kinship is fundamentally bilateral in that both male and female belong to the deme of their parents and both men and women have the right to pass on membership to their descendants. The same applies to the inheritance of land. Although the deme as a whole can be said to have a common right over deme

35

land, effective rights of use, and to a certain extent of disposal, are vested in individuals in nuclear or extended families and these are the rights that are inherited bilaterally. Every marriage thus is a potential threat to the continuity of the deme because if the children of such a marriage are outsiders they might inherit deme land.

The Merina try to overcome the problem by enjoining in-marriage within the deme, and especially between co-heirs of neighbouring land. This strong preference means that demes can be thought of as largely endogamous descent groups in which membership is ideally obtained through both father and mother. Demes have many attributes in common with cognatic descent groups, but are marked by a strong tendency to endogamy, explicitly and emphatically intended to ensure the non-dispersal of people and rights to land. Allegiance to the tomb and the duty to regroup in it the bodies of the ancestors is complemented by the duty not to dissipate the land of the ancestors; this too can be achieved only through in-marriage. To the Merina all these elements are merely different sides of the same categorical duty to the ancestors.

While the deme is an important and continuing element in Merina social organisation this does not mean that it has continued unchanged during the historical period that concerns us. The nineteenth century was dominated by a continuing struggle between the centrifugal pull of the state and centripetal pull of the demes (Bloch 1983). Throughout this period the demes tried to maintain their political independence and to protect their members from the growing exactions of the state, whether these took the form of taxation, corvée labour or military service. The state on the other hand tried to control the demes in order to ensure an increasing supply of these and to eliminate possible foci for rebellion. By and large, the whole of the nineteenth century seems to be characterised by a stalemate between these two competing forces.

The effect of Merina expansion on demes was far from neutral. As the Merina kingdom grew territorially, more and more deme members became involved in military and administrative service outside their ancestral territory. Meanwhile, in order to ensure continuing agricultural production in Imerina, the freemen away on government service were being replaced by a growing number of slaves. This meant that as time wore on, the demes were no longer just groups of people living and cultivating a demarcated area of ancestral land but, rather, groups of people who had rights in common to land they did not cultivate themselves but that was cultivated for them by slaves. Such a development, one would have thought, would have led to a diminishing importance for the demes, and there is no doubt that this was partly the case. During the twentieth century, however, deme unity was given new significance that in many ways reversed this trend.

The French conquest led to the further geographical dispersal of demes as many deme members became involved in trade and professions and began to rise in colonial society. This success was due to the educational advantages many free Merina possessed at the time of the conquest. It occurred however in a political context that was generally hostile to the Merina, who were identified with nationalism and anti-French feeling. Part of the Merina reaction to this hostility was to maintain traditional group ties for mutual support and mutual advantage (Bloch 1968b). As a result, demes and group membership have continued to have sociological importance and their corporate ideology with its focus on ancestral land and ancestral tombs has been maintained as a focus for a dispersed group of people.

The present-day situation is fairly complex. It is no longer the demes themselves that are strongly valued but, rather, the ideas associated with them, today applied to much smaller effective groupings, usually focussed on one tomb. These ideas include the importance of attachment to the tomb and the placing of the dead in the ancestral tomb; the maintenance of continuity; the recognition of the authority of elders, the avoidance of marriage to outsiders, which might lead to dispersal of assets; and the rule that ancestral land and houses on that territory should not be sold to outsiders.

The day-to-day manifestation of this concept of descent is extremely varied. It is totally different for middle-class urban dwellers than it is for peasants. In the rural area where I did field-work, local people identified with a vaguely delineated group of a few hundred people, often scattered over several localities. All members of this group were believed to belong to the same deme. They shared two or three tombs built close to each other in the ancestral territory of the deme and each local segment (local family) recognised the authority of one or more elders. The local family and the larger groups were seen in terms of the values of the deme: dependence on the ancestors, of whom the elders, called 'fathers and mothers', were the representatives, the need to keep together and to keep resources together against the threat of outsiders and of the divisive tendencies within the group.

Descent groups are only one side of Merina kinship, both theoretically and in fact. In contrast, local groups and individual households have a patrilineal bias that goes against the undifferentiation of descent, owing to the fact that marriages should be, and in most cases are, virilocal, even though the marriage ritual elaborately, if unconvincingly, denies this (Bloch 1978). This means that closely related households in any one particular locality tend to be related to one another by cumulative patrifiliation, and also that effective elders, those who have authority over a local grouping of the deme, are usually senior in the patrilineal line.

The other aspect of kinship that goes against the cognatic emphasis of the descent group results from the Merina theory of biological kinship. The Merina traditionally believe that at birth humans, like plants and animals, are only matrilineally related. This 'biological' kinship links children to their mothers and to their siblings, and exists irrespective of any conscious action. It explains why children of two sisters, that is, matrilateral parallel cousins, are thought to be particularly close, and why as a result sexual relations between such cousins are particularly incestuous. For the Merina, biological kinship stands in contrast with the kinship of descent, which is not the result of birth but the product of the blessing that flows mystically from the dead in the tomb, via the elders, to the new generation. The contrast between these two types of kinship is elaborated in many Merina rituals, especially, as we shall see, in the circumcision ceremony.

The most common representation of this contrast is in the symbolic opposition of the house to the tomb. The tomb is the symbol of unity and permanence of descendants of the deme, of its lack of differentiation and division, and should be made of stone to stand for ever. The house, however, is the focus of individual nuclear families, whose very existence threatens the unity of descent and in theory, if not always in fact, should be made of perishable materials. The house, and the household it contains, is focussed on an individual married pair and marriage is always a potential point of dispersal and change. The fact that it leads to patrilineal groupings that have relations of affinity between them is one aspect of the divisiveness of households; even more stressed is the fact that it is the site of individual birth. This makes the house the focus of matrilateral biological kinship, which forges individual ties that disrupt the unity and permanence of the group.

The household and the house, therefore, are seen as divisive of the unity of the deme: They represent a more limited focus of interest, which is antagonistic to the egalitarian united deme. Individual houses are associated with particular lines of filiation, as they are associated with individual nuclear or extended families. Individual households are further identified with individual rights to land, which are potentially antagonistic to the communal right of the deme.

If, by and large, the tomb stands for descent unity and corporateness and the house stands for kinship and division, there are none the less several qualifications to be made. The most important, from the point of view of this book, is that a similar kind of contrast exists within the house itself. Merina houses are traditionally oriented so that windows and doors face towards the west, with the door to the south of the window. Furthermore, the internal organisation is such that the hearth is to the south of the house, while the holiest part of the house is the north-east corner, because the north-east is the direction of the ancestors and the tomb. The north-east is the direction of the ancestors and the tomb. The north-east corner of the house is therefore a little like the tomb itself. Invocations to the ancestors are addressed to the north-east corner. Medicines and other highly valued objects are kept there, often including the first fruit of the harvest. People should sleep with their heads pointing towards the north-east, with the head of the house sleeping closest to the north-east corner and other people further away in descending order of precedence. The same applies to sitting arrangements: The more respected and more senior people always sit to the north-east of less important and less senior people. (See Figure 3.1.)

The holy north-east corner contrasts with the south part of the house, where the hearth is associated with women and heat. As the house is to the tomb in the

38

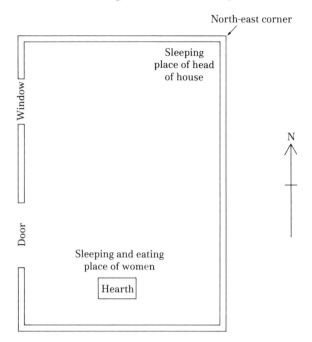

Figure 3.1.

primary contrast, so here the south of the house is to the north-east, and this opposition carries the same association of sanctity and order on the one hand and division, women, kinship and heat on the other. This is all elaborately acted out in the circumcision ritual.

Merina religion

The most important feature of the religious life of present-day Merina is that they are Christians. The great majority of Merina belong to one of a number of churches, the two most important being the Protestant heirs of the Congregationalists, and the Catholics.

In the preceding chapter I noted how church attendance has varied at different periods during the twentieth century, but only a very few Merina would describe themselves as other than Christian. This declaration is borne out by relatively high church attendance. For example, in 1962 more than 40 per cent of the people of Ambatomanoina were regular communicants. These people also held fairly orthodox Christian beliefs, although they differed from a European congregation in the relative emphasis placed on particular aspects of those beliefs. The only feature of their religious life that an outsider might consider clearly unorthodox was that they held non-Christian, as well as Christian, beliefs.

39

From blessing to violence

Whether or not these beliefs and practices were understood to be in conflict with Christianity varied from person to person, and a similar divergence was found among ministers and priests. On the whole, in the countryside, no conflict was seen to exist between Christianity and most of the non-Christian beliefs and practices, and this is still the case today. This is in part due, as we saw, to the history of the conversion of the Merina; it is also due to the fact that these non-Christian beliefs and practices seldom directly contradict or clash with Christian ideas. When they do clash, everybody recognises that there is a problem, but such conflict is rare because these beliefs and practices are, and are seen to be, part of family life and kinship. They cannot be challenged without challenging the very principles on which normal existence rests.

The rituals where these beliefs are manifest are beyond question for the ordinary Merina, and so Christianity could not honestly oppose them. In any case most of these rituals by now incorporate Christian elements such as hymns and prayers, proving clearly to the participants their compatability with the teachings of the various churches.

The non-Christian beliefs and practices stand in contrast to Christianity in only one way: They are non-sectarian. That is, they are shared by everybody and although they differ from family to family, these differences are not the basis of disagreements. As a result, in looking at these ideas, it is largely possible to ignore differences between Catholics and Protestants and even between different classes and social groupings.

The first and most important concept that we must look at when we consider these non-Christian beliefs and practices is the one that underpins the notion of the deme and of descent; this is what might be called the cult of blessing.

The central notion of the cult of blessing is the image of the continuity of the undivided deme associated with its undivided territory. Every generation is seen as a caretaker of the deme and if it maintains it, by avoiding division, its force will continue; in other words, this force or creative power will be passed on from generation to generation as a blessing.

The Merina word for blessing is *tsodrano,* which literally means blowing on water, and to understand it, it is best to look at the simplest possible *tsodrano.* This occurs whenever a junior asks to be blessed by a senior member of the deme, for example, a grandchild asking a grandparent. The causes of such a request are varied. The grandchild may be going off on a long journey, perhaps to study abroad. More simply, the grandchild may feel that things have not being going his way for a while and that he therefore requires the blessing of the ancestors.

First, the elder invokes the ancestors. Normally this does not mean calling on specific ancestors from the near past, for to do this would be to stress particular lines and would, as we saw, be divisive. Instead the elder invokes the ancestors as a whole, often naming only particular ancestral localities or tombs rather than individuals as the source of blessing. The invocation may take place anywhere,

40

but if the blessing is of particular significance it will take place at the communal familial tomb. The person giving the blessing first asks God and the ancestors to transmit all the blessings of the good life to the person being blessed. He lists strength, health, wealth, good crops, large herds and, above all, the power to continue the kinship group through many children. He therefore asks for seven boys and seven girls, the number seven standing for a fortunate number in general.

After the invocation at the tomb the elder takes water, which may have been left some time on the ancestral tomb, and puts it in a container. He then places a coin or silver with it. These objects are all associated with the mystical force of primacy called *hasina* (Bloch 1977a). It is a force of excellence, of essence, and is associated with high rank and even royalty, but also with the power of blessing in general. The elder tells the person being blessed, 'May you be rich, may you be strong, may you have seven boys and seven girls.' Then he either takes the water in his mouth and blows it on to the person blessed, or simply blows over the surface of the water so that it sprays the receiver. This is the *tsodrano* proper, the blessing, literally the blowing on of water.

The central element of the blessing is the transference down the line of generation of the power, the life force and the fertility of previous generations. These previous generations are in the tomb; they are the source of the blessing. For those for whom Christianity is really important, God, rather than the ancestors, is the ultimate source, and this is often noted in the speeches of blessing. The blessing coming from the ancestors is transmitted by the elder, who, because of his age and seniority, is an intermediary between the dead and the young. It is experienced as the purest manifestation of the love of the ancestors for their children. Blessing is essentially hierarchical, and although the hierarchy is one of age, it is also seen as one of authority because the two things are ideally indissoluble. Since all hierarchical relationships are merged in the one idiom of filiation, it is natural for political superiors to bless their subjects in the way that grandparents or parents might bless their offspring.

There are, however, other elements in blessing that are not connected to the relation between succeeding generations. Those other elements are represented by the water itself and by the coin. The coin, as we saw, is associated with the virtue of primacy and supremacy and therefore simply strengthens the power of the blessing. The symbolism of the water is, on the other hand, more complex and significant.

In Merina symbolism water is associated with the unappropriated fertility of the land. This may be contrasted with the rather different notion of the fertility of the deme and its appropriated land. The opposition is represented in terms of tombs. At one level the Merina consider each deme to be eternally associated with a given piece of land, and the proof of this association is the presence on this land of tombs used by the living, but containing the remains of previous generations. The maintenance of these tombs and the duty to place and regroup

41

the dispersed dead in them ensures the continuation of life-giving power; they contain the fertility of blessing. But the Merina also admit that ultimately they are not the autochthonous owners of the land. They are really conquerors who came from elsewhere and took the land from the people living on it. This notion contradicts the primary symbolism of the tomb, which emphasises the eternal link between the deme and its ancestral land. It demands recognition of a distant and mythical past when other, non-Merina, people lived on the land and had *their* tombs in its soil. Indeed their tombs are often believed to be found whenever anybody comes across the remains of an ancient tomb with no living owners. A large number of natural sites, especially streams and lakes, are also believed to be the tombs of these ancient peoples.

These autochthonous but defeated peoples are called Vazimba, and any early inhabitant to whom no genealogical link is claimed is classed as Vazimba. This belief has caused a lot of trouble for innocent historians who have tried to discover exactly who the Vazimba were (Berg 1981), not realising that any dead person who does not have descendants to continue his line is by definition a Vazimba. Thus rulers who are known to have existed in the distant past but who are not thought of as direct predecessors of the present royal line are termed Vazimba rulers. Similarly, groups quite recently displaced by invading Merina are called Vazimba. This is also true of demes that do not fit in the overarching genealogy that in the far distant past connects all Merina. In any given area any tomb not kept up by a group of living people is a Vazimba tomb. But tombs that are not kept up tend to become overgrown and sink into the ground, according to the Merina, and there is therefore danger that wherever one goes one might inadvertently step on a Vazimba tomb, the worst thing one can do to a tomb.

The notion of Vazimba carries with it certain implications. Vazimba are really the first owners of the land; so they must be the ultimate masters of fertility. But because they are not connected genealogically to living groups and because they have been defeated militarily by the ancestors of the Merina, they cannot transmit their life potential in an orderly way to pious descendants. Vazimba power is random, unregulated and potentially disruptive. As a result, one may inadvertently cause offence to Vazimba, especially by stepping on their forgotten tombs, and they then send disease and above all barrenness. By contrast, with luck and offerings, one may end the negative influence they exercise in retaliation for a breach of taboo connected with them, and thus effectively coax them into curing or giving fertility. This means that throughout Imerina there exist a whole variety of Vazimba cults and it seems that these have been gaining in importance. In comparison with Christian practice, these cults are a matter of individual and largely instrumental devotion and, with a few notable exceptions, they are not organised. Vazimba cults are especially concerned with fertility or rather the lack of it, caused by something somebody has done, probably unknowingly, of which the Vazimba disapprove. The fertility they withhold is of all kinds – crops, cattle, and so forth, but above all children. In particular women who are barren

42

Merina social organisation and religion

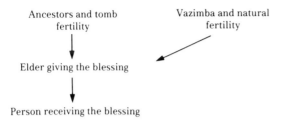

Figure 3.2.

or have an insufficient number of children, either through low fertility or high infant mortality, are often thought to be afflicted by the Vazimba. As a result, Vazimba cults are usually dominated by women.

The Vazimba, however, represent something more. Because of their generalised asociation with territory, they are rather like nature spirits. They are associated with the fertility of all uncultivated things, whether plants or animals, and particularly with wild cattle, which it was the monarch's privilege to hunt. These cattle, the *omby mahery*, or strong cattle, are seen as a typical symbol of certain aspects of the Vazimba strength, power and vitality. Above all, the Vazimba are associated with water, which like them is seen as powerful, active and unbounded, and symbolically stands for everything to do with them. This explains why streams and lakes are the sites of so many Vazimba cults.

It is this element that enters into the symbolic construction of the blessing, because the blessing is not simply a matter of establishing contact between different generations; it also involves blowing on water, water that is often specifically taken from Vazimba cult sites. It is this element too that is added to the ancestral fertility. The power of the Vazimba element is a wild and dangerous power of amoral forces; amoral because the Vazimba are unconcerned with the welfare of other peoples' descendants. In the blessing, however, their power is controlled and contained by the ancestral power. The Vazimba element in the blessing augments but cannot disrupt fertility and blessing, because it flows along such powerful lines of authority. The logic of the blessing can therefore be described in diagrammatic form as shown in Figure 3.2. We shall see that this simple logic underlies all the rituals that the Merina class as being *tsodrano*, or blessings, circumcision being one of the most important, where the element of the violent conquest of the Vazimba comes to the fore.

In order to understand further the implication of the central symbolism of blessing it is necessary to look briefly at two other rituals that are said to transmit *tsodrano*, the funerary rituals and the ritual of the royal bath.

Merina funerary rituals have been extensively discussed elsewhere (Bloch 1971a and 1982) and the reader should refer to these studies for details. Here I shall mention only those aspects relevant to an understanding of the circumcision ceremony. Merina funerals are often double. First the corpse is temporarily interred,

43

and much later a more important ceremony, the *famadihana,* involves exhumation of the corpse and its entry into the communal tomb.

This entry into the communal tomb is what makes the *famadihana* a ritual of *tsodrano.* It is a regrouping of the dead in the ancestral land and therefore it is a supreme act of maintaining the deme, since avoiding its dispersal is a key theme in the deme or *tsodrano* cult.

The *famadihana* is an act of *tsodrano* not just because it involves blowing on of water, which is only marginal here, but because the placing of the deme member in the tomb strengthens the eternal existence of the deme. The placing of the corpse in the tomb canalises the force of the dead and transfers it to the living so that they may receive the blessing: wealth, happiness, strength and above all children. This is made explicit at various stages in the ritual and is acted out clearly when, at the end of the ceremony, young women, desirous of children, steal little bits of the mats in which the dead had been wrapped and hide them under their beds in order to conceive quickly. In Merina symbolism, therefore, the entry into the tomb represents the victory of the continuity of the deme over the death of individual members.

In the funerary rituals the image of the enduring potency of the deme is dramatically constructed by contrast with its symbolic antithesis. This antithesis is, as we might expect, represented by women and houses. Women and houses are linked in Merina symbolism and the inside of the house is seen as a particularly female, maternal type of place. The first funeral, which occurs immediately after someone dies, is focussed on the inside of the house. The corpse is placed to the north-east of the house and is cared for and looked after principally by women mourners during the lengthy wake. After the wake the corpse is usually temporarily buried to 'dry', as the Merina stress. At the time of the second funeral, which normally takes place several years later, the disinterred corpse is again brought back to the house, and again it is surrounded by mourning women. When the time comes for the corpse to be taken to the tomb, it is carried out of the house on a journey of rejoicing. Here again the role of women is crucial. They have to carry the corpse until it enters the tomb, but for this to happen they have to be ritually driven forward by men. The whole journey seems to involve a physical and emotional assault on women. It is as if the journey to the tomb is achieved over and against the world of women and all it represents. Finally, when the tomb is reached it is dominated by men. Normally only men stand on it and go inside it. The actual entry therefore acts out the transferral of the body from women to men.

The role given to women is explicable in terms of the symbolic opposition of the unity of the deme represented by the tomb, and the division of kinship represented by the house. This division is brought about by individual filiation and marriage, both thought of as associated with birth and women.

This representation of women in the funerary rituals, which is also clear in the ritual of the royal bath and the circumcision ritual, does not mean that women have an exceptionally low status in Merina society (see Bloch in press c). In fact, in many ways the opposite is true. Because Merina women inherit and because they do not normally marry outside their group, they have, compared with many people in the world, exceptional political and economic power. This, however, is not reflected in the symbolic role they are given in ritual.

In these rituals women act out the symbolically constructed femininity of houses associated with division, maternal kinship, death and decay. They are, however, acting only an element that is present in all human beings, male or female. In the same way men at certain critical stages represent the blessing of the ancestors as opposed to the kinship of the flesh, but they too are composed of both elements. It is therefore essential to remember, as is all too often forgotten in anthropology, that the roles that people act in rituals do not reflect or define social status. Rather these roles are part of a drama that creates an image and that needs to be created because in many ways it contradicts what everybody knows. For the actors too, the humiliation of women is bounded by the role they act in the ritual; it is not 'all of themselves' that is involved. Indeed in so far as the rituals under discussion are a drama that creates the enduring entity of the descent group, and since women are both members of the descent group and transmitters of membership in the descent groups, the victory over impermanence and death that the rituals as a whole represent is also their victory. None the less it would be misleading to ignore totally the fact that it is because of the ambiguity of the status of women especially in relation to the patrilocal group that they are particularly suitable actors for the negative role, and we shall return to this point.

The *famadihana,* the ritual of the entry into the tomb, is first of all a ritual of *tsodrano* where the blessing is largely constructed by antithetical symbolism. It is important also to consider briefly how such a ritual act co-exists with the Christianity of most of the participants. It is impossible to give a history of funerary rituals in the way that will be attempted for the circumcision ceremony in Chapter 7, as the research for this has yet to be done. However, it is clear from my field-work that as far as ordinary Merina are concerned, there is little conflict between *famadihana* and Christianity. The *famadihana* does not imply any clear belief in ancestral spirits as such. It involves practices like the return of corpses to the land of their ancestors, which the Merina know are not entirely absent in the European countries that serve them as Christian models. The *famadihana* can and does accommodate moments for prayers, hymns, even readings from the Bible. More important, however, it deals with a world of experience, emotions and beliefs that does not seem to compete or correspond with the experiences, emotions and beliefs of Christianity. This is the product of the religious history examined in the first part of this chapter.

The other great ritual of blessing we must briefly consider in order to understand the circumcision ritual is the ritual of the royal bath (for a full study see Bloch in press b). Until French rule this was an annual ritual occurring at the turn of the lunar year. Its central aspect involved the ruler taking a bath in water

45

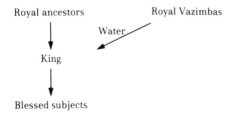

Figure 3.3.

brought from lakes where Vazimba queens were believed to have been buried. The water was brought to the palace by a group of youths 'whose father and mother are still living' (see Chapter 4), who symbolised the continuation of descent. Because they are important in the circumcision ritual, their significance will be discussed later.

Once the water had been brought the ruler, having visited the tombs of his predecessors and taken some earth from them, took a ritual bath just at the time when the new year was to start. After that the monarch filled a sacred horn with the water from the bath and blessed his assembled subjects with the water by spraying it on them.

The royal bath was followed by somewhat similar practices in every household in Imerina. Taking part in the ritual of the royal bath was a mark of political allegiance as well as an occasion for the paying of taxes (Bloch forthcoming b).

The ritual of the royal bath follows, on a larger scale, the logic of the simple blessing already discussed. The king similarly invokes his ancestors at the tombs of previous rulers. He places water associated with the Vazimba in contact with his body and later sprays his subjects (spoken of as children) with this water. In this way, as the ritual speeches make explicit, he passes on to them the benefits of blessing (see Figure 3.3).

It is important, however, to note here the transference of the symbolism of the blessing from the deme to the state. The equation between the two is very close. Of course the political effect of such a transference is to link the ruler to his subjects by a system of ideas that are at the very centre of their familial emotions and beliefs. This use of deme rituals for royal rituals is something we shall find again in the circumcision ceremony, where the ruler is paralleled with the elder and the state with the deme in a highly significant way.

The historical development of the ritual of the royal bath is again largely unstudied, but from the little we know it is clear that its history parallels the history of the royal circumcision given in Chapter 7. In particular, we know from numerous sources that the royal bath was greatly elaborated during the reign of Ranavalona I (Ayache 1976). Unlike the royal circumcision this ritual certainly continued after the conversion of the Merina monarch. The symbolism of the royal bath, like that of the circumcision ceremony, was recalled and emphasised in the revivalist aspects of nationalist revolts, especially the *mena lamba* and the 1947 revolt.

The circumcision ritual to be examined in the next chapter is therefore part of a ritual and religious configuration centred on the notion of blessing and is intimately linked with the concepts underlying Merina ideas of descent and kinship. All the ideas, beliefs and emotions linked with this complex configuration have a history and political significance. It is in order to gain more accurate insight into this wider history that we shall be examining these ideas, beliefs and emotions in detail in our focus on the circumcision ceremony.

The reason the circumcision ceremony rather than the ritual of the royal bath or the funerary rituals enables us to do this is simply that it is the only major ritual of blessing that has both had an uninterrupted history for the two-century period under examination and also had a continuing direct link with the wider political context.

4

Description and preliminary analysis of a circumcision ritual

The Merina circumcision ceremony is always described as a ritual that, like the second funeral and the royal bath, dispenses blessing or *tsodrano*, and as we shall see, its overall form is indeed governed by the pattern of Figure 3.2, which represents the notion of Merina blessing.

During field-work among the Merina in and around the village of Ambato-manoina (Bloch 1971a), I attended nine circumcision rituals, and of these I have detailed notes on five. All were different, but they shared the same fundamental symbolic structure. The significance of the variations between these different occasions will be discussed in Chapter 7. In order to examine the basic structure of the ritual, the present chapter concentrates on a description and preliminary analysis of just one such ritual, which took place in 1971. This particular occasion has been chosen because it was the most elaborate of the rituals I witnessed and because, since I was by then familiar with most aspects of the circumcision, I was able to understand what was happening more fully and to record it in more detail. In Chapter 5 a more general consideration of the overall pattern of the ritual will be undertaken.

All Merina boys are circumcised between the ages of one and two, and almost as soon as a boy is born people begin saving to organise a circumcision ritual. It is inconceivable to the Merina that boys may not be circumcised but it is precisely because it is inconceivable that it is difficult to get people to tell you why it has to be done. It is rather like asking people in Europe why they do not eat dogs.

Some sort of answer can be obtained or implied, however. People may simply say that it is the custom of the ancestors and leave it at that. In another context people say that circumcision makes boys 'sweet or beautiful', *soa*, or 'clean', *madio*. The ceremony is sometimes called *mahasoa*, that is, making *soa*. This is a euphemism for the proper word for the ceremony, *fora*, which, as far as I know, has no other meaning.

More explicitly, I was sometimes told that the ceremony made the children involved into men, and once I was told that before the ceremony the boys are like girls. I was also told several times that the ceremony is essential to make

Description and analysis of a circumcision ritual

boys potent sexually, but this was after much prodding. However, I could get no explanation why the prepuce was cut and there seems to be no folk rationalisation for the specific nature of the practice. There was much comment and amusement about the fact that the Europeans they knew, the French, were not circumcised, but I never heard any suggestion that this means they do not function properly sexually or in other physiological ways.

The most common answer I received to the question of why people practise circumcision was quite simply that circumcision is a blessing, a *tsodrano*. At first sight this has nothing to do with the practice itself, and so for a long time I ignored its significance, thinking it little more than a pious generality designed to put me off some more precise reason. However, it is clear to me now that this is indeed a very direct and profound explanation and one that should have led me to the central characteristics of the ritual. A Merina whose work has only recently come to light, long after my field-work, says precisely the same thing in writing generally about circumcision in the 1860s: 'That night is to be used in invoking of blessings for the children' (Raombana 1980, p. 47). The first task in explaining the ritual is therefore to show what is meant by saying that the circumcision ceremony is a 'blessing'. First, as will be demonstrated in more detail later, the ritual as a whole follows the same pattern as that given in Chapter 3 for the *tsodrano*, in that it involves the transfer of ancestral power by water. This is also true of *tsodrano* or parts of *tsodrano* performed during the ritual. Second, pointing out that circumcision is a *tsodrano* is a way of relating the practice to other rituals of *tsodrano*, of which the second funeral, the *famadihana*, is the most prominent. Once an informant, despairing of making me understand the essence of circumcision, actually said that it was 'like a *famadihana*'. By this he meant that the *famadihana* and the circumcision ceremony were both rituals of *tsodrano*. In fact, as we shall see, even more was implied, since the two rituals continually cross refer to each other in their symbolism and also at certain key points in the actions they require.

When the parents of the child have saved enough money, and when the right season has come, they go to an astrologer to choose a propitious day and night for the ceremony. The astrologer in choosing the date takes into account the 'destiny' of the child, that of both his parents, and possibly several other factors of lesser importance. He always chooses a time during the cold season in the months of June, July and August. The idea of cold is extremely significant, but this period is in any case the period for all major Merina rituals of *tsodrano*, and it occurs conveniently after the harvest has been brought home, when people dispose of significant amounts of money.

More than one child may be circumcised at a time, and in the case that I describe here two boys were circumcised. This is not exceptional; it occurred because two closely related boys happened to have been sufficiently close in age to make it possible and so diminish the expenses for those involved.

The circumcision took place in a small hamlet some thirty kilometres east of

49

From blessing to violence

Ambatomanoina. The hamlet was entirely composed of members of the Andria-mamilazabe deme, who are numerous in this area. The people attending the ritual numbered approximately two hundred and fifty and were, with few exceptions, members of this deme. They had come from all directions and included people from Tananarive and other distant urban centres, as well as from rural areas where Andriamamilazabe were then living.

The geographical heterogeneity also reflected class heterogeneity in that amongst those present there were teachers and traders and one graduate student from Paris, who was visiting his family. The bulk of the participants, however, were relatively well-off peasants and they dominated the proceedings. All the people present considered themselves to be close kin and knew each other well, mainly from similar ritual gatherings.

I had come with a group from a hamlet near Ambatomanoina and I also knew nearly everybody present. Two of the people I had accompanied were to take leading roles as elders in the ritual and some of the girls were to act as 'mothers of the child' (I explain this phrase later in this chapter). On our arrival we were received by the people of the hamlet who had, as usual, prepared a reception centre. This was a roughly built marquee of branches and banana leaves in which benches and a table had been set up. Here we went, like the other guests, to hand over our contribution towards the cost of the proceedings. Most people gave some rice and between fifty and one hundred Malagasy francs per household. All this was carefully noted down so that the recipients could reciprocate at a future date.

Some people have to contribute much more lavishly but they tend to do this in advance so that their money may be used to buy the rice, coffee and above all the cattle that will be consumed during the ceremony. These major contributors are close relatives of the parents of the child, or children, to be circumcised. A son-in-law who has taken his wife to live away from her parents' home and a son who similarly lives away from his parental locality have a special duty to contribute heavily, to make up for the division of the family they have caused (Bloch 1978).

This duty on the part of those who have left serves to emphasise how the circumcision ritual is, like all rituals of *tsodrano*, a ritual of kinship unity and indivisibility. All these rituals are premised on the idea that the group undivided will go on for ever, because its unity will canalise and transfer fertility to the new generations. In spite of the importance of the notion of group unity, however, it is often not clear what 'group' is involved. At one level this undivided unity seems to apply to the deme as a whole, but in fact rituals of unity and blessing that genuinely involve all the deme are practically non-existent. The deme is only a vague ideal of an undivided group. The other level that might be referred to is the group that gathers at rituals such as the one under examination; it is composed of members of the deme but is only a small fraction of it. This group, in spite of the idea of unity and boundedness that dominates the notion of

50

blessing, is actually a fairly fuzzy and indefinite one. The fuzziness is obscured, however, because the group is talked of throughout the ceremony as if it were the deme as a whole. It is rather like a street party in England on a day of national rejoicing. Through the force of rhetoric and emotions, the crowd in the street becomes the nation united beyond its usual divisions. On such an occasion it is not the unity and distinctness of the street that is celebrated by the gathering but the unity and distinctness of the whole nation, for which the empirical group stands.

In Imerina a similar feeling holds for the smaller groups that are composed within the deme. For example, members of a group who have buried their dead in one tomb talk as though that tomb were the only tomb of the whole deme, although there may be several hundred. Thus, when asked in general terms, people assert that any member of the deme may be buried there, though in fact this is not so.

All rituals of *tsodrano* like the circumcision give dramatic emphasis to unity and indivisibility, although what is united remains relatively unspecified. As a result a child's move on marriage away from the parental home, and usually to another village of deme members, can in some contexts be represented as an offence against the indivisibility of the deme as a whole and requires compensation in the form of larger contribution.

The group that gathers at a circumcision ritual represents the whole deme and the undivided extended family at the same time, although it corresponds to neither. From the time of arrival all act in a united way, eat together, prepare their hair and their clothes together and, above all, cook together; so far as they are concerned they are, for the time being, the deme as a whole.

The cooking at such a ritual is very different from everyday cooking. This is not only because of the luxuriousness of the food, which is referred to as 'drinking cattle fat together' – fat being the most highly prized food – but also because the cooking is done communally outside and by men. Normally cooking is done inside the house for each individual household and is almost exclusively a task for women. By contrast, at a ceremony such as this, a big hearth is set up outside tended exclusively by a large group of men who cook in large cooking pots, which are usually old fifty-gallon petrol drums. The cooking is accompanied by bawdy joking and has much of the atmosphere of a stag party. When, as in this case, there are very many guests, the cooked food is distributed to them on trestle tables outside.

The contrast between the united men cooking outside and the divided women at their hearth inside is, as we shall see, one that underlies much of the symbolism of the circumcision ritual because the outside is associated with the deme together as an undivided unit whereas the house is associated with women, individuals, kinship and division.

In the case of the circumcision I am describing nothing much happened the day we arrived apart from participation in the party atmosphere, which developed as more and more people arrived, food was cooked, served and eaten and coffee and rum was drunk. As the evening drew on, songs were sung in a progressively more sleepy way. The night passed as people snatched a bit of sleep, gossiped, drank, sang and no doubt found all kinds of other ways in which to enjoy themselves. The next day was for the most part much the same and people kept on arriving. It was taken up by and large with the immediate preparation for the ritual itself, which only properly began at around three in the afternoon.

The preparations therefore take place in an atmosphere of growing excitement and revelry, heightened by the promises of the smell of roasting coffee, the taste of rich food, the intoxication of rum and the exhilaration and tension of familial reunion. Both the places where the ritual is to occur and the people who are to play a role in it have to be made ready for the occasion.

In a ritual like the one I witnessed in 1971, which took place in a fairly small hamlet where everyone is related, the whole hamlet was cleaned up and the houses tidied and perhaps even repainted to receive the many guests. Two houses, however, always receive special attention. The first is the house where the circumciser, called the *ray ny zaza*, 'father of the child', hides during the night of the ritual. The circumciser is usually an expert, who performs the operation for a fee. This means that he is usually an outsider, although generally a deme member, and this is heightened by the fact that he must not be seen by the child or children to be circumcised. He hides in his house during the night, comforting himself with food and drink and occasional visits from elders or other men, who may see him so long as they do so discreetly. The other special house is much more important because this is where most of the ritual occurs.

Preparation of the house of circumcision

The house where the circumcision ceremony is to take place is usually that of the parents of the boy to be circumcised. The preparations of this house are externally much like those for any large gathering. In general there is only one living-room inside the house, measuring, as in this case, eight metres by five. The room is prepared, as it is for all ceremonies, by placing clean mats on the floor and also probably on both walls and ceiling, while any impedimenta are stored out of harm's way.

More significant is the preparation at the north-east corner, the corner of the ancestors, which is the holiest part of the house analogous to the tomb. All ritual occurring inside the house is actually directed towards this corner, and there a set of important plants is placed.

These plants fall into three categories, according to who is responsible for bringing them. Some are brought or specified by the astrologer, who has been consulted to find the right day. Some are brought by the parents of the child. Others are stolen by a group of youths 'whose father and mother are still living'.

52

Description and analysis of a circumcision ritual

All are placed carefully in the north-east corner the day before the night of the circumcision.

The plants supplied by the astrologer are 'medicines' and are intended to ensure that the operation will be successful and that the whole event will be trouble-free. These plants are part of recipes based on the complex pharmacology of Merina ritual experts. They are secret, not part of the public symbolism of the ritual, and therefore they need not concern us here.

The plants obtained by those in charge of the preparation of the ritual, often the parents of the child, are all wild. The ones that are to have an important part in the circumcision ritual are the following. First, a large number of long strands of a type of rampant grass that sends out suckers from already growing strands: This grass (*triticum repens*) is called in Malagasy by the word *fandrodahy*, which literally means 'which ties the male', a term referring to its role in the circumcision ritual. The strands selected for the ritual must be long, approximately thirty centimetres in length if possible, but most importantly they must be strands with a 'living mother'. What the Merina mean by this is that the strand must be an offshoot of another living strand.

The symbolism involved in the notion of 'being of a living mother' is central to the symbolic role of several other plants used in the circumcision, and indeed central to the ritual itself. This grass, like all other plants chosen in the ritual, is thought of as highly prolific, and this aspect is continually stressed by informants. Equally significant, however, is the notion that the plant is of a 'living mother'. This relates to the belief that natural fertility is almost exclusively matrilineal, a belief that recurs throughout Merina and indeed Malagasy thought (Huntingdon 1973). We have already seen it to be relevant to Merina notions of kinship, and we shall return again to it later.

Apart from the grass, which is essential, almost any other wild plant that is both prolific and 'of a living mother' may be placed in the north-east corner. At the 1971 ritual there were several. There were papyrus shoots (*zozoro*), especially chosen because they were offshoots of large plants, 'of a living mother'. Another reed, *fotatra*, which is similarly thought of as prolific (Razafimino 1938, p. 37), was also added. The pods of a tree whose name I failed to catch were added; these too, I was assured, were 'of a living mother' and particularly fruitful.

The reeds brought as young shoots are associated with the notion of quick growth, but some reeds, *bararata* in Malagasy, are brought fully grown. These reeds are associated with water, in which they grow, but also more directly with the autochthonous water spirits, the Vazimba, because they are believed to have sprung up in the lakes where the Vazimba queens were buried. These are also the places where the kings obtained the water for the royal circumcision. *Bararata* reeds are used in the ritual of measuring the child but are also made into *fototra*. *Fototra* are *bararata* reeds, one end of which is dipped in cattle dung so

53

that they look like gigantic matches. In the circumcision rituals I observed they were just left with the other plants in the north-east corner. The name *fototra* is, however, significant. It means the root, or the source of life of a thing, or a person. The symbolism of the *fototra* seems to be complementary to that of the young, prolific plants in that it stresses the origin of the source of fertility. In the past these *fototra* were burned, but I never saw this done (Richardson 1885, p. 207). Some bark from a tree called *somangana* was also collected in long strips and placed with the strands of grass.

In this ritual, but in no other I witnessed, a stick of a plant called in Malagasy *hasina* (Latin *Dracaenae*) was also included. The word *hasina* is highly significant in that it means 'holy' and 'powerful' and is associated with the essence of superior rank that differentiates demes (Bloch 1977a, p. 124, Délivré 1974, pp. 140–63). In this case its significance came from the fact that it originates in the east coast forest, where the Andriamamilazabe believe themselves to have lived in the past. I was told that this bit actually came from near one of their tombs in the forest. Be that as it may, it is an example of one of the more individual touches that groups and individuals add to the basic elements of the ritual. In powdered form the plant is often used in medicines for reviving vitality (Razafimino 1934, p. 37).

There is a third category of plants that must be put in the north-east corner. These are cultivated plants, which share the characteristics of many of the wild plants; they are also thought of as particularly prolific, and they, too, must be 'of living mother': They are a special gourd, bananas and sugar-cane.

The gourd is of particular importance in the ritual performance. It is a small gourd with a narrow neck approximately twenty centimetres high and dried in advance. It may have been grown for the purpose or bought from a market stall selling traditional medicines. The Merina call this gourd *arivo lahy*, the 'thousand men'. One thousand is a symbolic number signifying many. 'A thousand men' is a phrase customarily used to describe a large and powerful army. The name indirectly refers to a famous proverb and I was told occasionally that the full name of the gourd itself was actually the whole proverb: *Arivo lahy tsy maty indray andro*. This means literally 'a thousand men do not die in one day', which is taken to mean roughly 'unity is strength' (Houlder 1960). It is the motto of Tananarive, the capital of Madagascar, whose name literally means 'the town of a thousand'. It is none the less important to note exactly what kind of unity is implied in the typically Merina sentiment expressed in the proverb. It is unity through the continuity of the group, which transcends the discontinuity of the individual. The proverb is commonly quoted in speeches and homilies about the unity of clans or tomb groups, where it is used to express the famous principle that 'corporations never die'. This gourd is normally prepared and dried by the parents of the boy, who hang it over the hearth many months before the ceremony. It thus becomes an ever-present promise of the coming of the ceremony and Merina often become quite lyrical over this aspect.

54

Description and analysis of a circumcision ritual

A similar gourd is also used by the Merina for a whole set of other minor ceremonies concerned with the fertility, health or productivity of cattle and rice fields. These rituals will be analysed in a future publication but what is important here is that they too are formed around the symbolism of the *tsodrano* and that the gourd acts as the container for the water with which the cattle, the land and perhaps the people will be blessed.

The remaining two kinds of cultivated plants are banana and sugar-cane. Unlike the other plants supplied by the astrologer or the parents of the child they are supplied by a group of young men who are to play a significant part in the ceremony. The name that denotes these young men means 'of living father and living mother,' and, indeed, to be selected for the role a young man must have both his father and mother alive. He must also be unmarried. These young men are significant in many myths and rituals but nowhere as prominently as here. I shall return to this subject later.

Different, too, is the way the young men 'whose father and mother are still living' obtain the plants: They must steal them from unsuspecting neighbours. They first obtain a supply before the beginning of the ceremony on the preparatory day but they may continue to steal more, if necessary during the night. In all cases, however, they must steal them from nearby gardens and so start a chain of violence that characterises the fate of the bananas and sugar-cane during the whole proceedings.

The youths must obtain first of all a young banana tree with a large head of unripe bananas. These must be particularly numerous. The fronds of the tree are usually chopped off so that only the trunk, a few unsullied leaves and the head remain. The tree, like the grass, must have a living mother; in this case it means that the parent tree of which it is an offshoot must still be living. The youths must also bring several sugar-canes with the fronds still on them. These should be chosen because they have many knots on them ('eyes' in Malagasy); the knots are compared to children because from each one will come a sprout when the canes are planted. Again, therefore, as in the contrast of young reed and *fototra,* fertility is emphasised from both ends: in terms of fruitful progeny and in terms of a 'strong' origin, in both cases visualised matrilineally. In this instance, however, a new theme is added: that of the need to do violence, by stealing, to this natural, mother-focussed, power of reproduction.

Special roles connected with the circumcision ceremony

The day preceding the night of the actual circumcision also involves allocating the roles various people are going to play during the ritual.

The main role is that of the circumciser himself. As we noted before, he must not be seen by the child until the very moment of the operation and he is not usually a close relative but simply an expert, although normally a member of the deme. Often he is an expert in several paramedical practices and an astrologer.

From blessing to violence

In this instance, as happens often, he was the astrologer consulted for the auspicious date of the operation. The most symbolically telling aspect of his role is that although he is not closely related to the child or children to be circumcised, he is called 'father of the child'.

This role parallels that of another group of people who are allocated a part in the ritual, that of the 'mothers of the child', *reny ny zaza*. They are a group of young women who have special responsibility for the child during the proceedings, seemingly often taking over from the real mother, dancing with the child on their backs throughout the ceremony. They must be virgins, I was told, but clearly this is not taken seriously, given the choice made on this particular occasion. People however, were emphatic that at the least they must abstain from sexual intercourse during the ceremony, which meant that they were not allowed to go out of the house where the ceremony took place unchaperoned. They had their hair done in a distinctive way. It was bunched in four separate pinnacles from which hung plaits. The top of the four pinnacles was joined by rows of beads, and beads also framed the forehead. I obtained no clear statement as to the meaning of this hair fashion but special hair-styles are often used in other rituals to signify special states. This is, however, the most distinctive hair-style, and as we shall see, in doing their hair in this way the 'mothers of the child' are following a very old custom. Although these girls have no specific ritual acts to perform except perhaps to comfort the child, they take a leading part in dancing and singing and often seem to dominate it. It is believed that their vigour in participation will lead to their fertility, and they seemed to enjoy the proceedings greatly.

At this stage the main point to note is that the role of 'mothers of the child' is emphatically non-biological. The first written reference to the 'mothers of the child' (Callet 1908, p. 788 n. 1) already mentions the taboo on sex associated with the role and this reflects well the emphasis of people during my field-work. Furthermore the non-biological aspect of the 'motherhood' of the 'mothers of the child' goes well beyond their non-sexuality. As we have seen, they should theoretically not have borne children and equally, in contrast to the real mother, they should be more than one, thus representing group motherhood rather than individual motherhood. Of course the 'father of the child', the circumciser, is also a non-biological parent. Indeed, this non-sexual, non-biological nature of the 'parenthood' of circumcision, to which we shall return, spreads to all the participants in that they should all avoid sexual contact during the ceremony, and this is so especially for the real parents of the child, who should, I was told, avoid such contact from seven days before, and until after the wound of the child has healed.

The preparation of the 'mothers' of the child – especially their elaborate hairdressing – naturally takes a long time and it was a main concern during the preparatory day. The other main role in this ritual involves much less preparation. This is the already mentioned role of the *velonraiamandreny*, the 'youths

Description and analysis of a circumcision ritual

whose father and mother are still living'. They must be, as we noted above, precisely this. They are normally adolescents who have not married. The idea behind their role seems to be that they are in the middle of the flow of life between the generations. They are also visualised as being in a stage of their life when they are particularly strong and, equally importantly, free from domestic commitments. At the particular ritual I am describing, the auspicious number of seven such youths were chosen. Their role is not limited to the circumcision ceremony and they are of great importance in Merina symbolism generally. These young men had a role in the annual royal ceremony of the bath when they fetched the holy water of the bath, a parallel with the circumcision ceremony. They killed the sacred bulls (*volavita*) in the sacrifices that preceded many state occasions. They also had roles at royal funerals and other ceremonies. Their task in these rituals is nearly always linked with carrying the water of blessing as it is here.

Perhaps the most central aspect of their ritual significance is, as is so often the case in Merina symbolism, to be found in their name. They are intermediaries between the generations, and it is as intermediaries that they have their greatest part to play. There is, however, even more to it than that. Their name stresses bilateral descent, both mothers and fathers. The significance of this double stress is that it is associated with the unity of the deme, where both sides are joined. The same idea is expressed in the Merina name for elder, *rayamandreny,* which means fathers and mothers (*aman* is an emphatic 'and'). Elders are called by this name irrespective of their sex; it is the fact that both sexes are present that is important because it represents that in the elders the deme is already undivided by sex and marriage, as it will be undivided when in the tomb the living will be merged into one substance. This notion of emphatic bilaterality is also found in invocations to the ancestors, which stress that the ancestors are from *both* the father's *and* mother's side. By their name the youths, too, are identified as agents of this ancestral unity, undivided by time, gender and sex and therefore standing in contrast to the fertility of the plants which are *only* 'of living mother'.

The beginning of the ceremony

At the particular ceremony I am describing, the preparations continued throughout the morning and were followed by a rich meal, consisting of beef and rice, for all those present. After this the atmosphere began to change and clearly the significant part of the proceedings was truly beginning.

The clearest sign of this change was that people began to greet each other in the traditional way appropriate for the circumcision ceremony and stopped wearing hats. Both these acts are particularly significant. Normally it is as difficult to part the Merina from their hats as it would be to part English businessmen from their shoes. The reason for this shedding of hats was, I was told, because they brought bad luck, but more specifically, in private, because if hats were worn

57

the prepuce would not come off easily during the operation. This is clearly an example of Frazerian sympathetic magic, as was the less strictly enforced taboo on wearing red, which I was told ensured that the blood would not flow for too long.

Equally significant was the new greeting. Greetings are of great importance among the Merina. They are never omitted and they always specify with great precision the social relation existing between people. In particular, different ranks greet each other differently. The greeting used at the circumcision must, however, replace all other greetings. It is *arahaba ririna,* which literally means 'we greet the cold season'.

The fact that the circumcision ceremony must take place during the cold months of the year has already been noted, and the symbol of cold is central throughout the ceremony. The cold is said to diminish the danger of the operation and throughout the ceremony people come up to each other and say 'Isn't it cold?' or words to that effect, whatever the weather might actually be like. The symbolic significance of cold and hot is of major importance among the Merina.

Heat is associated with birth; the whole vocabulary associated with the mother about to have a child, and having had a child, involves reference to heat: for example, to look after a newborn child and its mother is 'to make warm' or 'to make to be warm' (Richardson 1885, p. 154). The expectant mother and the mother who has had a child must be kept warm by all means, to the extent that fires are kindled under the bed of the mother in labour and have to be kept up for a period of up to two months after the birth so that both the child and the mother will on no account be cold. For the same reason a little house of mats is built above the bed. The mother and child live in it during this period. It is called the 'hot house' and it is indeed very hot inside one of these.[1] This theme is also found in the medicines for threatened miscarriage, which are intended to be warming through the use of various spices, especially ginger.

The symbolism of cold is perhaps less clear. The notion of cold is associated with tombs and is often mentioned in discussing what death in the tomb is like. Malagasy tombs are massive stone structures partly under ground, and are therefore very cold, especially when entered during the heat of the day. The Merina often mention as a reason for carrying out the *famadihana* that the deceased appeared to them in a dream and that he asked of them new shrouds because he was cold. The stress on cold in the circumcision ceremony therefore associates the ritual with the world of the tomb and thus deme unity; at the same time it opposes it to heat and natural birth.

The beginning of the central ritual

By three o'clock in the afternoon the meal had been eaten, everybody had arrived and people began to gather together outside the house in which the circumcision

Description and analysis of a circumcision ritual

was to be performed in such a way that it was a sign to all that the main ritual was about to begin. What had brought everybody together was that all preparations had been made for a *tsodrano:* a blessing ceremony.

The whole circumcision ceremony is seen as a form of *tsodrano,* but this does not mean that there are not also rituals of *tsodrano,* which by themselves would be complete, incorporated in it. One such is the initial *tsodrano,* which precedes, in roughly the same form, all major rituals such as marriages, new year ceremonies, and so forth. It involves asking for a blessing on the proceedings and the killing of a bull, which will be eaten during the ceremony, although some parts may be distributed to the visitors to take home. The killing of the animal is preceded by a kind of corrida in which the bull is chased, tripped and repeatedly wounded with considerable and apparently unnecessary cruelty. I would hesitate to call this killing a sacrifice, as the actual killing of the animal is not directly connected to the main purpose of the ritual, which is the asking for a blessing; rather it is a demonstration of the fact that a ritual is in progress and is being celebrated with appropriate splendour.[2] None the less, as we shall see, the violence involved in the actual killing, and the subsequent consumption of the meat is of central significance to the ritual in general.

The initial blessing marks the beginning of the ceremony and the period of special contact with the ancestors that it institutes. Thus at approximately three o'clock in the afternoon at the ceremony I am describing the people gathered on the hillside outside the house where the circumcision was to be held. To the north-east of the crowd a bull had been tied up ready for slaughter and to the north-east of the bull a mat had been laid on the ground, held down by a peg in its north-east corner, the corner of the ancestors. By this peg the contact with the ancestors was signified. On the mat was placed a bowl of water in which were submerged uncut silver coins (*ariary tsy vaky*). Uncut silver coins are symbols of purity and holiness, since in the past the Merina obtained smaller currency than the Maria Theresa thaler, their principal coin, by chopping the thalers up into fractions. Uncut silver coins became extremely rare and are kept preciously to this day in all families. Their 'holiness' is still suggestive, as is the holiness of silver, which is associated with the notion of *hasina.*

Once all the arrangements for the initial blessing had been set up – Figure 4.1 shows the spatial organisation – three elders, fathers and mothers, stepped forward in turn to make the speech asking for a blessing. These elders had been chosen partly because of their age, partly because they were important people both politically and in terms of wealth (see Bloch 1971a). They were, however, also selected according to rules that should always be applied at circumcisions and to a certain extent at most large rituals. There were two male elders and one female elder. The two male elders, who spoke first, were respectively associated with the father's side and the mother's side of the boys' family. As is usual, this was something of an arbitrary choice because the two elders were each related on both sides. Also, since there were two boys, although closely related, the

59

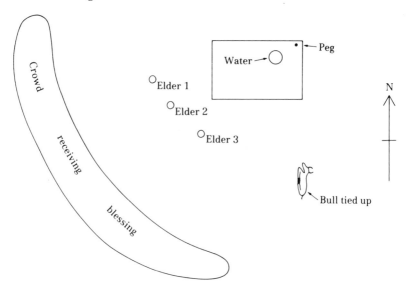

Figure 4.1.

'two sides' were even more artificial. There is, as far as I know, no pattern of strict precedence for the elder 'from the father's side' over the elder 'from the mother's side', although usually it is the former who asks the blessing first, as was the case here. The female elder is always last and is often mildly ridiculed, as she was on this occasion. This is, however, not always so; for example, when the female elder is an influential woman it would be unthinkable.

The explanation the Merina give for the need for these elders is that all sides of the family/deme should be represented: the father's side *and* the mother's side, the men *and* the women. This demonstrates once again the emphatically bilateral and balanced character of Merina demes and it shows also that women, as well as men, are members of demes. This equal membership irrespective of gender is, however, not unproblematic because of the other representation of women as dividers of the deme. It is this contradiction which, I believe, may lie at the back of the fact that a woman is necessary but nevertheless often ridiculed. This is so especially at circumcision ceremonies where, as we shall see, the negative representation of femininity is particularly prominent.

Although the moment when the three elders stepped forward was the beginning of the ritual for those who had gathered at the village, this was not so for the three elders themselves. The previous day they had gone to the ancestral tomb of the family and had already invoked the ancestors. This was a private ceremony with only a few persons present and I did not attend it on this (or any other) occasion. I was told, however, that they had addressed the ancestors with almost the same words as those with which they began their invocation in the more public forum of the village.

The first elder therefore stepped forward and made the following speech (the translation is as close as possible for such characteristically Merina rhetoric):

> To start off with, I must beg your forgiveness for speaking out of turn before you. There is a proverb that says, 'You should not parade in borrowed clothes in front of their owner.'[3] [You should not assume leadership when others present are better qualified.] Since 'I am not a father, I am not an older brother but I am a child, I am a younger brother'. I ask the elders, whom I hold the equal of the sun and the moon, to help me, and I ask of them and of all living beings on earth and below the heavens, all of you present, even all of you who are not present, grant me God's strength. God who created the world, we all invoke him; all of us here who are part of his work. 'We invoke you, God, and your power.' Come quickly! Oh come and see what is being done here! We implore you! We call you that you might be present! We ask for Your help! Oh, hurry, hurry here in answer to our prayers and to our call!
>
> After calling on the power of God we also call on the Ancestors; since although human beings were created in heaven there was a beginning, and they did not come from the sky directly. We therefore invoke you too! We call on you. We call to you to come from the forest.[4] We call in all directions! We call towards the hills! We call Ambohimilatsara, Amboniavaratra, on the tops of the wombs of Anjohy, Fahasihana and also Tsolondrano and Papango. [These are the names of the most important ancestral villages (*Tanin Drazana*, Bloch 1971a, p. 105) of the deme although the emphasis is on those where the people gathered actually have ancestral tombs.] Come Ancestors from these villages! 'Come all of you, for we are calling to you!' Come! Come and join and participate here with us, your descendants! Come and join and grant the demands we make! 'Come and celebrate your strength!' Come and listen to your descendants! Come you trees! [The ancestors are being addressed by the names of the hill villages where they are buried and so the trees that grow on them are used as metaphors for the descendants of the villagers.] We are all your children gathered together here. We know that you do not come because of our power or the power of our asking but you come because of the will of God and of your own volition; Ancestors!
>
> Of this we must remind ourselves whenever we are gathered together, that 'we are but children mindful of our powerlessness'. But let *your* power be here!
>
> We have gathered before you not without reason, but with one aim in mind, to ask for blessings. We ask for your blessing, for your gift of blessing. We ask you to use your power to grant us your blessing. O, come quickly! O, hasten! Forestall our prayers! We beg for your help! The reason why we are here is that we ask for your blessing on us all and more particularly the blessing which you destine for our child [to be circumcised]. O, come quickly! O, hasten![5]

As the speech ended the elder himself blessed first the child and then the onlookers. This consisted in his picking up the plate with water and spraying it either with the hand or by blowing on it. This is the action that gives the word for blessing, *tsodrano*, which literally means 'blowing on of water'. This is what God and the ancestors have been asked to do, via the mediation of the elders of the deme.

After the first elder had performed the blessing he was followed by the other two, who made very similar speeches. The speech of the third female elder was, as we have noted, much curtailed by ridicule. She did however perform the action of blessing. Then the bull that had been tied up after the corrida was killed without any special ceremony and prepared for cooking.

There is one last act in this part of the proceedings, which again is found in all major Merina ceremonies. After the killing of the bull, the mat on which the water of the blessing had been placed is thrown to the women and some men, who fight for it to obtain greater fertility. They tear it as they fight among themselves. This is so that they can put the bits they obtain either on the wall or under their beds.

Discussion of the initial blessing

Before proceeding further with the description of the ritual a few preliminary points should be clarified.

The fact that the invocation begins with asking a blessing of God was of course seen as highly appropriate by the Merina of 1971, all of whom considered themselves Christians, though with varying degrees of commitment; and the Christian element was pointed out to me by a few of the people present who did not know me and feared that I might consider the proceedings as particularly pagan. There is however no question that this part of the speeches was put in for my benefit. It is always present in all Merina invocations.

On the other hand, it would equally be wrong to attribute these references to God as necessarily Christian. The pre-Christian Merina had a notion of one or several creator gods located in the sky and they were often included in blessing invocations (Callet 1908, p. 85, Freeman and Johns 1980, pp. 51–9). What is perhaps somewhat more Christian is the fact that the beginning of the invocation refers *only* to God and to no other pre-ancestral supernatural beings. Such a multiple invocation is often made and includes with God several vague supernatural entities such as 'holy earth'. None the less, as here, the ancestor and tombs are usually the focus of blessing invocation. God is given as an ultimate origin, a kind of ancestor of the ancestors, not directly connected, at least genealogically, to the living.

The other point to note at this stage is the value of the mat for fertility. This is an aspect of the general fertility-giving power of blessings, but it shows that anything connected with the fertility-giving power of the ancestors and its transmission gains, as a result, this life-giving potential. As we shall see this is true of anything used in a ritual such as the circumcision ceremony.

Finally, the anonymity of the ancestors in the invocation should be noted, as it is typical of all Merina religious notions. No ancestor is named, instead we are given the names of ancestral localities, that is, localities in which tombs are placed, and tombs have communal, not individual, reference. The blessing that is asked is from an undifferentiated group of ancestors to an undifferentiated group of descendants. This illustrates well the Merina notion of descent and makes the opposition of descent to 'genealogy' and individual filiation comprehensible.

The beginning of the rituals specifically concerned with circumcision

After the blessing there was a short period of wandering about, greeting old friends and perhaps final preparation of the house and of the hair-styles of the 'mothers of the child' until around six o'clock, when the circumcision ritual itself began. The father and mother of the child sat in the north-east corner of the house in front of the plants that had been gathered. The head of the local kinship group, followed by other people who were to attend the ceremony, approached in a procession as if to visit the parents of the child. After the usual exchange of greetings suitable to such a visit, the head of the local family congratulated the parents on having produced a male child. He then blessed the parents again after a shorter invocation by blowing water on them, and informed them in an eloquent speech that it is the custom of the ancestors to circumcise male children and that is why they have all come.

This second blessing is very similar in form to the one already described and was also briefly repeated by two other elders. The speeches were, however, more specific in their reference to the circumcision and the children who were to be circumcised. The elders tended to adopt the method of speaking called *teny drazana,* 'ancestral speech', which means that they appeared to speak for the ancestors and not for themselves to the extent that sometimes they took on the role of the ancestors, saying 'we the ancestors have come to bless you'.

The father of the child answered by saying that he was aware of the customs of the ancestors and thanked them all for coming and giving their blessing. Everyone then went out of the house and very soon the 'youths whose father and mother are still living', followed by a typical Merina band of pipes and drum, proceeded in a triumphal procession around the village, carrying the banana plants they had brought with them and had previously placed in the north-east corner. Half-way round the boys to be circumcised were introduced to the banana plants for the first time. The children had been dressed in white smocks, perhaps inspired by christening robes, and they were photographed near the banana tree by a rich relative from Tananarive and myself.[6]

After this photographic halt, the real fathers of the children, soon joined by the mothers and the elders, began a traditional Merina dance, which I was told they performed in thanks to the ancestors. As the dance proceeded they scattered sweets to the crowd. These sweets were pounced on by everybody but especially the young women present. As so often in this ritual, it was explained to me that eating these sweets led to increased fertility. The dance was said again to be *tsodrano* and the sweets seemed to be a substitute for the scattered water. Sweets in Madagascar are signs of luxury and plenty and eating the blessing of plenty

A child being shown the banana tree before the beginning of the 1971 circumcision. Note the headdresses of the 'mothers of the child'.

64

inevitably leads to the supreme gift of continuing life: fertility. This dance was particularly significant in that it marked the beginning of the dancing, singing and music that was to go on uninterrupted till dawn the next morning, when the actual operation was performed. Such dancing will be discussed later.

After a period of parading round, the banana plant was carried back into the house and placed in the north-east corner again. From then on dancing continued in the house till morning. If the child is old enough he will take part in the dancing, but if not he will be put on the back of his mother or the 'mothers of the child' and jigged up and down to the rhythm of the music. The Merina deliberately try to tire him out and prevent him from sleeping, as they consider this to have an anaesthetic effect. Be that as it may, very soon after the operation the child falls asleep and sleeps on for a very long time afterwards.

Singing, dancing and music until the ceremony of the fetching of the powerful water (7 P.M. to 3 A.M.)

The singing, which dominates the proceedings throughout the ceremony, is usually accompanied; on this occasion there were also a few periods of purely instrumental music when the singers seemed exhausted. The form of such accompaniment varies according to what the organisers can afford. The simplest ceremonies are merely accompanied by clapping supplemented by home-made instruments such as blankets bundled to form drums and a castanet arrangement of three spoons, two held tight one against the other and a third being pushed between them to produce a rhythmic clicking. Sometimes accordions are played, as they were intermittently on this occasion when the band wanted a rest. Most of the time, however, a traditional Malagasy band of flutes and drums played with varying degrees of vigour throughout the night.[7]

As the music is almost exclusively an harmonic accompaniment to songs, it is like the songs themselves, an endless repetition of never more than two phrases. The songs, the words of which will be considered later, are rarely more than two lines and are for the most part sung in the question-and-answer form characteristic of not only Malagasy but also African music.

All the songs are accompanied by dancing. It is little different from other forms of Merina dancing except that it is nearly all done facing the plants placed in the north-east corner. The child who is to be circumcised may well join in the dancing or will be carried on the back of 'the mothers of the child'. Throughout he will be in front, facing the plants.

Traditional Merina dancing principally involves rhythmic feet movement and movement of the shoulders and arms in a way that is said to imitate the flight of birds. During the circumcision ceremony this dancing is often modified so that the usual arm movements are replaced by a rhythmic pointing towards the north-east corner and the plants placed there, with one arm following the other. All men and women continue dancing and sing as they dance. At certain moments a higher pitch of excitement is reached. This is produced by the musicians increasing the speed of the rhythm and does not mark any special high point in the ritual. Often this higher level of participation is introduced simply to wake people up.

Interspersed in this dancing in which everybody participates there are also interludes of somewhat different dancing by only one, two or at most three people of the same sex. This type of dancing too is not special to circumcisions, but it only occurs at rituals of blessing. The most common form of this 'display' dancing consists principally of shoulder and hand movements while the rest of the body is held tight. This rather static dancing is interspersed with freer, more flowing movements of the arms and legs. It also involves graceful use of the *lamba*, a kind of toga worn by both men and women. This display dancing is similar for men and women but women and men never dance together, only men with men and women with women. Again, this dancing is said to imitate the flight of birds and when the dancers have danced a long time the 'flight' aspect becomes more obvious as the dancers make sounds like that of birds' wings in the wind.

Sometimes this dancing induces something of a trancelike state, and the dancer dances particularly well with his or her eyes closed. When this happens, the chatter and laughter that normally continues along with the music dies away. The other dancers fall away and everyone watches this display of what the Merina call 'ancestral dance'. The dancer is said to have been entered by a *zanahary*, a word that may refer to almost any supernatural being. There is no attempt to find out the identity of this spirit and nobody seems interested. It is simply a moment of grace and mystical beauty for which everyone is grateful.

Another type of occasional display dance is that called the 'fighting bulls', but this is done exclusively by men. Again this type of dancing occurs at all rituals of blessing. The feet movement is freer than in the other dances and the main feature consists in the men raising ther arms above their heads in imitation of horns. The dancing involves a repeated coming forward and retreating that mimes bulls fighting. It is much enjoyed and clearly involves a display of virility and aggression. It is said with relish to be a 'dance of males' (*lahy*).

Dancing is nearly always accompanied by singing throughout the whole ceremony and a great number of different songs are introduced during the night. These fall into two categories. On the one hand there are songs that are specific to the circumcision, and on the other there are songs that might be sung at any other ceremony, or even on no special occasion.

This second category consists of a mixed bunch including folk songs sung largely to while away the time in a pleasant manner, songs learned from the radio, which may be Merina folk songs recorded in the countryside and which the people already know, or folk songs from other parts of Madagascar, or popular songs, the creation of various radio singers. It would be impossible and totally artificial to separate those out; as far as people are concerned these are

Description and analysis of a circumcision ritual

just good songs, fun to sing, to pass away the time, and that is all there is to them.

The first category is different. It consists of songs that are only sung at circumcision ceremonies and whose words clearly refer to the ritual. This is not to say that they are not also considered fun and it would be misleading to suggest that they are viewed with anything like religious awe. These songs are however an integral part of the circumcision and some are essential.

They usually occur roughly in the order listed, but not much importance is attached to a little shuffling. They are often repeated for no very special reason, simply because people like them and cannot think what to sing next. These songs always follow a similar pattern. They are one- or two-line songs repeated again and again with the words often distorted and unclear, although often with some words clearly emphasized by the music. Words emphasised in this way are printed in bold type in the texts. Each song continues from five to ten minutes, sometimes longer. This means that the lines are repeated again and again and again. Then another song is started by somebody, and if the singers are tired of the one they have been singing the new song will be taken up; if not it is drowned in renewed enthusiasm for the old one.

The following list includes most of the songs that were sung between 7 P.M. and 3 A.M. The songs that are specific circumcision songs are marked with an asterisk.

1. *Tsodrano no ilaina:* It is a blessing that we seek.
   (A song that nearly always opens rituals of Tsodrano)
2. (A hummed song with no words)
3. *Tsara ny ani'e fa mijoro tsara:* A good day and I am feeling good.
4. *Faly aho letsy fa tera dahy:* I am happy for you, for you have borne a male child.*
5. *Ani'e! zana m'iray:* Oh! Our child.*
6. *E Azony leroa:* We [are happy] to have got you.*
7. *O'ry mama / De mba hilalao'e, etc.;* O mother, play children, etc.
8. *E nan kaiza / Razana mahalala, etc.*
   (Not understood but refers to famous ancestors)
9. *Ari e! Zana m'iray*
   (A variation of song 5)*
10. (Same as song 8)
11. *Tonga ny zaza indrina e!:* The desired child has come.*

After all these songs had been sung there was a period from 9.30 until 11.30 when no new songs were introduced. It was really a matter of filling in time by repetition. During this time the most important people had left the room with only the 'mothers of the child', the real parents of the children, and the children themselves being present all the time. The men were drinking outside for much of this time.

At 11.30 P.M. things began to become more exciting again. The room filled up and new songs were introduced.

67

12. (Same as song 7)
13. *Voasary lalao:* Play with an orange.
14. *Isy mirahavavy, sambatra ve hianareo?:* O sisters, are you feeling well?*
    (This is addressed to all the *reny ny zaza.*)
15. (Same as song 3)
16. *Tsara ny zaza indrina:* The desired child is well.*
    (A variation of song 11)
17. *E ' loha rano:* [Literally] O head of water [or source of water]
    (This may refer to the living descendants of ancestors)
18. *Maka aiza Razanamala:* Where are you going, Razanamalala?
19. (Same as song 13)
20. *Sevalahy iry manakinky avo:* Male *seva* are growing up.*
    (*Seva* (Budleia fusca): a fast-growing plant associated with masculinity by its name)[8]
21. *Anay' e no mahery:* To us the strong one [the boy].
22. *Godogodon' ity tany ity* / *Any aminay indray raha taona any:* We beat this earth [by dancing] that we shall be here again next year.*
    (This song is accompanied by vigorous stamping, especially by women of child-bearing age. It is understood that by their intense participation in the ceremony they will bear more children and therefore have many more circumcisions to participate in.)
23. *Tsy mamboly, voky ragoika' e:* You do not cultivate yet you are full, O Crow.
24. *Le mahery no anay' e!*
    (Variation of song 21)
25. *E le mahery e e le mahery O'* *
    (Variation on the word *Mahery: Mahery* means powerful and wild)
26. *E 'le mahery tsy azon tsanfona:* Nothing can stop the powerful one, I say he is powerful!*
27. (Same as song 22)
28. *Mazava Atsinanana ny aninnay*
    Anio ahy mandray eto rampitso aho
    Ma maraina e'. Raivo Hiaraka
    Hiany isika izao
    Zozoro tokana e am ny anosy
    Anio . . . etc.
    The East is getting light as we are together
    Today I shall remain, tomorrow I shall leave.
    Raiva we are now together
    But only I shall remain
    A lonely papyrus reed on the shore of the lake
29. (Same as songs 24 and 25)*
30. *Zanak boromahery* / *Manan'atody am bato:* Child of the powerful [*mahery*] bird [*Falco communis*] / Who lays his eggs on a stone.

This song is probably the most important of the whole circumcision ceremony. It recurs most often in the more charged moments and is most often mentioned by Merina when they talk about the ceremony. The name for the bird mentioned is made up from the word for bird, *vorona,* and the word for strong or wild, *mahery.* The birds named in this way are types of falcons and are often given as examples of power. This bird was adopted as a sign of royalty in the nineteenth century. It is believed that it lays its eggs on stones without making a nest, and this is seen as a sign of strength and of disdain for feminine comfort.

31. *Zanakay* **mahery** / *Manan' atody am bato:* Our powerful child [*zanaka*] / Who lays eggs on a stone.* (A variant of song 30)

The word for *child* is transposed with the word for *bird* from time to time in song.

32. (Same as song 25)
33. (Same as song 26)
34. (Same as song 22)
35. (Same as song 28)
36. (Same as song 21)

Discussion of the early songs, 1–36

Several of the themes that have already been touched on emerge from the text of the songs. First of all, the centrality of the notion of *tsodrano* is spelt out clearly in the introductory song 1. It is picked up explicitly again in song 22. This states that participation in the ceremony will make the women fertile, and human fertility is probably the first and clearest manifestation of *tsodrano*. In fact all the songs are seen as being linked to *tsodrano* simply because they are songs of joy, of thanksgiving and of expectation of future success. They look forward to the life of the child to be circumcised and backward to the source of that life: the ancestors. The continuation of life within the group is *tsodrano*.

Second, the songs begin a subtle dialectic around the notion of *tsodrano* that will be further elaborated in what will follow. This argument is centred around the notion of *mahery*.

Mahery is the word that occurs by far the most frequently in songs that are specific to the circumcision. Moreover the singing so emphasises it that if one is not listening carefully the first part of the ceremony may sound like an almost continual repetition of this single word.

Mahery is derived from the root *hery*. It is translated in the standard dictionaries as: strong, robust, mighty, heavy (Richardson 1885, p. 254), vigour, energy, potency, efficacy, surplus, violence, and so forth (Abinal and Malzac 1963, p. 238). I would add to these meanings the notion of 'wild' as opposed to 'domesticated', since wild cattle are called *omby* (the word for cattle) *mahery*.[9] Other animal names may also be qualified in this way to mean 'wild'. Délivré makes an interesting distinction between the word *mahery* and the word *hasina*, which can also be translated as 'powerful' but equally and more centrally as 'holy'. '*Hasina* consists therefore of two elements', concludes Délivré,

one of which is positive and the other is negative; the first is a beneficial force since it contributes to the maintenance of the classical hierarchical superiority of beings who

From blessing to violence

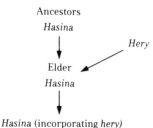

Hasina (incorporating *hery)*

Figure 4.2.

are 'powerful and sacred'. This is the real meaning of *hasina* (the word *hery* can be used to signify it occasionally). The second element is fearful and has the potential to destroy the social order if one does not take care. (That is the usual meaning of the word *hery*.) [1974, p. 147, my translation.]

This extremely carefully phrased passage seems to me to capture exactly the Merina notion in all its ambiguity. I believe the apparent puzzle can be clarified by going back to the explanation of the notion of *tsodrano* given in Chapter 3. There I pointed out that the notion of blessing is principally the canalisation of the power of the ancestors via the intermediary of the person administering the blessing. This was legitimate fertility, which can be described as *hasina;* but I also pointed out how another element, associated with the power of nature as a source of uncontrolled amoral vitality and with the amoral (because they have no descendants) Vazimba, has to be added to the ancestral blessing; but added under violent control. This amoral and therefore potentially destructive force was symbolised by water, itself associated with the Vazimba. Before the water can contribute safely to the blessing, it has to be contained by the elders; then, and then only, can it be blown on to the descendants.

It will be apparent that it is this power that is designated by the word *hery* and, not surprisingly, the word, as we shall see, is associated in the ritual with wild water and wild bulls, both associated with the Vazimba. If we therefore transpose Figure 3.2 to describe the *tsodrano* on to the notions of *hery* and *hasina,* we can see that it illustrates Délivré's point well. We can see how it is possible for the words *hasina* and *hery* both to be opposite at one level, because they represent different sources of fertility (the holy, moral, ancestral as opposed to the wild, dangerous, natural), and to be almost synonymous at another level, because the *tsodrano* merges the two elements.

We shall return to this central point but at this stage it explains what the word *mahery* stands for. It stands for wild, uncontrolled, fertile nature symbolised by water, and bulls. However, after they have been violently mastered *mahery* entities can be used and consumed to contribute to *masina* entities. The ambiguity explains why the water, the fetching of which will form the central part of the ceremony, can be alternatively referred to by the words *masina* (from *hasina)*

70

and *mahery,* although the latter word dominates the first part of the ritual, before the water has been mastered by the spear.

Another animal qualified as *mahery* is the falcon, referred to in song 30. On the one hand it shares with wild bulls and wild plants the uncontrolled vigour of nature, hence the use of the adjective, but in another respect it contrasts with the Vazimba/natural world. One of the most stressed aspects of natural filiation, especially in the circumcision ritual, is its matrilinearity, the fact that it is of a 'living mother'. In contrast, the falcon, according to the song, spurns motherhood and the nest and this is what is emphasised in the second line of the song. In other words, the falcon is a *mahery* creature that has turned away from natural matrifiliation, and as we shall see, this is the process that will be acted out for the circumcised child by the ritual. Because of the falcon's antimotherhood, it becomes a suitable equivalent for the about-to-be circumcised child. This parallellism is stressed in songs 30 and 31, where the child and the bird are deliberately equated by substitution of the one for the other.

Ritual acts in the first part of the ceremony

Even though most of the time between 7 P.M. and 3 A.M. was dominated by singing and dancing several other things happened. Once the singing and dancing was well under way, women crept up to the banana tree and attempted to steal the unripe bananas to take them outside and eat them there. In this, however, they were always interrupted by other women and some men, and a mock fight developed, during which the bananas were broken into little pieces. It was only these little pieces that they managed to take outside, where they swallowed them. Eating these pieces of unripe banana increases fertility, according to the Merina. The fighting involved here, like all other fighting involved in the ceremony, was quite violent but not vicious, and clearly was enjoyable and exhilarating. Parallel to the stealing of bananas by the women was the stealing of the sugar-canes by the men and sometimes by the women also. This was likewise accompanied by a fight as people tried to take the canes outside the house; as the fighting occurred on or near the threshold the canes were broken up and ultimately eaten outside the house. This stealing and fighting was repeated throughout the night.

The pattern only varies if one of the dancers becomes semi-possessed by a *zanahary,* or spirit of an unspecified kind. When this happens, the dancer simply takes either a banana or sugar-cane and goes out of the house unhindered at the end of the dance. Taking of sugar-cane or bananas goes on throughout the night, and so, not infrequently, the supply runs out. When this occurs the young men 'whose mothers and fathers are still living' will be sent out to steal more from nearby gardens in the way that they had done originally.

The symbolism of the taking of the bananas and sugar-cane was never explained to me, but some elements are clearly implied if we put various ideas together. As we have noted, for many other plants used in the circumcision, the

71

qualities that are stressed are that they are (1) prolific and (2) 'of a living mother'. As such, they relate to the prolific fertility of the wild, which they illustrate by the number of their progeny and also by their matrilineal descent. It will be remembered that Merina ideas emphasise that natural descent is entirely matrilineal and that a degree of patrifiliation is achieved only by the transformation of the progeny brought about by a degree of violence, as in the circumcision ceremony.

When we consider the fate of the sugar-cane and the banana plants it will be seen that they have to be violated twice before their blessing or fertility potential can be safely released. First they are stolen from someone's garden, and then they are taken, fought over and broken into pieces; only then can swallowing them lead to fertility. In this they parallel the child, who is described in the early part of the ritual as *mahery*. He too is already powerful and wild (*mahery*), but he has to be fought over and cut before his inherent potential has been turned into true blessing. The parallel between the fate of the child and the sugar-cane and banana plants is even closer in that they, like him, as we shall see, must be violently taken out, from inside the house to outside the house, before their life-giving potential can be released in such a way that it is of value to the descent group.

Two other ritual acts always take place during this part of the ceremony. As the dancing and singing build up, the child who is to be circumcised is handed over to any man present and, to the child's delight, is thrown up in the air while the others present shout joyfully. The significance of this act lies in the fact that an uncircumcised boy should never be raised above the head of a man. If he should, it is believed he would not obtain a penis erection during intercourse and would therefore be infertile. Actually, doing this at this stage slightly anticipates his change of status, but apparently with no ill effects. The throwing into the air is repeated several times during the night, sometimes to wake the child up and sometimes perhaps because he asks for it.

Another ritual act consists in one of the elders taking one of the *bararata* reeds from the plants in the north-east corner and cutting it with a knife, first once then twice so that it falls to the ground in three pieces. This is again accompanied by whooping. This action is called 'measuring the child' because the cutting is done first at knee level, then at shoulder level and then at head level. It is said that unless the reed is cut in this way the child will not grow. The symbolism that seems to lie behind this practice is similar to that behind the banana and sugar-cane ritual. The reeds are, as we have seen, both highly prolific and 'of a living mother'. The reed is made to parallel the child when it is placed next to him. However, before the reed's potential can be released and passed on, it must be cut. Only after the reed has been mutilated does its natural power change from a threat to growth into a cause of growth. The antagonistic yet complementary relationship of natural and ancestor fertility that underlies Merina kinship is once again revealed in all its complexity. The one leads to the other after violence.

72

Description and analysis of a circumcision ritual

At the performance I am describing, the most elaborate that I have ever seen, another ritual sequence occurred at around midnight – one that I witnessed in no other ritual performance. Three elders came in from the house reserved for the circumciser, where they had been drinking. The came in clearly intending to raise the level of the proceedings as everybody seemed to have become rather quiet and sleepy. The began to perform a 'bull' dance with extreme intensity. As always on such occasions the clapping and drumming took on an extremely monotonous hypnotic quality. They danced with great agility, especially considering their age, changing after a while to the bird dance, making sounds like that of birds' wings in the wind. Sweat ran down their faces and in the end they were faltering on their feet. As they danced, which they did for nearly half an hour, the elders were handed a bottle of water. This, I was told, had been placed on the tomb a long time beforehand. They danced with it until one of them entered into a state of apparent semi-disassociation. He spoke in a surprisingly neutral and unemotional voice, addressing the children to be circumcised and all those present. It then became clear that what was planned was another *tsodrano* and rather a dramatic one at that. His speech, which was difficult to hear, seemed much like the invocation of any *tsodrano* and corresponded fairly closely to that already given.

I was told that he was speaking the 'words of the ancestors'; this was clearly an instance of something close to possession, for I was also told that the ancestors were speaking in him. The elder seemed in a trance state, although this was marked by extreme calm and not by any ecstatic behaviour. It is important to note, however, that the formal speaking of elders at a ceremony is always referred to as speaking 'with the words of the ancestors' even when this could be described as simply an oratorical device. It seems to me that it would be wrong to assume that for the Merina this type of possession is sharply different from the type of speech making by elders already described for the earlier part of the ceremony. It is but a further stage in the process whereby, as the ritual takes over, the living elders become more and more depersonalised and their role as representatives of the ancestors comes to the fore. Possession is simply the logical culmination of the proper behaviour for an elder; it is nothing special or in any way set apart from normal ritual behaviour.

The speech of invocation made by the possessed elder was extremely difficult for me to hear as it was principally spoken to the child. It was, however, not being kept secret so that only one person would hear. On the whole the child was addressed in a kindly, loving, grandfatherly tone. He was given recommendations to good behaviour and exhortations to follow various ancestral customs, to go to church, to obey elders and the government. The elder then also gave general advice to several other people present who consulted him on the preparation of medicines, on what foods to eat and avoid and how to deal with a wide range of interpersonal, financial and practical matters: for example, how to avoid hailstorms. After this the elder blessed the child with water from the bottle in the usual way, and then blessed everybody present. The same thing was done briefly by two other elders.

Although the possession episode was obviously of some significance, it followed the same pattern as all other *tsodranos* and was described as such. The use of water from a bottle that has been placed on the tomb for a considerable time is not exceptional. It only emphasises the association with the ancestors, who are the prime source of blessing. Similarly, possession is simply a further step in the association of elders with ancestors that lies behind the notion of blessing. Blessing is the canalisation of the power of the deme through the generations, or rather the perpetual maintenance of the deme, by the transference of its life potential from one group of caretakers to another. In this logic all generations are equivalent. The elders of one moment are the ancestors of the next and it is the power of the ancestors that they dispense. Possession simply acts this out. It is significant, however, that after this particularly charged *tsodrano* I was told that the child had been made *masina,* the strongest possible description of the transcendent power he had been given.

The ceremony of the fetching of the powerful water

What in many ways can be considered as the core of the ritual began around 3 A.M. This was the ceremony of the fetching of the powerful (*mahery*) water.[10] It began when the 'youths whose father and mother are still living' burst into the house, where everyone was singing and dancing and where, up to then, the proceedings had been taking place. They hit the door violently with a rice mortar to gain entry. Their entry was resisted by the real father of the child and all the other men and a mock fight ensued. In the end the youths crossed the threshold, the first acting as a powerful or wild *mahery* bull; this he did by imitating its horns with his arms and hands. He was immediately followed by another youth, who brandished a spear threatening the 'bull'[11]. Finally they all arrived and danced, while the other participants sang a song almost identical to the first line of song 31, except that the phrase *zanakay mahery,* 'our powerful child', had been replaced by 'powerful [wild] bull', *omby mahery.*

After the entry of the 'bull', the ordinary singing and dancing reasserted itself until the next stage, the preparation of the gourd. The gourd, *arivolahy,* the 'thousand men', was taken out from amongst the plants at the north-east corner and seven elders gathered round.[12] Two of the elders took a strip of the *somangana* bark and a strand of the 'living mother' grass, which they held together; another elder held the gourd upright and put his finger over the hole left by the removal of the stem at the top of the gourd. Then all the elders intoned the following verses and were joined by everybody for the exclamation that follows each phrase:

> *Baba zato O! Baba arivo O!*
> *Velondreny O! Velondray O!*

Description and analysis of a circumcision ritual
which means

Father of a hundred! Father of a thousand!
Of living mother! Of living father!

This was recited three times and each time the strip of grass and bark was brought a little nearer to the neck of the gourd until at the final repetition they were rapidly tied round the neck as if capturing a wild animal. The whole process, including the speaking of the spell, was repeated seven times so that in the end seven pieces of bark and grass were tied round the neck of the gourd.

Once the gourd had been 'caught' it was slowly lowered to its side with the finger still kept on the only opening. The movement of lowering was itself divided into three and each part of the movement involved reciting three times the same phrase as for tying. Then the spear brought in by the second youth was held poised threateningly over the lowered gourd, the seven elders each placing one hand on its shaft. The same phrase was again repeated seven times, and each time the spear was lowered, until at the seventh time it actually pierced the head of the gourd and thereby opened it. Immediately someone slipped an uncut silver coin into it. As the gourd was pierced all present whooped loudly.

The next phase of the proceedings involved placing the pierced gourd on the head of the 'bull'. This again was done in three stages, and was preluded by the triple repetition of the same *Baba zato . . .* incantation. The gourd was first raised to the knee of the kneeling 'bull', then on to his shoulder, then on to his head. As soon as it reached the head, the youth acting the bull rushed out, followed by the youth who brandished the spear, still threatening the bull and the gourd, and all the other 'youths whose father and mother are still living'.

They rushed out of the house into the night, leaving not only the house but the village as well and went a considerable distance to a waterfall. Such running water is called living or powerful (*mahery*) water, and is thus also associated with the fertility of nature and of the Vazimba. In the case of circumcision water, the notion of the purity of such water is added to the notion of its power. The water the youths go to obtain must be taken before dawn, because, I was told, this ensures that it is unsullied by contamination, even by birds, who in flying over it might desecrate it with their droppings. Before dawn, rushing water is thought to be perfectly clean, *madio,* or sweet, *soa,* the state that, as we noted above, circumcision is said to bring about for the child. In the ritual, the water so obtained is called *rano mahery,* from the word *rano* for water and the word *mahery,* which we have already discussed. From this point the word *mahery,* in the songs that are sung and in the name of the objects referred to, completely dominates the ceremony. But as the ritual proceeds in some lines of the song *mahery,* 'powerful', is replaced by the word *masina.*

Having reached the waterfall, the youth with the gourd, always threatened by the youth with the spear, must scoop up water in one clean scoop, and thereafter he must not spill any of it. He must carry the water back to the village and the house of the circumcision, which may be quite a distance. He holds the gourd on his head, and is followed by the spear-carrier, still threatening him, and the other youths.

Meanwhile, at the house, the departure of the 'bull' was followed by the participants' splitting up into two groups, one group consisting of the 'mothers of the child' as well as his own mother and the child himself, all of whom stayed dancing in front of the plants in much the same way as before. The others went outside the house, preparing themselves as if to stop the youths returning by arming themselves with dry cattle dung. As they did this they began to sing a new set of songs, 37, 38, 39, 43, which, although they all have slightly different words, are dominated, as a result of the musical stress, by the simple phrase *rano mahery*, 'powerful water'.

Going outside into the night after such a prolonged period cooped up in the house, where many people had been singing and dancing in a small space, made this a very dramatic moment. This was especially so since the cold offered a striking and much remarked sensory contrast with the heat of the inside of the house, heightened for me at least by thoughts of the cool waterfall where the youths had been to fetch the water. It was obligatory to comment on the cold at this point, and indeed in the cold season in the middle of the night it can be near freezing. In this way the stress on cold already discussed came dramatically to the fore.

As the returning youths crept towards the village, they teased those who were waiting for them with taunting fragments of song and, armed with switches, they tried to creep up to the house of the circumcision unobserved. When at last they emerged from cover, another mock fight ensued between the returning youths, who had to run round the house three times before entering it and defended themselves with their switches, and those who had remained and threw cattle dung at them. To be hit by one of the switches in this fight is again said to promote fertility and to be a 'blessing'.

In the end, however, the youths who had been to the waterfall managed to force their way into the house. Once they were inside the fighting stopped and they went to the north-east corner and danced with the filled gourd in front of the plants. They were joined by everybody else in a dance that took the form of mimed pointing at the children and the water and plants in the north-east corner. The youth carrying the spear performed this dance, still as if threatening, with a slight throwing movement of the spear. As a result the threatening of the *mahery* water with a spear and the pointing to the child by the participants became associated in a single rhythmic act. The whole episode was accompanied by the following songs:

37. *Tonga soa rano **mahery**:* The powerful water has arrived safely.*
38. *Alefaso rano **mahery** / Rano **mahery** no ilaina:* Come on powerful water, / Powerful water which we desire.*
39. *Alefaso rano **mahery**:* Hurry powerful water.*

40. (As song 30)
41. (As song 31)
42. (As song 38)
43. *Ataovy soa rano* **mahery:** Achieve well powerful water.*
44. (As song 30)
45. (As song 31)
46. *Rano masina masindrano /*
    Rano mahery no manory: Holy water. Holy Water / Powerful water that overcomes.*
    (N.B. the use of the word *masina* from *hasina* to describe the water here.)
47. (As song 30)
48. (As song 42)
49. (As song 30)
50. (As song 45)

Ultimately the gourd with the water was put down at the foot of the plants, and there it rested until it was used.

In many ways the fetching of the water was the main focus of the ceremony and little of significance happened after this episode until the actual operation. The dancing and singing continued accompanied by occasional scuffles when a man or a woman stole a banana or a part of a sugar-cane. No new songs were introduced, athough many of the songs previously given recurred in no particular order.

The symbolism of the ceremony of the fetching of the powerful water

The ceremony of the fetching of the powerful water clearly involves extremely rich and complex symbolism, and some aspects of it must be discussed before continuing with this description.

It is in this part of the ritual that the symbolism of the house first comes clearly to the fore. As we noted in the previous chapter, houses are symbolically linked to the world of women, but much more specifically to matrilinearity. This is because the aspect of houses emphasised in such rituals is their association with heat, and therefore with natural birth, which is seen as leading only to matrilineal filiation. This warm woman-focussed house is here for the first time assaulted and penetrated violently by the young men coming from the cold outside. This occurs twice: during the initial entry with the pestle and during the re-entry when the youths return from the waterfall carrying the powerful water. This breaking into the house is said to cause fertility, especially the second entry and its associated mock fight. In a sense these entries reverse the trajectory of the bananas and the sugar-canes. Violence occurs when they are taken out of the house; for the water it occurs when it is taken into the house. In both cases, however, it is the breaking of the boundary that leads to fertility and, as we shall see, this is not the end of the journey for the water.

It is also significant that this breaking into the house is done by 'youths whose father and mother are still living'. The 'non-domestic' status of these youths

77

(they must not be married) makes them appropriate 'opposites' to the home. Second, because they have *both* their mother and father, they represent the bilateral unity of the deme as against the unilineal nature of the woman–house. Third, because these youths are of *living* mother and father they represent both strength in this life and the continuing existence of the descent groups, as opposed to the individual disruptive and impermanent nature of the birth-focussed house, which contrasts with the eternal life-giving tomb. This element is also heightened because, as we saw, the very name of these youths also links them with the elders, the earthly representative combination of motherhood and fatherhood.

The conquest of matrilinearity and natural birth is also acted out in a number of ways in other parts of this sequence. First of all, the two roles given to some of the 'youths whose father and mother are still living' are significant. One youth acts as a wild, powerful bull, *omby mahery*, which, as noted earlier, is associated with wild fertility and the Vazimba (Ramilisaonina 1974). This bull is therefore linked with all the other elements associated with the fertility of nature, also defined as *mahery*. However, the bull is *threatened* by the other youth with the spear; the fate awaiting it is like that of the bull killed for the ceremony of *tsodrano*. The reference is surely to the essential initial capture of the bull in a violent corrida, which leads ultimately to its being tied up and killed during the opening *tsodrano*.

The same symbolism underlies the preparation of the gourd. The gourd is first caught and bound by grass and bark. Then it is threatened. Then it is broken open and cut by a spear held by the representatives of the ancestors and the bilaterally united deme, the elders. As they perform this act, the elders, followed by everybody else, repeat the formula 'Of living father, of living mother. Father of a hundred, father of a thousand'. This stresses, first, the complementarity of both sides of descent and, second, the continuing flow of life and fertility through the generations: from the previous generations, through the present generation, to the future generation. The central symbolic element of this part of the ritual is of course the powerful water itself. It is, however, better to leave consideration of this until we have seen what happens to it.

The actual circumcision

Reverting to the particular ceremony, after the fetching of the powerful water nothing much happened, and people continued to dance and sing much as before. They were waiting for the actual circumcision, which took place at dawn, around seven o'clock, although the actual time had been kept secret by the circumciser.

In fact, the circumciser had come long before but he was waiting hidden in his house, only to appear at the time fixed by the astrologer. When the time finally came for the operation, the child's grandmother danced one final time to prepare for the operation, then a place was made ready on the threshold of the house, that is, to the west of the house. The ground was scattered all over with cattle dung, and a rice mortar was placed at the threshold; this was also filled with cattle dung, forming a seat for the person who was to hold the child. It is extremely important that blood should fall on the cattle dung and mortar, although I could discover no explanation why this should be so. Cattle dung, however, has many symbolic associations; above all it is associated with vigour and wealth. It is considered a sign of wealth to let the dung accumulate in the cattle pen and one often finds cattle left deep in the stuff.

The time having come for the circumcision, all the men went outside the house to form a semi-circle facing the door. The women stayed inside the house. The child himself was taken outside to the threshold. The man who held him (it is usually a grandfather), sat on the mortar with the child on his lap. The other men stood at a distance and the circumciser performed the operation, cutting off the prepuce with an old razor blade. As he was doing it the youth who had been carrying the spear banged it against a metal winnowing tray standing for a shield, making a deafening row while the assembled men shouted at the top of their voices *lahy' lehy lahy'*, 'A man! He is a man!' until the job had been completed. The effect of all this is usually so to bewilder the child that he thinks of crying only after the event.

While all this was going on, the women inside were taking part in a special dance involving crawling on hands and knees and taking up dirt from the floor with their hands and throwing it on their heads. At the same time some women made as though to get outside, but were restrained. As soon as the end of the operation was marked by the ending of the shouting, however, the women took some strands of a reed called *sandrify*, which is normally used in weaving fruit baskets, and started to weave tiny baskets, which in fact they never finished. As they did this, they sang the following question-and-answer song:

51.   Q: *Mandrary inona ianareo?*
            A: *Mandrary sandrify izahay*
            Q: *Atao inona izany?*
            A: *Asim bola sy voangy*

            Q: What are you plaiting?
            A: We are plaiting *sandrify*
            Q: What is it for?
            A: It's to place silver and pearls in*

Meanwhile outside, as soon as the operation was finished, the prepuce was taken and given to a senior relative, who swallowed it there and then in a piece of banana. The *rano mahery* was handed from inside the house to an elder, who poured it over the child, especially over his penis. As he did this, the elder repeated phrases that often accompany blessings: 'May you be strong! May you be rich! May you have possessions! May you have cattle! May you have seven

79

boys and seven girls!' Then the circumciser, the 'father of the child', anointed the child's penis with a black paste, which was a medicine he had prepared that ensures quick healing.

Immediately after the water had been poured on to the child, and the silver had been taken out for safe keeping, the gourd was thrown far away by one of the elders. As soon as this was done everybody, men and women, rushed after it, grabbing at it and each other, fighting over it in the hope of escaping from the ensuing melee with at least a little piece of it. These pieces, like the pieces of the mat from the original *tsodrano,* are carefully put under their beds by both men and women in order to increase the chances of conception.

After this the terrified and crying child was handed back to his real mother through the window, which is normally to the north of the door in a Malagasy house. This is significant because an uncircumcised child should never be handed through a window into a house. If the child is handed through a window before circumcision he will not be able to penetrate a woman during intercourse.

The child was comforted by his mother inside the house and was given a chicken to be cooked for him later.[13] The guests then prepared to leave, congratulating the parents and the elders with a special greeting, *Aperina ny zaza:* May the child heal. After a few weeks it is usual for the family to celebrate with a meal the fact that the child's penis has healed successfully; it is usual too for the elders to again bless all present.

Analysis of the final part of the ritual

The final part of the ritual that has just been described is based on the symbolic meanings established in the earlier parts. First of all, we may consider the symbolism of the house and the outside, a contrast that is linked to the symbolism of hot and cold. Up to this stage in the ritual, the main emphasis had been on the assault on the boundary of the house, especially on breaking out of the house. This is emphatically illustrated in this part of the ritual by the exit of the child, who breaks out from the inside of the house to the outside and thereby becomes fully potent. It is significant that this breaking out of the house should involve violence to mark the transition and that this violence, the operation itself, involves the 'breaking out' of his male part. Equally significant is the fact that this violence occurs exactly at the point of transition between the inside and the outside: on the threshold. This liberation and conquest over the world of the house, heat, birth and matrilinearity is again emphasised by yet another transition, the parallel symbolism of the passage from night to day. The operation occurs at dawn, and dawn is central to much Merina ritual symbolism, especially in the ritual of the royal bath.

It is also important to note that the circumcision of the child, who is sitting on a dung-filled mortar on the threshold, itself elaborates further the significance of the passage from the inside to the outside of the house. The ritual up to that point has been most concerned to define the significance of the inside of the house with its association with women, birth, heat and matrifiliation and the need to break out of, and to transform, this complex. Its opposite, the outside, has so far been weakly elaborated. The outside is where fertility can be transmitted, as is shown by the fact that this is where the sugar-cane and banana can be eaten. This is paralleled by its also being the place where the child has to be taken to become potent. When this occurs, however, the outside has been symbolically constructed because there, outside, to receive the circumcised child, are the men gathered together, representing the united deme, the 'thousand men' of the proverb. This association of men and deme unity is further filled out by the already discussed notion of cold. Cold, as was suggested earlier, is not just the opposite of the heat of matrilineal birth. It is also associated with the tomb, the symbol of deme indivisibility and permanence. This associated notion is strengthened by the way the child is seated on the threshold during the operation. The position of the child re-echoes the traditional way in which a corpse, on its way to the tomb, is washed in this position on the threshold, as it is taken out of the house after a period of mourning, a time dominated by women. The entry of the child into the world of men, which is so dramatically acted out at the moment of the operation, is therefore also his entry into the world of the tomb and therefore of the deme united.

This last point, however, only serves to emphasise that another element seems to be involved in this last part of the ritual, an element that had so far been much less explicit and that goes beyond the simple contrast between the outside of the house, standing for deme unity, and the inside of the house, standing for deme division. This other element is illustrated if we look carefully at the role of women. In the earlier part of the ritual, as for most Merina symbolism, the representation of women is dual. On the one hand, women are associated with individual kinship and division through the notions of birth and houses; on the other hand, they are represented as an essential part of the deme, which includes both the father's and the mother's side, as is emphasised in the words of the blessing and the name for elders ('fathers and mothers'). At the actual moment of circumcision, however, it is as if this second representation becomes obliterated by the first. Only men represent the united deme and masculinity is equated with the descent group, an idea strongly revealed in the fact that as the child leaves the divisive house filled with women he is welcomed into the world of tomb and deme by the words 'He is a man.' On the other hand women are represented in a *totally* negative light at this point. The action of the dance they perform during the actual operation, the throwing of dirt on their own heads, implies in Merina ideas the most complete form of self-pollution because contact of the head with dirt is the worst possible offence that can be committed against the self or anybody else. Even more significant is the fact that it is also the action of women mourning after a death when the body is still 'wet' and decaying and before it has entered the tomb. Women mourn the dead by sitting on a rubbish heap, their hair undone, throwing dirt on their heads from time to time. This is perhaps their clearest association with the negative aspects of bodily existence (Bloch 1982). By doing the same thing here the women are not only polluting themselves but also in a sense mourning the death of the child as a 'wet' creature. This occurs at the same time as the men are welcoming him into the world of the dry, cold tomb.

At the moment of circumcision it is as if the rather subtle opposition unity–tomb, division–house had been replaced by a simple male–female opposition. This second element, I feel, is never totally absent from other parts of the ritual, but up to this point it has not been spelt out. It is because of this playing down of the male–female opposition that I have not so far discussed what might appear as the obviously sexual side of the operation. The erotic aspect of the penetration of the house by the pestle-wielding youth at the beginning of the ceremony of the fetching of the powerful water is relatively clear and caused knowing giggles when I discussed it with the participants, but it was never fully admitted by my informants.

This reluctance is significant because it reveals the contradiction that becomes increasingly apparent as the ritual proceeds. This is a contradiction between two sets of contrasts. One of these is the tomb–house contrast. The other is the simple men–women contrast that comes to the fore by the end of the ritual, when as a result the sexual meanings appear much more openly, as in the re-entry of the circumcised child through the window. At that moment, it is as though a different but related interpretation of the ritual has partially subverted the central message, concerned with unity and division.

This aspect of things, however, should not be exaggerated. At the critical moment, women throw dirt on their heads, but they also sing the song (51) about pearls and silver and plait little baskets to put them in. There the reference is to a myth of the origin of the ritual (see Chapter 6), when princes were believed to have thrown pearls and silver in the lake from which the *rano mahery* was first taken (Callet 1908, p. 789). The song is one of thanksgiving and, like many other parts of the ritual, it shows that the women, too, are beneficiaries of the blessing of circumcision. However, it is principally in the central part of the ritual, that concerned with the powerful water, that the orthodox line comes out most clearly and is reasserted.

The powerful water comes from a place associated with the fertility of nature and the Vazimba. It is scooped up in a container prepared by the violence of the elders and carried by their agents. The elders have previously invoked the ancestors and they have put the holy silver in the gourd. Then, after the operation, the child is blessed by the water poured by the elders in the same way as for any other blessing. In fact, the Merina quite unproblematically say that this is blessing – a blessing that contains the two essential elements of all blessings, the water from nature, and the contact with the elders/ancestors.

It is significant that after its preparation the powerful water, *rano mahery*, can

82

also be referred to as holy water, *rano masina* (song 46), and in the same way the child has been transformed by the ritual from a wild 'natural child', *zanaka mahery,* to a 'holy' child, *zanaka masina.*

The whole ritual is thus revealed to be a *tsodrano,* a blowing of water. The final part of the ritual is really a continuation of the beginning. The first part was an ordinary blessing bestowed by the elders on the members of the deme. The last part is the carrying down of the blessing (water) by the agents of the elders, the 'youths whose father and mother are still living', to the youngest generation, that of the child, and even down to the future unborn generation by association with the child's penis. In order to receive the blessing of the bilateral and bisexual ancestors the child has had first to be violently separated from the unilineal (matrilineal) and the unisexual (female) world of the house, which although it may be *mahery,* is not *masina.*

This transformation reinvigorates the descent group as it introduces a new potent member. It is therefore a *tsodrano* and like all *tsodrano* it leads to the *general* fertility of all participants. Anything involved in this process is particularly good for fertility, whether it be the mat or the broken gourd, both of which are scrambled for by men and women.

5

The symbolism of circumcision

The preceding chapter examined a particular circumcision ritual and began the process of unravelling its symbolism. In the present chapter, this fragmentary interpretation will be pulled together so that a more general consideration of the meaning of this type of ritual can be undertaken.

The stream of blessing

Again we must start with the notion of *tsodrano*, of blowing on water, or blessing. This must be our starting point simply because of the informants' statements that the circumcision ritual is a *tsodrano*, and if we needed further confirmation, we would have it from the words of the first song: 'It is a blessing that we ask.'

The notion of *tsodrano* is inseparable from the Merina notion of descent. The notion of descent is central, but it is also vague in so far as it is far from clear which sociological group is identified with descent. In many ways it is a mystical experience.

In Merina rhetoric the whole kingdom is sometimes represented as a descent group. At other times, the semi-territorial grouping that I have called the deme is represented as a descent group. At still other times, the group of people associated with a tomb is talked of as a descent group. Even any apparently ad hoc group of related people can be talked of in the idiom of descent.

This vagueness can be explained partly by the nature of Merina kinship and especially by the nature of Merina demes, which, in spite of the fluidity we have noted above, seem to me to be the anchor of the notion of descent and to come closest to the sociological notion of descent groups (Bloch 1971a, pp. 46–50).

The deme is represented by the combination of three linked concepts: continual regrouping, corporateness and undifferentiation. The concept of continual regrouping is the corollary of a view of life as a continual potential dispersal (Andriamanjato 1957). In life people leave to live away from their ancestral (deme) lands; they form relationships with outsiders that might even lead to marriage. Marriage outside the deme is the worst aspect of dispersal because it leads to the possible loss of women and even men, whose procreative potential is thus dispersed. Equally dangerous, marriage to outsiders leads, as a result of bilateral inheritance, to the dispersal of ancestral rice lands.

Descent is the opposite of dispersal; it is the process of continual regrouping by in-marriage that leads to the retention of people and also of land, because only deme members will inherit when both their parents are deme members. Descent is also the regrouping of the bodies of the members of the deme, not in life, as this is unfortunately impossible, but as corpses. Thus secondary funerals bring the members back to the tomb.

The tomb is therefore regrouping par excellence, and by the same token it is the second aspect of descent: permanence. Permanence follows from regrouping because if the deme is not dispersed its life potential will continue. What this means, given the unfortunate mortality of human beings, is that the life potential of the deme must be transformed undiminished from generation to generation.

There is, however, another threat to descent permanence, and that is internal differentiation. For the Merina a stress on particular lines of descent and on particular kinship links is potentially disruptive of the undivided corporateness of descent, especially because such stress may, and indeed does, lead to hierarchical differentiation within the deme (for a discussion of this see Bloch 1981).

Descent is therefore a set of values mainly relating to a sociological idea: However, because it is a set of values it can easily be attached to different sociological phenomena. For example, royal rhetoric can represent the whole kingdom as one descent group and this was often done to encourage esprit de corps in exhortatory speeches or in more symbolic ways, as will be seen in the next chapter. Descent values can also be vaguely associated with any group of related people who by this rhetorical device become, for a moment, representatives of the deme. This is what happens at a ritual such as the one examined in the preceding chapter.

As we noted, there are three parts of the ritual that could occur by themselves as more ordinary rituals of *tsodrano,* and that I shall therefore call 'separable *tsodranos'.* These three parts are the initial blessing, the blessing that inaugurates the dancing and singing, and the special blessing by the elders in the middle of the night, which involved something like possession. The first two blessings are identical in most respects and can therefore be taken together.

The invocation given in Chapter 4 is apparently quite explicit about what is involved. First of all there is the invocation to God. This, however, is cut off from the rest of the invocation; it is before the 'beginning'.

The 'beginning' is the ancestors. The ancestors have previously been invoked at the preliminary ceremony at the tomb; they are invoked by the reference to the north-east to be found in the peg anchoring the mat on which the water will be placed, and they are invoked by the words of the elders. Indeed, their presence throughout the ritual is heightened simply by the fact that the whole proceedings are addressed to the north-east corner of the house. This fact marks the whole ritual as 'ancestor business', but the invoked ancestors are considerably different from the ancestors found in the classical loci of ancestor worship, such as Africa or China.

The first point to note is that the ancestors are anonymous. At no stage are particular ancestors honoured, even when they are believed to actually 'possess' those who give the blessing. The non-individuality of the ancestor is well illustrated by the simile that calls them 'trees', growing on the ancestral hills where the ancestral tombs are placed. It is also emphasised by the fact that the ancestors are actually referred to by the name of the location of their tombs, not by their personal names.

This last point brings to light another aspect of Merina ancestors. They are never one but many. This is underlined by the rule that there can never be only one corpse in a tomb. As a result old corpses have to be put in a new tomb before it can be used.

Ancestors are therefore an anonymous group, and this of course reflects one of the principles of descent: They are undifferentiated and corporate, which is stressed even further in that they are emphatically bilateral. In the speech of blessing they are spoken of as being 'on the father's side and on the mother's side'. In spite of this there is no idea that they do not share the same tombs, because they ideally form an endogamous and regrouped unit. The anti-individuality of descent and tombs is not only marked by certain practices during rituals, but is also stressed in proverbs such as *Miharo karam-doha Mihara taolon doha:* In the tomb bones and skulls should be mixed together.

If the ancestors are together and undifferentiated then, it is believed, the life power of the deme will be maintained, and therefore transferred from generation to generation. This transferral is the blessing bestowed by the elders, and furthermore what this blessing consists of is explicitly stated. It is the power to obtain wealth, strength and progeny – in other words, the power for a full life. The experience of this transference and of the continuity of one self with the ancestors is a key mystical emotion for the participants in all Merina ritual.

The elders are suitable mediums of this power of blessing because they possess certain attributes that they share with the ancestors, but unlike the ancestors they still also share with living people the fact that they are alive.

The elders are like the ancestors in the sense that they are old; that is, they are the ancestors of the immediate future. They are also like the ancestors in other ways. First, they are bilateral: They join the father's side and the mother's side. This is expressed in their name, which as we saw, means 'father *and* mother'. Second, this theme is further emphasised in the ritual by the fact that they are chosen from both the father's side and the mother's side, and they must include both men and women. This complete lack of differentiation makes them the personification of a group, not individuals; they are not anybody's own father, or anybody's own mother, they are the whole deme's father *and* mother.

The elders are therefore ideally suited to ask for the transference of the blessing from the ancestors, whom they in some ways resemble, and they pass this blessing on to their descendants, with whom they share substance and life. The elders are intermediaries by their very nature, and they are the inevitable channels of the transfer of the descent life force. This they transmit in a material sense by blowing on the water of blessing, the *tsodrano*.

The third instance of a 'separable *tsodrano*' that occurred in the ritual was different from the other two in only minor ways. It simply heightened the identification of the elders with the ancestors by means of possession. They held the bottle that had been 'held' by the ancestors and they spoke as ancestors. In other words, for the period of possession they had become the ancestors, or the ancestors were in them. I do not believe we can usefully separate blessings where possession occurs and where it does not. The point is simply that for the reasons already discussed the elders are, by their very nature, mediums between the living and the dead. Possession simply heightened their 'conductivity' as blessing givers. Thus the primary role of the possessed elders was to do what elders always do, to bless with water. However, because of their clarified conductivity, this was a particularly powerful, intimate and moving blessing.

Given the clarity of the channel that had been opened up by possession from the ancestors to their descendants, it was not surprising that people took the occasion to consult the ancestors on other matters of great concern, in the way that children are expected to consult their parents, and it is not surprising that the ancestor/elders, out of love for their descendants, helped them.

This type of possession offers a total contrast to certain other types of possession found in Madagascar and elsewhere in the world, which involve a struggle with dangerous amoral spirits (Ottino 1965, Estrade 1977). The possession of blessing is only an extension of the love of a parent for a child and this is shown by the calm and relaxed atmosphere of the occasion, which contrasts so much with possession by other types of spirits.

If the three separable blessings were similar, the 'central' blessing of the circumcision – the blessing of the powerful water – was different; and, indeed, it is unique to the circumcision ceremony. The difference lies in the fact that in an ordinary blessing the elders bless the living together without distinction as to generation, but in the circumcision a number of distinct generations *below* that of the elders are hinted at or specified. The point is that the ritual of circumcision is the *bringing down* of the blessing to the generation of the circumcised child. In order for this to be done several intermediaries must be established between the elders and the child. These intermediaries correspond to those previously established between the ancestors and the mass of the living, by the existence and the actions of the elders. As a result these lower intermediaries must be *in between*, and also worthy channels of the blessing of descent.

The next generation after the elders to be realised in the ritual is that of the 'mothers' and 'father' of the child. The actual parents of the child would be unsuitable vessels for the transmission of blessing because they are individually associated with the child; they imply lines of kinship differentiation and are anti-

87

thetical to the descent group and therefore to blessing. Rather the real parents must be replaced by non-lineal antecedents. This non-lineal, non-biological and non-domestic aspect of the 'parents' given by the circumcision is emphasised by the fact that the 'mothers' of the child should be asexual and in theory not have borne children, while the 'father' of the child must never have seen him before.

If the 'parents' generation is hinted at as part of the chain of intermediaries between the elders and the child, this aspect of succeeding generations is much more emphasised in the generation below that of the 'parents': the generation of the 'youths whose father *and* mother are still living'. Their name is highly significant in a number of ways. First of all the name specifies them as being of the next generation after the 'father' and 'mothers'. Here, however, there is an ambiguity, in that their names could also mean that they are the children of the elders (whom, it will be remembered, are called 'fathers and mothers'). This ambiguity seems to me revealing because it shows that the symbolism is not meant to convey a precise sociological picture of a number of generations but rather the general image of generations following each other in a continuing chain of moral life and blessing. For this reason there is no need to specify exactly where any particular person or group fit in; what matters is that they represent an intermediary generation.

As a result, we find that like the elders, they have to be defined as sharing something in common with the generations on either side of them, and as being suitable transmitters of blessing. Their suitability is, as is to be expected, expressed in the same way as for other intermediary generations. First of all, like the elders, they unify the deme by their emphatic bilaterality. They are of living fathers *and* mothers, and again the emphatic *and* is used. They have a clear relationship to the preceding generation; they are their children but in a *general,* non-lineal way because they stand as a group in relation to a previous undifferentiated group.

On the other hand, the youths are also, in part, like the about-to-be circumcised child, the youngest generation. They are children who have as yet had no chance to produce a generation to follow them. They are simply full of promise. Furthermore their vitality is emphasised because of the association of the concept of 'living' and the celebration of their strength required by the proceedings. As an intermediate generation the youths therefore look both ways; they are agents of transfer for the blessing down the generations.

In this role, they take the container for the water of blessing – the container prepared by the elders – on a journey that comes to its end when the blessing is poured on to the new generation. Like the elders the youths are intermediaries, although they are intermediaries between the boy and the parents or elders.

This is what marks out circumcision ceremonies from other rituals of blessing. It is a blessing, but one that is carried right down to the new generation through continuing intermediaries. Perhaps nothing stresses this more clearly than the formula that endlessly accompanies the preparation of the gourd 'a thousand

88

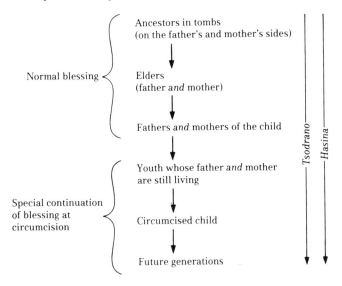

Figure 5.1.

men'. The gourd will be carried by the youths. It is therefore not surprising that what is being said, as it is being tied and then pierced, is 'Father of a hundred, father of a thousand. Of living father, of living mother.' The incantation stresses the continuity of the intermediate generation between those who have generated and those who will generate. It establishes the necessary continuity for the transmission of blessing from those who have produced to those who will produce.

This brings us to the final generation hinted at in the ritual, the generation to be fathered by the child himself. By the transfer of the blessing to the circumcised child, he will achieve legitimate potency, which will therefore create yet further generations. Once again the nature of the blessing is made plain. This explains why the blessing of the child is also a blessing for all and a source of fertility for all. The blessing of the child is the celebration and creation of the success of all and so all who participate will benefit; the blessing of circumcision produces new generations in general for the descent group. As such it marks the extension of conquest by the ancestors of the vitality of the young who are still 'wet'.

Figure 5.1 depicts the line of blessing from the ancestors to the circumcised child and beyond, as apparent in the circumcision ceremony. We can see how the element of ancestral authority and vitality is differentially allocated within the generations with the circumcised child receiving blessing for the first time and being removed from simple matrilineal vitality (*mahery*).

To this line of descending blessing is added another essential element through the symbolism of the silver coins and silver generally. As has been discussed in

89

From blessing to violence

several places (for example, Bloch 1974), the Merina hold the notion that demes are possessors of a virtue that creates rank hierarchy. This virtue is transmitted from generation to generation within the deme and is therefore a constitutive element of *tsodrano;* it is referred to by the word *hasina.* As we noted earlier, the notion of *hasina* (adjective *masina*) implies holiness, purity, pre-eminence. The word however also refers to the uncut Maria Theresa thaler, partly because of its wholeness and partly because silver itself is thought to partake of *hasina.* It is therefore fitting that the blessing of the ancestors, which itself is *masina,* should contain a silver *hasina.* This is added to the water of the three separable blessings and to the powerful water for the specific blessing of circumcision. The significance of this addition is simply that because the blessing is the transference of the life power of the deme, it also should transfer what we might call its 'unique excellence'.

The devalued entities

We have so far considered the line of blessing activated by the circumcision, but this line is not only represented positively, it is also strongly represented antithetically. Indeed, it could be argued that the symbolism of the circumcision ceremony is much more concerned with what is *not* ancestral blessing than with what is. The antithesis can be seen in the ritual representation of the world from which the child must break out and be freed before he can receive the blessing of the ancestors.

The central symbol of this negated complex is the house. The house has to be left so that the child can receive the blessing of circumcision, and significantly this he receives on the threshold, on the way out. Similarly, the sugar-cane and the bananas have to be taken out of the house in order that their fertile potential can be released.

The symbolism of the house is central, but, perhaps because it is so central, it is never discussed by participants. When I suggested my interpretation to my informants they casually agreed with me but moved on as if uninterested. This contrasts with the way they were willing to discuss exegetically more specific and also more arcane symbolism such as that of measuring the child.

The significance of the house is much more subtly if subexplicitly constructed. An essential part of this construction is the allusion to the hot/cold contrast. Some of this is explicit. As we noted, the initial greetings that dramatically replaced the normal ones on the occasion of the circumcision ceremony literally mean: 'We greet the cold season.' Similarly, at the time when people go out of the house to challenge the 'youths whose father and mother are still living', they must also comment on and emphasise the fact that it is cold outside the house. The fact that people say it is cold is, however, of less significance than the fact that one really does feel cold on coming out of the house at that moment, because the house has become dramatically overheated by the continual dancing of the

90

The symbolism of circumcision

large crowd inside. The sensory awareness of the difference in temperature inside and outside gives meaning to the contrast in a much more direct if non-linguistic way, and also it gives meaning to the symbol of the inside of the house. Again, informants have little to say about this contrast, and the reason is probably that, as with the house, the meaning and power of the symbols is not conveyed principally by words. What is achieved, however, by coming out of the house in the middle of the night is that the symbolism of the inside and outside of the house and that of hot and cold are collapsed together, each giving meaning to the other.

Fortunately many aspects of the hot and cold symbolism are explicit, but this is in contexts other than the actual circumcision ceremony. The association of the tomb and cold was discussed in Chapter 4. What is significant here is that the use of the notion of cold in the ritual brings the tomb just outside the house, and therefore focusses on either side of a threshold a fundamental Merina symbolic contrast of house and tomb.

The area just outside the door, marked as a cold area during the fetching of the powerful water, becomes the place where the men stand at the time of the operation, ready to welcome into their midst the newly circumcised child. By this means they not only welcome him out of the house and into the world of men among men, but also into the world of the undivided, undifferentiated and eternal tomb and deme.

The associations of heat are explicit in a different way from those of cold. As we saw, all the vocabulary of childbirth involves the notion of heat. This is also true of the practices that accompany childbirth, which involve keeping the mother and child hot. It is especially revealing to note that such practices traditionally involved the building of a small house, inside the house, for the newborn child. Heat therefore links the symbols of birth and the house, but it also more specifically links birth with the inside of the house, for it occurs inside a house that is itself inside a house. Heat, the inside of houses and biological birth are therefore three facets of the same symbolic notion, a notion created partly in the ritual of circumcision and partly in other rituals. In the circumcision ritual, however, this notion represents the negated totality from which the child must break free. It gives meaning to what the child leaves as he crosses the threshold.

The crossing of the threshold, which has been given meaning by the symbolic construction of house–birth–heat, reveals two further points of importance. The first point is that if the house must be left in order to obtain fertility and blessing, this exit must be accompanied by violence. In the case of the sugar-cane and the banana this violence involves a mock fight and the breaking up of the plants into bits. In the case of the boy it is the operation itself. This violence marks the importance of the transition between the inside and outside of the house and also the difficulty of penetrating from one side of the threshold to the other. The other significance of this violence is that it links the exits from the house with the entries into the house in a way that will be discussed later.

91

From blessing to violence

The second point that emerges when we bear in mind the symbolism of house–birth–heat, and the fact that it must be left behind in order to receive blessing and fertility, is that circumcision is in one sense an antibirth ritual.

Such a conclusion might appear paradoxical for a ritual so clearly concerned with fertility. This paradox, however, is at the centre of the ritual because it is concerned with defining 'true' fertility and opposing it to the mere 'biological' fertility of the house–birth–heat complex.

The construction of 'mere biological' fertility, and its devaluation, is further elaborated by associating women with the house–birth–heat complex. In Merina symbolism, women are associated with natural birth in a number of ways that go beyond the obvious. As we have already frequently noted, 'biological' links between parents and children are represented as purely matrilineal. Second, the process of birth and the minor ritual acts that accompany it are attended only by women inside heated houses. Women, houses, heat and birth therefore become part of the same symbolic whole. Furthermore, this devalued whole inevitably connects up with the antidescent notion of internal differentiation and division. This is because birth, houses and women form the symbolic basis of individual kinship ties. Houses represent the particular interests of the household with its private property against the merged interests and the communal property of the deme. Women and birth signify the branching and divergence of individual lines, which lead to possible hierarchy within the deme and possible division and loss of land and people. As a result, the house and women as birth-givers in the house are not only separate and contrasted with the cold tomb world outside, they are also a threat to its unity, indivisibility and permanence.

The linked contrasts between unity and division, on the one hand, and descent groups and women, on the other, is elaborated even further in the ritual, to the detriment of the 'divisive women'. This is achieved by emphasising yet another opposition: that of cleanliness and dirt. The symbolic association of women, birth and dirt is most marked during the actual operation, when women put dirt on their bodies in the most intimate way by throwing it on their heads. The dirt itself contrasts with the water of the blessing, the powerful water, which must be super-clean, unsullied by even that remote possibility of the passage of a bird. This further contrast, which is added to the original contrast of the inside and outside of the house, explains why the circumcision ritual can also be described as a cleansing.

There is, however, an even more funadmental aspect to the 'dirt' of the house: It is associated with death. Putting dirt on one's head is, as we saw, a sign of mourning for the recently dead, a willing taking-on of pollution that comes from the decomposing corpse. This in the symbolism of the funerary sequence is also linked with the house, in contrast to the tomb, where the dry, clean body is housed. Dirt here becomes an allusion to death and decomposition and the association of women and houses with them. The biological link between parents and children through birth becomes, as a result, also linked with the decompo-

92

sition of the corpse before it has been finally placed in the tomb. It is as if all aspects of the transience of human life were contrasted with eternal existence in the tomb.

The circumcision involves the child being taken out of the world of women and houses and introduced to that of the cold tomb. In many ways an opposition between women and tombs seems strange in that, for the Merina, women are also deme members and have a right of entry into the tomb, yet women are represented at certain moments of the ritual as though they had to be expelled from the world of the tomb. The contradiction is there, and it must be fully understood to appreciate the role of women during the operation.

The circumcision ritual principally contrasts women alone in individual houses as against men *and* women together. The world of descent, of the tomb and of blessing, is emphatically a world of men *and* women. This we saw emphasised in the way the ancestors must be both from the father's and the mother's side and elders too must be from the father's and the mother's side, and include both men and women, and be father *and* mother.

It is because the ritual acts out an opposition between women alone, on the one hand, and men and women together, on the other, that women are willing and even eager to participate in a ritual that so clearly humiliates them. Throughout the ritual, women are represented as rejoicing in the gaining of ancestral fertility in which they participate, for example, in the fighting for the mat at the beginning, in the fighting for the gourd at the end and most explicitly in singing such songs as song 22. But they are also represented as dirty creatures to be transcended. This contradiction is, as is to be expected, most apparent at the critical point of the ritual, the time of the operation, when almost at the same time women throw dirt on their hair but also rejoice by singing song 51, 'We plait baskets for silver and pearls', which means 'We are receiving blessings.' Women are willing to participate because if as women they are humiliated, as deme members they are blessed.

But we should note here, as in the preceding chapter, that in the emotions aroused by the ritual and in some of the symbolism the subtlety, or perhaps the casuistry, of the contrast is obscured by the expression of a much wider ranging and less integrated male/female antagonism. This seems apparent in the behaviour of men at such rituals and in the fact that the party outside the house, which welcomes the child to the world of the tomb and therefore to the world of men *and* women, consists only of men, who celebrate their shared virility.

But even though the simple element of gender antagonism creeps in at several points, it is not the main focus. This becomes apparent when we turn to the final aspect of the devalued entities, the notion of individual biological parenthood, whether motherhood or fatherhood. One major aspect of the circumcision ceremony devalues the notion entirely by the simple device of replacing both the father and the mother of the child by a different father and several different mothers. The role of these 'mothers of the child' is best understood when con-

93

trasted with that of the biological mother of the child: They are many, while she is one. It is therefore the notion of individual mothering, with its divisive implications, that is attacked. There is yet more that contrasts the 'mothers' with the real mother. The 'mothers of the child' negate natural motherhood in an equally fundamental way in that they are emphatically non-sexual.

It will be remembered that the 'mothers' should ideally be virgins, certainly should not have borne children, and at the very least should avoid sexual contact during the ritual. The new 'mothers' reproduce, not through the force of biology and real birth, but through the force of blessing. Unlike the real mother, the 'mothers' are symbols of women as members of the undivided deme, while the sexually active mother, who relies on that uniquely female process of biological fertility, is a symbol of division and all that is negative in femininity.

We can therefore understand why the circumcision ritual is both a fertility ritual and an antibirth ritual. We can also understand why it is also an antisex ritual, as the need for abstinence on the part of the participants demonstrates. The circumcision celebrates descent, which in Merina terms is the procreation of new undifferentiated generations (men and women) by preceding undifferentiated generations (fathers and mothers) by means of blessing. This is contrasted with the dirty generation of individuals by mothers in houses; a result of the polluting processes of sexuality, parturition and individual parenthood.

However, in order to replace birth, descent has to borrow from birth and biology a symbolism which in some ways almost undermines the whole basis of the ritual. The 'non-biological' birth acts out metaphorically a birth that inevitably has to be indicated by ways which refer back to biology; in this way the coming of the child out of warm woman–house into the cold is often recognised as mirroring the process of biological birth, although in this case, it is a birth under the authority of men. The symbolical problem is thought-provoking: even in a ritual process dedicated to negating the material process of existence there are, in the end, no resources available for doing this other than the process itself.

At this stage I can summarise in Figure 5.2 what we have considered so far, showing how the stream of descent that was illustrated in Figure 5.1 has been further defined by means of the specification of its antithesis.

Adding the power of the wild

The devalued world given by the antithetical column in Figure 5.2 is not simply a matter of negation. This is shown by the fact that the next to last element, matriliny, is an aspect of many symbols that are actually sought after in the circumcision ritual in order to *increase* the vitality of the child and the group.

This section will examine the aspect of force or vitality *added* to strengthen the power of blessing and then will go on to discuss the ambiguous relationship of this element to the devalued entities considered in the preceding section.

The 'matrilineal' elements brought to the circumcision ceremony are mainly

94

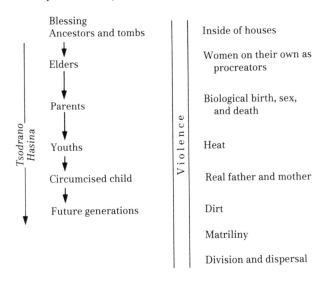

Figure 5.2.

plants and animals, which unlike deme members receiving ancestral blessing, are *only* matrilineal because they are merely 'natural'. Nature, however, is not without its own power. This is a notion that, as we have seen, is expressed in a number of ways but finds one expression in the belief in the Vazimba. The Vazimba are not in themselves directly important in the type of circumcision ritual analysed, but indirectly their power is continually implied, in that they are associated with the force and fertility of nature. This is because the Vazimba are the ultimate masters of the earth, the first possessors of tombs on the land and therefore the ultimate vessels of its life-giving potential. However, unlike the ancestors who have less ancient tombs, the Vazimba have no living descendants. This means that there is no orderly transmission of their power through the flow of blessing to particular groups of living beings. As a result, their power is wild or strong: *mahery*.

This power of nature, or of the Vazimba, is to be found in all nondeme living things and especially in wild things.[1] It is extremely potent because of its vitality, yet it is disruptive because it is not under the canalising influence of blessings and circumcision. It is only transmitted through natural filiation, matrilineally.

The natural/Vazimba world therefore presents a problem. It is the ultimate source of vitality and therefore necessary for the living, but it is uncontrolled and therefore anarchic and dangerous.

The solution to this problem lies in the use of the strength of wild Vazimba nature but under violent control. The attempt to achieve this is the aspect of the blessing that has not so far been examined in this chapter. In Chapter 3, however, we noted how this aspect is involved with the notion of the water of the blessing and therefore also with the water of the circumcision, since it too is water for blessing.

Water is associated with the Vazimba especially when it is clean and flowing, because then it is most *mahery,* powerful. Because of this, before it can be beneficial to people in an orderly way, it has to be *canalised* by the authority-dominated process of blessing. In order for this transformation to be achieved it must literally be *contained* by the power of descent.

This containment can, as we have seen, take several forms. It may be achieved by the water's being placed in a bottle on the tomb of the ancestors for a considerable time. In this way the water is held by the great power of the ancestors and so controlled. The water can also be contained in the mouths of the elders who, by the power they have obtained through contact with the ancestors, can 'hold it' before spraying it on to their descendants. Third, the water can be held in a gourd, 'a thousand men', before being safely poured in blessing on the penis of the child in the ritual of circumcision.[2]

The preparation of the gourd is itself revealing of the complexity of the ideas involved in the control of wild power and fertility. First of all, the gourd is a cultivated plant and therefore, like the other plants it is linked with uncontrolled nature. On the other hand, this particular gourd is unlike other plants in that some of its features relate it not only to the matrilineal world of natural things but also to the bilateral 'descent' world of the tomb and blessing. These aspects are alluded to by its name, whether in the short form, 'a thousand men', or in its long form, 'a thousand men do not die in one day', which stress the notions of permanence transcending the impermanence of generations, the notion of unity and non-divisiveness, and even masculinity.[3] In different ways these are all, as we have seen, characteristics of descent, a notion that contrasts sharply with natural filiation. The gourd by its very name shares something of descent, and by the fact that it is a plant it is something of wild nature. It is therefore a mediating object and this of course is precisely its role in this ritual, as indeed it is in the other rituals in which it is used.

The intermediate character of the 'thousand men' gourd is further transformed and stressed by its preparation. The gourd is first bound by a grass and a strip of bark, which are 'of living mother' and which therefore clearly belong to the world of matriliny. This binding is however only a preliminary to the 'liberation' of the gourd from this influence. It is the first stage of the violence that the gourd, and the water it will contain, undergo at the hand of the elders, the catching and binding that are also inflicted on cattle before they are made ready for killing and eating. The violence is continued in a similar idiom when the head of the gourd is broken open by the spear held by the elders. In other words, the gourd, having first been moved on to the side of nature by being 'bound' with matrilineal grass, is then dramatically received back into the world of descent so that it can contain the blessing. The fate of the gourd clearly foreshadows the fate of the child in two ways: First, having been associated with matrilineal nature, the child will

96

also be moved from the world of women and of nature to the world of descent by having his 'end' opened up by the elders, and second, as the violent process of the preparation of the gourd is taking place, the central doctrine of descent is being repeated again and again in the incantation. This central doctrine consists of the celebration of the unity of the father and the mother's side, the celebration of the transference of blessing through the generations and hence of the permanence of the descent group, and finally the celebration of the generative power caused by undivided transference. These three elements are perfectly combined in the repeated formula 'of living father, of living mother, father of a hundred, father of a thousand', which accompanies the preparation of the gourd.

The gourd is therefore dramatically obtained for the side of descent, but this is so that it can continue the violent process and *contain* the vitality of water. The importance of the *rano mahery* is obvious from its prominence in the songs and indeed in the actions of the ritual. The fetching of the water forms a major sequence, of which the preparation of the gourd is merely the preliminary. Its strength is what will strengthen the child, but for it to be of value it must be conquered. This explains the spear with which it is continually threatened and the violent way in which it is obtained. Its vitality is necessary and beneficial, if it can only be mastered and so transformed.

The notion of the violent mastering of natural fertility is perhaps the most acted out notion of the circumcision. It explains why plants 'of living mother', especially the sugar-cane and banana, may give fertility to descent beings. The plants are strong and fertile in themselves (*mahery*), and they confer these virtues on those who consume them, but *only* after they have been mastered by the double violence involved: first, stealing them in order to place them in the north-east corner and, second, stealing them again in order to take them out from the north-east corner. The stealing is itself significant in that the notion of individual household property held against the corporate ownership of the deme is a theme that continually recurs in Merina thought. The stealing is a denial of private property within the group, a denial of the separateness of the household and therefore an assertion of deme unity.

The power of natural fertility, 'of living mother', is something to be sought but also something to be overcome. The same idea underlies the use of the reeds in the ritual. They are thought to be particularly vital and fast growing, and what is more, they are associated with the water in which they grow. But at least in the case of the reed, which is repeatedly cut to 'measure' the child, its growing power can be transmitted only by its being cut down.

The symbolism of the 'measuring' shows particularly well what is involved. The fast growth of the reed 'of living mother' taken from the water is passed on to the child through contact, but this power binds the child and can only be transferred when it has been cut or like the water 'caught' by the elders. This kind of notion also explains the burning of the *fototra,* the reed covered at one end in cattle dung. Rather than promising a strong progeny, the *fototra,* meaning 'source'

97

or 'root', is the demonstration of strong maternity. However, like the reed of measurement, it can only pass on the vitality that created it after violence has been done to it.

The same notion lies at the back of the symbolism of the mime of the wild bull, the *omby mahery*. Wild cattle are thought by the Merina to be associated with the Vazimba and also to display the unpredictable, fearful yet enviable vitality of the wild. This, I believe, explains the significance of killing them at the beginning of rituals of blessing and why this act does not really correspond to the ideas usually conveyed by the word 'sacrifice'. Cattle produce the richest of food, the eating of which is a supreme manifestation of well-being and therefore of blessing. The killing of a bull or cow is the same conquest and reconversion of natural fertility that we saw in the case of the sugar-cane and bananas. This explains why the killing is often preceded by a brutal corrida, which establishes dramatically the mastery of men over the animal.

This notion also underpins the dance threatening the *omby mahery* during the ritual of the fetching of the powerful water, when the youth acting the bull is followed by the one holding the spear. The dance conveys that in spite of the animal's vitality its fate awaits it; the fate of having its life force transferred into blessing.

Consideration of the bull brings us back to the central word of the ritual: *mahery*. The elements we have just considered are all qualified as *mahery;* the plants, the cattle and above all the water. They are all wild, vital, unpredictable. They all share the same fate in the circumcision ritual: They are to be tamed, broken, violated so that their vitality can be captured for the power of blessing, or, to put it another way, so that the power of matrilineal filiation can be turned into the power of undifferentiated asexual bilaterality. As the *mahery* element is captured it therefore changes, it becomes controlled, and can then even be called *masina,* or holy. This is so for the water; once it has been brought back in the gourd it is no longer referred to simply as *mahery,* but is now also said to be *masina.* As a result of its capture the water has retained its *mahery* element and this is transferred to the child, but now the *mahery* element has also become *masina.*

The transformation through violence of *mahery* things into *masina* things defines in advance the journey of transformation through which the child himself is taken on circumcision. This type of substitution occurs most frequently, however, in songs referring to the only *mahery* element yet to be discussed, the *voronmahery* or 'powerful bird', which because of the emphasis laid on it in the songs, is clearly important.

The *voronmahery* shares with other *mahery* things the vitality and potency of all wild things. However, unlike other *mahery* things it is a non-human being in clear opposition to the biological ties of mother and child. This is stressed in the song concerning the powerful bird in the phrase 'it lays its eggs on a stone'; in other words, it spurns the nest. As such the *voronmahery*, together with the *omby*

98

I		II	III		IV
Strong Vital Elements *Mahery*		Intermediaries	The Tomb		Devalued entities
Sugarcanes		The gourd	The regrouped ancestors		Inside of houses
Bananas		The falcon			
Water	Violence		Blessing	Violence	Women on their own
Cattle			Cold		Heat
Plants growing in water			The 'fathers *and* mothers' circumcision		Real father and mother
Prolific plants of 'living mothers'			Undifferentiated descent		Dirt
					Matriliny
Vazimbas			Unity and regrouping		Division and dispersal

Figure 5.3.

mahery, is, like the gourd 'a thousand men', an intermediary between the world of blessing, which spurns the nest, and the world of the Vazimba and of wild things; it shares something of both. It is therefore highly significant that the *voronmahery* is the *mahery* element most closely associated with the child in the songs preceding the operation. By the continual replacement of the phrase *mahery* bird for *mahery* child (see song 31) the transitional or intermediate status of the one is given to the other. Having been made 'like a *voronmahery*', the child is therefore already on his way on the journey from the inside of the house to the outside, from the world of matriliny to that of descent.

In this section we have considered the wild *mahery* face of nature that must be added to the blessing to give it vitality. Because of its wildness, however, this can only be done under control, which is exercised first by violence and by containment. We can therefore add a new column to the diagram we have been building on, a column of *mahery* things that contribute to the blessing in the same way as water does. Before their contribution can take place, the *mahery* elements must first be subdued by violence. This violence takes the form of scooping, cutting, breaking, burning or, in the case of cattle, even killing.

The transformation of *mahery* things into blessing is a difficult one, but it is facilitated by intermediaries that share something of the *mahery* things and something of descent. For the sake of clarity these intermediaries are shown separately in Figure 5.3. This is somewhat misleading, however, in that they are merely a mixture of items in the two columns on either side. If we add to the two columns of Figure 5.2 the column of *mahery* things and that of *mahery* intermediaries, we produce Figure 5.3.

Figure 5.3 represents the argument so far and includes all the symbols of the ritual. It has reduced these into three (column II being merely intermediary). Even this reduction, however, is misleadingly complex in that it hides the intimate connection between columns I and IV, which so far has not been discussed.

The connection between desirable *mahery* things and the devalued entities

The most obvious connection between columns I and IV lies in the fact that they both relate to natural, matrilineal fertility. The elements from column I are all 'of living mother'. Their vitality is brought in and added to that of descent, although this is only possible after violence has been done to them. The elements in column IV are also focussed on the biological mother–child relationship, but they are violently expelled. This connection is also revealed in a vague way in relation to the Vazimba. The Vazimba are closely associated with the vitality of nature in column I, but they are also associated with column IV in their connection with women. The Vazimba are often worshipped by women; they are the cause of the barrenness of women, and they were ruled over by women. In fact the connection between columns I and IV is total: Columns I and IV are really the same element represented in a positive and negative light. That the same element should be represented in an opposing way reflects the ambivalence to be found in the Merina notion of the force of nature, an ambivalence that characterises the Vazimba. The Vazima are powerful, but they are neither good nor bad since their power lacks direction because they have no legitimate descendants. As a result they can be seen at the same time as both beneficial and harmful but, in either case, as dangerous.

Because columns I and IV are two aspects of the same entity, it is possible to transform Figure 5.3 into the circle of Figure 5.4, where descent (III) is first established by expelling the negative aspects of vitality (IV); however, this same force under its positive aspect (I) is then reintroduced to descent by way of the mediators (II) although after having been conquered violence. In other words, the relation of descent to natural fertility is a forward and backward movement, first throwing away what is then recuperated.

The journey starts with the expulsion of the matrilineal force of nature and ends with the reintroduction of this force after its conquest, so another way of representing this movement is by Figure 5.5. What has to be driven out in order to obtain the blessing of descent must at a later stage be recovered to give vitality to descent, although this is possible only after violence has been done to it.

The circumcised child

All this may sound very abstract until we realise that this is exactly what happens to the circumcised child in the ritual both symbolically and physically. The ritual

The symbolism of circumcision

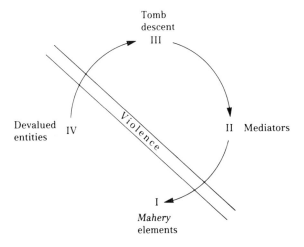

Figure 5.4.

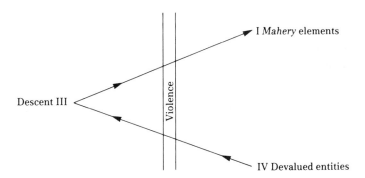

Figure 5.5.

starts with an uncompromising association of the child with the world of women, matrilineal fertility, heat and biology: For the night preceding the operation he must remain in the house. Then little by little his separation from this maternal world is achieved. It begins with his being thrown up in the air, and then with his being 'measured', a practice that already requires the violation (the cutting) of the matrilineal reed. His journey of removal is continued in his association and equation, through the songs, with first the 'wild' bull and then the 'wild' bird. The wild bull is significant in that although he is a supremely strong and fertile animal, he is, in the ritual, continually threatened by the spear that follows him; he is 'about to be killed' or, in other words, to be violently made into blessing. The wild bird with whom the child is also equated is an intermediary in that although *mahery* he spurns the nest; 'he lays his eggs on a stone'. Finally,

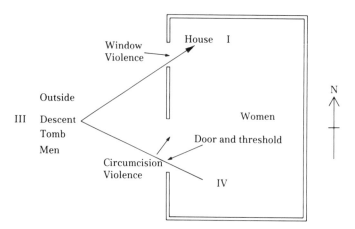

Figure 5.6.

when the inside of the house is defined as most polluting, as the women are throwing dirt on their heads, the child breaks out at the beginning of the new day, after having been done violence to on the threshold. He can then join the world of descent, of the cold tomb, which is represented by men. Once, however, he has achieved this transition, the child then recovers the female world of the house and natural vitality. He *re-enters* the house as in Figure 5.5, but he re-enters it not in the appropriate way, but through the window and therefore violently, with clear sexual overtones of conquest.

The necessity of the re-entry into the tamed feminine world is in fact made clear by the sexuality of the symbolism. This re-entry is necessary for future natural procreation, which the child, having obtained the non-biological side of blessing, must still achieve. This explains the celebration, by the throwing in the air, of the child's future erections. After the operation, however, these erections and the penetrations they will lead to will be for ever transformed and marked by blessing because the penis will have been permanently marked by the circumcision. These erections will no longer be merely natural but also ancestral. The ritual proclaims that sexuality is destructive when unconquered by authority, as it is in the case of women, but constructive when, after having been conquered and marked by the purifying violence of the circumcision, it can then be openly celebrated, as it is by the sexual re-entry into the house.

This last element shows well the circular nature of the symbolism, which drives out matrilineal sexual nature only to reintroduce it. The child is driven out of the house and the world of women at the circumcision, as he crosses the threshold, but this exit is only a prelude to re-entry through the window. In this way the circular Figure 5.4, and even more clearly the zigzag Figure 5.5, is revealed not to be an abstraction but a description of the child's trajectory at circumcision as shown in Figure 5.6.

The symbolism of circumcision

The same diagram can serve to describe the trajectory of other ritual elements that make their journey before the child, although in a somewhat different way. The powerful water is first 'caught' by the gourd, which is an intermediary between blessing and nature. The water is not just outside but far outside, quite beyond the ritually created space of the ritual. It is then violently brought into the house (Figure 5.3, column IV) but is then taken out again to the outside of descent (Figure 5.3, column III) to strengthen it.

The trajectory of the banana and sugar-cane also shows the same coming and going. These are taken violently into the house after having been stolen and are taken violently out, so that they can strengthen ancestral fertility.

This continual forward and backward movement serves to reveal the limitation of the dialectic of the ritual. It is as though the ritual was an attempt to establish a source of fertility free from nature, women and biology and based entirely on descent blessing and authority, but it has to recognise in the end that this cannot be done, in this world at least, because of the inevitable reliance of the living on natural fertility. As a result the symbolism seems to be forever chasing its own tail, recovering what it has thrown out and celebrating what it has denigrated.

The same theme is revealed in the notion of birth. The whole circumcision ritual is, as we stressed, antibirth by women, yet in the end it acts out a birth by bringing the child out of the female house. In this way the circumcision ceremony not only defines itself as a 'new' birth but it does so with imagery borrowed from what it appears to revile most, the biological process of parturition. Of course, the symbolism of the ritual insists that this second birth is different because it is directly under the control of the ancestors and the elders, yet significantly it cannot get away from the nature of birth in its less 'elaborated' form.

This second aspect, like the hot and cold symbolism, no doubt adds to the emotional and sensual power of the proceedings, but it also brings us back to another central ambiguity: The opposition between the wild and descent is operated through the identification of women with the wild, while women as deme members are also part of the descent side of the equation. As a result, for a moment during the operation, the opposition of the wild and descent is acted out as the opposition between men and women, but this can only be a hint of a new direction and it is immediately discounted.

This ambiguity explains the reason why there is no parallel initiation ceremony for women. Merina women have the potential to reproduce matrilineally by their very nature. Without men they would therefore take over the descent group. Men on the other hand need to transform their natural potential because even in them the potential of their uncontrolled sexuality is female. They have therefore to operate this transformation by expelling the female element and then recovering it in a way that can be expressed at the same time as a sexual victory over women and a recovery of strength.

In fact the ambiguity that is revealed here is inevitable and central. It is clear in even the most concise statement of the symbolism of the circumcision ritual

103

that can be given. *Circumcision is the demonstration that blessing is the true transcendental source of eternal life through descent. This is established by the denial of the value of sexuality, birth, women and nature; however, this refined solution although suitable for the ancestors is not suitable for the living. In this world women, sex, birth and nature cannot be finally expelled; they have to be reintroduced if life is to be life, but violently conquered.* For the living, descent must therefore be continually complemented by strength; only the dead, re-grouped, united and having transcended the distinctions of genealogy and gender, can afford to drive out the natural forever and live (or, rather, not live) by blessing alone. The circumcision ceremony is therefore partly assertion and partly compromise.

What is asserted is clear enough. It is that through the blessing of the ancestors true fertility can be achieved and that natural existence is a dangerous cheat of which the participants must rid themselves. It is there to be conquered violently. As such the circumcision ritual is like other rituals of blessing, a statement that nothing new of value is ever created; that the order of the deme should be maintained forever unchanged and unchanging by the transmission of the power implied by the very notion of descent. The political significance of this is clear and is quite obvious to the Merina. Only by obedience to ancestral custom, only by reproducing what has always existed, only by maintaining an unchanging order will life be fulfilled. Blessing is a call to obedience, obedience to the past and the dead, and also by extension obedience to senior generation, in general, whether alive or dead.

The circumcision is therefore a ritual of legitimation of those in authority, especially of the elders. This, of course, does not suggest that the ritual is created by the elders to establish their authority. Such an idea is clearly preposterous; the elders, like everybody else, are most concerned to follow exactly the custom of the ancestors and not to create for their own purposes. This, however, is not to say that the elders and everybody else are not aware of the legitimising aspect of the ritual. I was repeatedly told that the effect of not participating in the rituals would be that children would not obey their parents any more, elders would not be honoured and the ancestors forgotten. The circumcision ritual is an assertion that the basis of authority in this life is a timeless order, transcending the flux of life.

The ritual is therefore perceived as totally non-creative; for the participants it is a matter of following a formula. Yet it performs a social function that is clear to the participants and this must have been created in the socio-historical process by people such as the participants who do not see themselves as creating at all. This is the puzzle that lies at the heart of much social science, as we saw in Chapter 1; we can begin to examine it in this case by looking at the historical process leading to the creation of the ritual examined in this chapter and Chapter 4. This examination will provide the subject matter of Chapters 6 and 7.

6

The myth of the origin of circumcision

The purpose of this chapter and the next is to trace the history of the Merina circumcision ceremony as far as the documentation makes possible. As we shall see, the historical sources on the ritual are limited and insufficient but clear enough to give us more than a general idea of what has happened since approximately the time of the reign of Andrianampoinimerina at the end of the eighteenth century. The circumcision ceremony existed before then in Imerina, and the ritual was already practised in the seventeenth century and probably long before in other parts of the island (de Flacourt 1661). It is likely that aspects of the circumcision ritual have been borrowed by the Merina from other peoples in Madagascar who practise related rituals, and no doubt a similar process has taken place the other way. It is also not impossible that borrowings go well beyond Madagascar. I do not feel, however, that such wide-ranging hypotheses can at present be more than empty speculation, and so I shall limit myself to the documented history of the circumcision ritual for the period from 1800 to 1971 in Imerina.

Before engaging in this historical enquiry, it is worth considering the mythical origin of the ritual, not because such myths have any historical value in themselves but because they again reveal and confirm the themes expounded in the two preceding chapters.

I obtained only the barest accounts of the mythical origin of the ritual from informants during field-work, but these fragmentary accounts correspond to the fuller version recorded by the Jesuit missionary Callet in the nineteenth century and published as a footnote to page 788 of the *Tantaran ny Andriana* of the 1908 edition. This book first appeared in 1873, and the account of the myth seems to have been collected in southern Imerina (Délivré 1974, p. 388 n. 16). The style of this account makes it clear that it was written directly from a spoken account, the only modification being that Callet did not take the myth down in its entirety, since he marks several gaps in his transcription by etceteras.

The main point of the myth, the attribution of the ritual to Andriamanelo, is confirmed in many places, the earliest being in Ellis 1838, vol. 1, p. 176.

Before examining this myth of the origin of circumcision in detail it is necessary to place the main participants of the story. As noted, the introduction of the ritual is attributed to the Merina king Andriamanelo, a king of great mythical significance as he was at the origin of the royal dynasty of the Merina rulers in power at the time when the myth was recorded, and he is still remembered as the founder of the royal line. Before Andriamanelo, rulers in the area of Imerina are qualified in the traditions as Vazimba and he is attributed with driving out the Vazimba. In contrast to the Vazimba, who are usually represented as being ruled over by queens, Andriamanelo begins a series of heroic kings.

Interestingly Andriamanelo's relation to the Vazimba is ambiguous. On the one hand, he is a hero who drives out the Vazimba. He does this by his control of an advanced technology, that of iron. Thus we are told in a popular myth that whereas the Vazimba only had spears of clay (which in Malagasy is called *tany manga*, 'blue earth' or 'baked earth'), he discovered the techniques of smelting and forging, and as a result he defeated the Vazimba with iron spears (Callet 1908, p. 67). Indeed, his metallurgical skills are often mentioned as being even more extensive, for he is also said to be the inventor of silver working. Not only is Andriamanelo represented as a master of superior technology, he is also represented as a master of astrology, an advanced technique of civilisation, which he is said to have discovered. Symbolically, therefore, Andriamanelo is the complete antithesis of the wild and uncultivated Vazimba.

On the other hand, he is also intimately connected with the Vazimba because he is the son of the most famous named Vazimba, the queen Rangita. Rangita has all the attributes of a Vazimba in the beliefs of people; she is, as we shall see, associated with water. She is said to be small and dark and her name means curly haired, and above all she is a woman and a mother. Her relationship to her anti-Vazimba son is not really clear in the myth collected by Callet or, for that matter, in any available version. The passing remarks made to me about her in the field did not suggest that Andriamanelo's wars against the Vazimba directly concerned her and I believe it is best to leave the matter at that.

The other two characters that occur in the myth, Ranoro and Ramasy, are even more hazy. Ranoro is the name sometimes given to a younger brother of Andriamanelo, sometimes to his son. Much more importantly, however, it is also the name given to another Vazimba queen, whose fame equals, and in some places in Imerina exceeds, that of Rangita. Ranoro, like Rangita, is the object of a major Vazimba cult, which is flourishing to this day. Ranoro's attributes are normally given as identical to those of Rangita.

In the myth Ranoro male and Ranoro female are interestingly merged. At first we are dealing with Ranoro male. Then we are told that Ranoro is related to Andriamanelo through female links. Then we are told that Ranoro female took on the name of Ranoro male and that she was dragged into the water by Ranoro male. By the end of the myth it is only the female Ranoro who is mentioned.

The other character in the myth, Ramasy, was not known by any of my informants, but he is referred to in the *Tantaran* as another son of Andriamanelo

The myth of the origin of circumcision

(Callet 1908, p. 72). Ramasy is also given with Ranoro as one of the ancestors of the Antehiroka deme, whose role in the royal circumcision ceremony and in other rituals is of great importance. However, when Ramasy is mentioned in that context I had always assumed that a woman was being referred to since the name Ramasy, like Ranoro, usually refers only to women.

The version of the myth given by Callet is as follows in my translation. The original is to be found in a long footnote to page 788 of volume 2 of the *Tantaran ny Andriana* (1908 edition):

Here is what is told concerning the sacred Andranomiry lake. During the reign of Rangita, the queen gave the following instructions to her subjects [children] and to her son Andriamanelo. 'The kingdom will from this day on be governed by Andriamanelo since I, myself, will enter the waters of this lake lying before us in order to render its water holy so that you might pray and bless us with it and thereby rule over this land.' To which Andriamanelo answered, 'What will this water you are preparing be used for?' And she said, 'This will be holy water, for whenever you bear a male child you must come and obtain this water with which to bless them.'

Her son then said 'Will it only be us, the rulers [the *Andriana*], who will take this water?' To which she said, 'No, all the people will take it; it will benefit everybody. Whenever there is circumcision people of high and low rank will come equally to obtain this water; but the manner in which the *Andriana* will take it will be different. They will take the water from the very centre of the lake, the ordinary people will take the water to the east of the centre and the black people [the slaves] will take it from the north; and this is all because this lake in which I will rest will henceforth be holy. Thus come here at Andranomiry to take the powerful water [*mahery*] that you desire.' And thus Rangita decreed how the circumcision should be. 'Take from me the holy water of blessing, here at Andranomiry, take the powerful [*mahery*] water here.' And thus it came to pass that a powerful ruler [*mahery*] entered the waters saying 'Here I shall be,' and from then on this lake was known as Andranomiry.

When Rangita died she was therefore placed in a canoe and another was placed on top and she was entirely immersed in the lake. Then Andriamanelo circumcised his male children and he simply obtained the water from this holy lake. But the children died as the rites for the taking of the water had not yet arrived, nor had the custom of using an *arivolahy* gourd been introduced, nor had it been bound up with silver, nor was there the shield and the lance, nor the preparation of the house, nor the banana tree. Ranoro spoke in the following terms, 'You do not know the proper way of fetching the water.' Andriamanelo then asked, 'What is the proper way?' To which Ranoro answered, 'The use of the gourd *arivolahy* is the proper custom,' and Andriamanelo asked, 'What is this *arivolahy*?' 'It is a gourd without equal.' Andriamanelo then answered, 'Show us what to do, that we may learn.'

And this is what Ranoro did. The neck of the gourd was bound with silver chains, then the gourd was carried, followed by one bearing a shield and a spear. Then those who were to carry it, which only the youths whose father and mother are still living may do, dressed themselves in silk [possibly shrouds].[1] They were driven forward carrying the gourd to the holy lake to the sound of gun-fire. When they got there they took the water by plunging the *arivolahy* gourd three times into the water. As they did this the people who were higher up holding shields and lances said: 'Be a man! Be a man, Be a man!' And when those who were taking the water by plunging the gourds had achieved their aim and even if the gourd was not full, they carried them back on their heads saying, 'This is holy water, the water of joy.' Once they had obtained the

107

holy water at the sacred lake they camped outside at Ambohibato. Then they obtained the trunk of a banana tree, sugar-canes and *bararata* reeds.

They appointed the 'mothers' of the child and the 'father' of the child. Then the 'mothers' and the 'father' had to abstain [from sexual relations], and they dressed themselves with shrouds [*lamba mena*, see Bloch 1971a, p. 145]. Then there was rejoicing and dancing as the holy water entered into the house. At Ambohimasina the water, the banana trees, the sugar-canes and the various reeds were placed on a holy stone. It is said that Rangita ordered this stone to be placed there in the village of Ambohibato. [The word *ambohibato* means 'the village of the stone' and the text suggests that the village got its name in this way.] She said that this stone was to be used in this way by her descendants for ever, when they hold a circumcision. Then in the evening the binding plant was used, so were the reeds and the fire and the child was 'measured'. Later, as the cock was about to crow [sometime before dawn], people sang 'We shall make our child be at peace, etc. . . .' When the time came for the child to be circumcised, brave famous men held a spear and said 'May you be like your father, May you be like me.' Then the small child was placed on a drum, etc. . . .

And when Andriamanelo performed the circumcision in this way the children did not die any more. He was pleased and said to Ranoro, 'Henceforth if any child of the ruler is to be circumcised you and future generations will follow this custom. You will tie the gourd, you will prepare the house, you will set up the banana tree; it will be your duty to prepare what has to be done from beginning to end.' And Ranoro answered, 'So it shall be. I shall divide the task between myself and Ramasy. I, Ranoro, shall go to the Antehilika, while Ramasy [Ranoro's elder brother] will go to the holy lake Amparihimasina where he will join Rangita after his death. And so, when you fetch water here call it not only holy water [*ranomasina*] but also joyful water [*ranomanoro*], [this is a pun on the names Ranoro and Ramasy] so that you remember us two men.' These two men were matrilateral parallel cousins to Andriamanelo, and Andriamanelo was the son of a woman, the son of Rangita. And so these two men taught the customs of the circumcision, especially that water was not enough. And these two men went their different ways; Ranoro went to the land of the Antehiroka and Ramasy remained here at Alasora. When he died Ramasy was submerged at Amparihimasina. And so it was instituted that whenever a child of the ruling family is to be circumcised, the descendants of these two men must officiate. This is the case for the members of the Andrianamasinavolona [the royal deme] or any other ruler. They may not proceed to do it without them.

Later, we are told in the story that, in the reign of Andrianjaka, Ranoro the man became Ranoro the woman. Ranoro the man took Ranoro the woman alive with him into the water of the Lake Andranoro in the land of the Antehiroka. Ranoro the man went into the water before Ranoro the woman. And from this day forth the Antehiroka have multiplied and have kept the memory of these events. This explains the cult of Ranoro the woman at Andranoro.

The holy lake lies to the north of Imerimanjaka. All the kings past and present have kept it holy. The slaves are not allowed to go to the middle of the lake. Ducks and geese are not allowed to go on to it. One may not set fish traps in it, etc. The princes must throw pearls and uncut silver coins at its centre. In the past Volavita cattle [especially associated with royalty] were killed there if the rain was insufficient. This is because Rangita is holy.

Before discussing the main aspects of the myth, a preliminary remark should clarify the obscure references to the various lakes where Rangita, Ranoro and Ramasy were submerged. The point of this is that different demes or different

The myth of the origin of circumcision

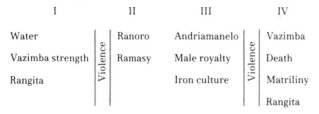

I		II	III		IV
Water		Ranoro	Andriamanelo		Vazimba
Vazimba strength	*Violence*	Ramasy	Male royalty	*Violence*	Death
Rangita			Iron culture		Matriliny
					Rangita

Figure 6.1.

sections of demes obtain their 'powerful' water from a variety of places and thus an attempt is made to explain the sanctity of several of these. It is clear that Callet obtained this myth from the village of Alasora in Antehiroka territory, and so the validation of the lakes where Ranoro and Ramasy are submerged refers to the places where that deme obtained its powerful water. The other lake mentioned, Amparihimasina (the holy lake), is where the royal family obtained its powerful water.

If we ignore these details the myth becomes fairly simple. The water of the lakes is the burial place of the Vazimba queens, the 'mothers' of the Merina king. On the other hand, the king to whom is attributed the institution of the circumcision is also the one who 'drove out' the Vazimba. The relationship of the royal line to the Vazimba/motherhood vitality/water complex is therefore ambiguous. Like descent in the circumcision ritual the relation is both antagonistic and complementary. Andriamanelo's link to his Vazimba mother is at first negative, because he drives out the Vazimba over whom she rules. However, once she has made way for him her power needs to be 'recovered' in order to bless his children; so the children have to be given the water of the lake in which she is buried. This recovery is nevertheless dangerous. Even though Rangita is dead, the power of her water is still too strong and actually kills Andriamanelo's son. It is only after Ranoro has stepped in and has taught the proper circumcision ritual for controlling the powerful water that it becomes truly beneficent. Ranoro in this myth is therefore a mediator, allowing the reintroduction of the power of water via the ritual, which puts the water under control – tames it, so to speak. It is not surprising that he/she should thus be of dual gender, sharing something of descent and something of nature, since he/she is the agent for the safe transfer of Vazimba/feminine power to the Merina/male children. He/she operates the transition by the violent transition techniques of circumcision on the doorstep. A similar role is given to the equally gender-ambiguous Ramasy, although this person is less developed in this version of the myth.

It is thus possible to schematize the myth by means of Figure 6.1 in the same way it was done for the circumcision ritual in Figure 5.3. The parallelism between the two diagrams shows how the same ideas underlie the ritual and the myth. Column III is symbolised by Andriamanelo, the founder of the royal descent line and represents descent and the tomb world generally. Column IV corresponds to the mother/nature entity seen in its negative representation and is symbolised by the Vazimba, with their lack of culture, especially metallurgy. Column I corresponds to the same entity but in its positive aspect, the power of nature, which must be reintroduced to vitalise the blessing. Column II is the mediating power of intermediaries which, by domesticating column I by violence, make it safe to be added to column III.

In this way the myth reveals the same type of pattern as is acted out in the ritual. Of course in other versions of the myth there may be slight variations, but the fundamentals remain. For example, in those parts of Imerina where the cult of Ranoro as a Vazimba queen is highly developed she replaces Rangita altogether in the story and is attributed her role. As a result, in these versions she is unambiguously female.

It is as if the myth at one level reflects the ritual. We find the three stages of the ritual. First, the caricaturing of the biological maternal – a world of rude, ugly people who are driven out by the beautiful, technologically sophisticated Merina. If in the myth the roles for acting this opposition are represented mainly in terms of the opposition indigenous/conqueror, this opposition is none the less also one of gender. The Vazimba are associated with femininity in a number of ways and are ruled over by queens, while the Merina are represented by their king and their warlike qualities.

Again, as in the ritual, the second act concerns the reintroduction of what had been driven out: the reintroduction of the powerful, *mahery,* water under the strict, restrictive and brutal control of the ritual. But despite this extraordinarily close similarity of structure, there seem to me to be a number of differences of emphasis, or perhaps of atmosphere, between the two.

First of all the myth, in a way that the ritual could not do, links the dramatic argument to an image of the past, to the accepted history of the Merina in general and the royal dynasty in particular. At the same time, the geography of the area is also introduced. The image created by the ritual gains greater reality by the evidence of the places and the peoples to which it is made to refer, and at the same time makes these places and people appear in the light created by the ritual.

Second, there is a more subtle and less clear difference between the myth and the ritual. While the ritual is a joyful and, in the end, unproblematic assertion of a representation of the world, the myth seems to dwell on unsatisfactory aspects of the construction. This feature is, I believe, typical of Merina myth as opposed to rituals.

The problem that seems to follow from the driving out of the Vazimba/natural/biological/feminine element is stressed particularly strongly in the failure that results from the first attempt at reintroducing it. This takes the poignant form of the death of the circumcised boy. Not only is there the contradiction of using what one has spurned, but so is the weakness of the control apparent.

The myth of the origin of circumcision

The powerful water of the Vazimba queen is necessary for the fertility of the boys, and so the enemy that had been driven out must be reintroduced in order for life to continue; but this reintroduction, done with insufficient violence, can kill from the inside to which it has been returned. The problem posed in the otherworldliness of the created ideal order and discussed in Chapter 5 is even less easily solved in the myth than it is in the ritual.

Third, the same ambiguity seems to be present in the transformation of Ranoro from male to female and in the indeterminacy of Ramasy. Instead of the myth smoothing over the problem of the mediation, one has the feeling that, instead, it emphasises it and its difficulty. The story of the relationship between the male and the female Ranoro is uneasy and yet quite dramatic.

Lévi-Strauss, in a number of recent works, stresses the contrast he sees between myth and ritual and this seems borne out particularly well by his South American examples. For him, myth is a speculation on the insoluble condition of man in nature. Myths bruise themselves on the contradictions of existence. Rituals for Lévi-Strauss, by contrast, smooth over and ignore problems by obscuring them in the very nature of the drama they involve. Such a strong contrast between myth and ritual is clearly not appropriate for a case such as this. The myth and the ritual are very close in structure. It is true however, that in so far as they do differ, they differ in the direction indicated.

There are also a number of aspects that are clearly to be understood in terms of Malinowski's very different theory of myth as a charter. This is so of the valuation of certain lakes by the myth and of the way it marks out different ranks in Merina society by minor variations such as where in the lakes the water is to be taken from. In addition the myth specifically validates many of the ritual practices: the use of the gourd *arivolahy;* the practice of tying it; the use of bananas and sugar-cane, spears, reeds and so forth; the 'measuring' of the children; the giving of the non-sexual roles of father and mother of the child; and so forth. In fact, it is striking how much the myth specifies the details of the rituals if only by allusion, and this includes giving the words of several of the songs to be sung.

In fact, the implied detailed specification of the ritual by the myth and the fact that this specification could apply to the ritual as it was practised in 1971 is of historical significance, even if this is not the case for the myth as a narrative. It shows well that at the time the myth was collected, probably around 1881 (Délivré 1974, p. 65), the ritual was substantially the same as now. The only three details that would not match are the fact that the *arivolahy* gourd was bound by silver chains instead of by plants; that a drum is referred to, which, as will become clear, was used at that time instead of the mortar as a seat for the circumcised child; and finally the use of shrouds for the youths whose father and mother are still living, which clearly associates them even more closely with descent and the tomb. These three elements will be discussed more fully in the historical account in the next chapter.

111

From blessing to violence

Beyond this mere 'charter' aspect, however, there is yet another element in the myth that we shall see is of great political significance. The myth indissolubly merges the metaphysics of the symbolism with the exercise of military violence and the conquest of the Vazimba – the setting for the whole story.

7

The history of the circumcision

If the myth of the origin of circumcision discussed in the preceding chapter is not of historical significance as regards the story it purports to tell, it remains of historical value by implication. It makes it clear that, at the time when the myth was collected, the details of the ritual were largely similar to what they are today.

From 1793 to 1825

Our earliest genuinely historical source, however, is a statement of the laws concerning circumcision. Like the myth, these laws are also found in Callet's collection of traditions, oral histories and manuscripts entitled *Tantaran ny Andriana*. These laws do not specify in detail how the ritual should be carried out and seem to take this side of things for granted; rather, they specify when the ritual should take place and what taxes should be paid. The laws take the form of a royal speech, as do all Merina laws. The speech is reported as spoken by Andrianampoinimerina and probably dates back to the period between 1793 (when Andrianampoinimerina installed himself in Tananarive) and the time of his death and the succession of Radama I, probably 1810. It is, however, possible that the so-called laws of Andrianampoinimerina are laws of Radama I, which were described as being the work of his father to give them greater legitimacy. This phenomenon is quite common in Merina tradition, and it has been described by Délivré as 'ascending anachronism' (Délivré 1974, pp. 177, 199). In this case, these would have to be laws concerning the very early part of Radama's reign and the difference is inconsequential for the argument of this book.

We can be reasonably certain that the laws represent a certain degree of innovation. This is because such memorised royal speeches in Merina history mark the introduction of new statutes.

The laws of Andrianampoinimerina concerning the circumcision are given in several places in the *Tantaran* collection without much variation. The fullest account is found on page 788 of volume 2 (Callet 1908). Here is a fairly free translation of the relevant passage:

113

Thus Andrianampoinimerina gave the laws concerning circumcision: 'Here is what I have to tell you my children [subjects]. When you have sons, do not let them remain strong [*hery*], let them be circumcised. We shall pay a *kirobo*[1] for each house in which the ritual of circumcision will take place, and an uncut coin[2] to sanctify the king and also another tax. As you see, my kinsmen, I do not change the ways of the ancestors; the Antehiroka, the children of Ramasy and Ranoro, will tie the gourds for the king and for the Andrianamisanavalona, and so on, down. For they are those who begin the ritual, who put up the banana trees, who prepare the house, who fetch the holy water from Ranoro in the sacred lake, indeed it is they who fetch the powerful water at Andranomiry.'

Andrianampoinimerina then said, 'If you want to circumcise sons each father will pay a *sikajy*,[3] and if there be some who want to adopt children they do so by this payment. Slaves pay a tax of *lasiray*[4] to the circumciser.'

And he said, 'We shall circumcise every seven years. Before you begin, the whole population will take the ordeal to clear the land of witches. O you Merina! You may not vary the interval of seven years because otherwise the children would be either too old or too young and their wounds would not heal. There will be the main circumcision and the minor circumcision. The main circumcision will follow the royal decision, which will be the signal to hold the ceremony.

'First there will be the royal circumcision, then the circumcision of relatives of the king,[5] then the circumcision of the people, and if there are any people who have not been circumcised by the end of this first period, they will be circumcised the next year at the time of the lesser circumcision. Then the people will perform the ritual of giving thanks.'

And Andrianampoinimerina went on, 'And if there be any who have not carried out the circumcision then they must wait seven years; for if any circumcise at other times, they shall be killed. If any are found not to have had their sons circumcised at the appointed time, they will be killed, even if their child be born during the period of the circumcision. All male children must be circumcised without exception otherwise the wife and children of the father of the boy will be sold into slavery and the same will apply to the wife and children of those who carry out the circumcision at other than the appointed time. And concerning the ordeal of the *tanghena*, customary at the time of the circumcision, the people shall give three *ariary* to all who survive taking the poison, but those who die will forfeit all their goods.'

Although, as we noted, this text does not tell us how the circumcision was to be carried out, certain parts of the speech make this clear by implication. We have reference to the tying of the gourd, to the fetching of powerful water, to bananas and to the preparation of the house. Clearly, then, the ritual Andrianampoinimerina is talking about is similar to that we discussed in the earlier chapters. That this is so in terms of the general symbolic structure is also confirmed by the reference to the notion of *hery*, the root of *mahery*, the word discussed at length in Chapters 4 and 5, which corresponds in part to our notion of wild and strong. Andrianampoinimerina says, 'Do not let your sons remain *hery*', thereby making it clear that the ritual involves the transformation of the child from a thing of the wild to a thing of descent through circumcision. The reference to the powerful water, however, enables us to complete the picture by hinting at the reintroduction of the wild element, which we saw was also an essential part of the ritual.

114

The history of the circumcision

Similarly the reference to the Antehiroka deme, whose central role in the royal circumcision is also emphasised, and to what is said about them and their ancestors Ranoro and Ramasy, tallies completely with the ideas expressed in the myth and discussed in the last chapter. This central role of the Antehiroka is principally relevant to the royal circumcision, as is the elaboration of the thanksgiving ritual that followed it and will be discussed later.

As far as we can tell, therefore, the ritual to which Andrianampoinimerina is alluding largely resembles the present-day circumcision. So, probably, did the ritual that existed before that time, if we are to believe the king himself, who says emphatically, 'I do not change the ways of the ancestors.'

There are none the less new elements, which explain the necessity for the memorised speech, and those are made very clear. They all concern what we might call the state orchestration of the ritual, that is, its correlation with the cycles and geography of royal power. These elements are (1) the obligation to perform the ritual, (2) the link of the ritual with the ordeal, (3) taxation and (4) the synchronisation of the ritual.

The obligation to circumcise has to be understood as the obligation to circumcise following the king's command. It is unthinkable now, as it was at the time of Andrianampoinimerina, for Merina boys not to be circumcised. None the less, nowadays the ritual can be carried out on the initiative of an elder, in consultation with an astrologer, at any time during the appropriate months, and this had also been true in the past, before Andrianampoinimerina's laws. His legislation, however, ruled out this possibility. He made it emphatically clear that the central ritual of blessing could *only* be carried out at the king's command. As a result of this apparently minor innovation, the ritual becomes a state ritual.

This is reflected in another way in the linking of the ritual to the ordeal. This was an ordeal whereby any person suspected of any crime or wickedness, but especially witchcraft, was made to drink a poison, *tanghena,* containing five or three bits of chicken skin. If the accused vomited the poison and the chicken skins, he was vindicated; if not, he died, either from the poison or by execution. At moments of crisis, or before state rituals such as the circumcision, the whole population was put to the test to clear the kingdom of witches. This will be discussed more fully later in this chapter, but Andrianampoinimerina's decision to require a *general* ordeal before the circumcision made the ritual a matter of state concerning the whole area of the kingdom, which had to be 'cleaned'. This was so even though the ritual was still carried out privately and independently in individual houses and concerned small, discrete groups of people. The same effect was produced by the ritual of thanksgiving that followed the completion of all the circumcision rituals in the kingdom. This involved the king travelling all round the country performing rituals at a number of specified sites to which were brought the children who had been circumcised during the appointed period. Again the many separate rituals were linked together by an act of the king.

The elaborate nature of the taxation instituted by Andrianampoinimerina is

115

also to be seen in terms of the linking up of the ritual with the state. Of course, there is no doubt that the money thus collected was of importance in itself for Andrianampoinimerina and his government, and indeed he took every opportunity available to tax his subjects. There is also, however, a strongly symbolic element in taxation. The differing amounts required of different groups demonstrates the unequal but homogeneous character of the state and is linked with our unequal regulations relating to the circumcision. Most important, however, is the gift of the uncut *ariary* for each circumcision house. This coin was called *hasina,* which as we have seen, can be partly translated as 'holy'. The notion of *hasina* is central to the concept of blessing, *tsodrano,* in that the power the blessing conveyed from ascendants to descendant can be called *hasina.* It is that which superiors have and pass on to their descendants, and so it is the essence of the power of the king. This mystical *hasina,* which I have elsewhere called *hasina* mark I, is counterbalanced by the material *hasina, hasina* mark II, which takes the form of the uncut coin (Bloch 1974). The fact that the coin is uncut is always, as in Callet's account, stressed as a sign of purity. In a blessing, while the juniors give *hasina* mark II to the elders, the elders bless by transferring *hasina* mark I to the juniors. The fact that the word covers both meanings shows well the inseparable nature of the two-way flow of *hasina.* He who gives *hasina* mark II receives *hasina* mark I.

If we bear this in mind the full significance of the giving of an uncut *ariary* (*hasina* mark II) for each circumcision house becomes clear. It is both a sign of allegiance and a sign of receiving the blessing of the monarch. This accords well with the general symbolism of circumcision, which as we noted, is a ritual that transmits blessing to the child. On the other hand, it also introduces a new element. The ultimate source of blessing ceases to be only the ancestors and comes to include the king as well, and this occurs as a result of the requirement to give this particular tax.

Finally, there is the synchronisation of the ritual, and this is the element most stressed in the speech of Andrianampoinimerina. Such synchronisation, also at periods of seven years, occurred in other parts of Madagascar whenever an organised, centralised state was established, and as such the requirement to orchestrate rituals so that they occur at intervals fixed by the ruler is the mark of the emergence of such a state. The number seven is chosen because it is propitious in nature and it can only be explained in the context of the symbolic uses of number throughout Madagascar and beyond. In fact, as is the case for this and other ritual intervals, or other numerical usage, the actual number of years separating royal circumcisions was of little importance. We know for sure that state circumcision rituals occurred in 1825, 1843 and 1868, and these dates do not fit in with seven-year intervals. The number is more indicative of the generally auspicious nature of circumcisions than it is a guide to the time when the ritual should be performed. More significant is the fact that the circumcision ritual had to occur at a time fixed by the ruler. This made the circumcision a declaration of allegiance to the particular ruler. Having one's children circumcised at the time set by the ruler demonstrated emphatically that one was part of his kingdom. Similarly, not to follow the time appointed was a declaration of independence. This explains the emphatic threats against those who might circumcise at times other than fixed by the state. To do so was tantamount to open rebellion, a refusal to recognise the authority of the ruler.

The absolute necessity of only circumcising at intervals fixed on a statewide basis explains what at first sight appears as an oddity: the fact that there was a major circumcision ritual and then a minor circumcision in the year immediately following the main one. The reason seems to be that there simply was not enough time to perform all the rituals in the proper season if the interval of seven years was to be maintained, given the many circumcision rituals that had to be carried out within a fixed period and had to follow one another in order of precedence (first the king, then the lower ranks one after the other). The problem was solved by having a small circumcision ritual the following year, and thus gave a second chance, which was nothing more than the continuation of the first. This allowed enough time, and above all, the circumcision rituals of all the kingdom could follow one another in hierarchical order and still be orchestrated by the performance of the ritual by the royal family. (Foltz [1965] interprets these facts differently.)

What Andrianampoinimerina did, therefore, in promulgating these circumcision laws was use what had previously been a descent group ceremony and orchestrate it so that it became at the same time a matter of state. First, it became an indication of allegiance. The ritual placed the family of the circumcised child in the state, while at the same time the ordered sequence constructed the symbolic representation of the state. This was so for both the spatial and the temporal representation of the kingdom, which became organised by long cycles of ritual. These cycles marked different significant sites and related them to one another and to the central power. These sites were associated with so-called different branches of the royal family, which were often in fact the remnants of the families of conquered rivals, and so the royal progress that marked the thanksgiving stage could be seen as the transformation of the image of territorial conquest into that of familial unity. It was within this temporally, geographically and morally ordered unit that the new child was placed in the overall system.

It was, however, not just the royal regulations instituted by Andrianampoinimerina that made it possible for the circumcision ritual to produce the effect of placing and constructing, it was also the very nature of the ritual. As we saw, the circumcision ritual places the child in a flow of blessings or in other words in a position in an authority structure. The regulating of the ritual by the state incorporated that structure, the descent structure, in the wider structure of the state. The two structures came to be represented as different levels of the one overall system and as a result coloured each other: The state took on the appearance of a large descent group, the descent group took on aspects of being a

117

constitutive part of a small kingdom. As a result, at the same time as the child received the blessing of the ancestors through circumcision, he also became a subject of the king. This explains the fact that the performance of the ritual and the paying of taxes it necessitated could at the same time be the recognition by the state of an act of adoption. As the adopted child received the blessing from his adopted parents' ancestors and thereby became a member of the descent group, he also received the royal blessing of the state and became a subject. The merging of the two processes is made clear by a quotation that applies to the period immediately following Andrianampoinimerina's reign. Thus the London Missionary Society missionary W. Ellis was able to write, in his *History of Madagascar* (1838): 'Before a youth is considered fit for the army, or capable of rendering any service to the government, and hence before any domestic establishment can be formed, he must undergo a ceremony practised by many nations . . . circumcision' (vol. 1, p. 176).

The fixing of the timing, the taxation, and the compulsion on all, which were introduced by Andrianampoinimerina, therefore brought about a change, if not in the nature of the ritual itself, at least in the social entities it concerned. Andrianampoinimerina's laws imply that the blessing, the life force that is transmitted through circumcision, comes in part from the ancestors and in part from the king. The group concerned is therefore not only as much the descent group joined by the ancestors' transmitted power but also the kingdom formed by the transfer of royal blessing to the new child. The orchestration of the circumcision ceremony implied a representation of the state as one large descent group carrying out its ritual together. Perhaps this is best indicated by the need to clean the whole kingdom symbolically by removing the witches, preparing it, like the circumcision house, for the ritual. The representation of the whole kingdom as one descent group was central to much of what we know of the reign of Andrianampoinimerina. It dominated the rhetoric of the royal speeches, which today form the main part of Merina oral history. This representation was also evident in the ritual of the royal bath, in which the whole kingdom received the yearly blessing of the king's ancestor via the king (Bloch in press b). The regularisation of the circumcision ritual was simply one aspect of that wider representation, although a very important one.

There is also another aspect to this representation of the state as a large kinship or descent group. Merina kinship comprises two elements: descent, with its stress on undifferentiation and equality within the group, and hierarchy, focussed on the unequal relation of parents and children, and of older and younger siblings (Bloch 1981). When it is represented as a kinship group the state may therefore be seen as being at once an undifferentiated unit *and* a hierarchy. This latter notion being derived from the kinship model, it therefore shares the same moral character as the corporate representation.

The hierarchical representation of kinship means that the whole kingdom can be represented as one family with the king as the elder, or representative of the generation nearest to the ancestors, and the other constituent groups and statuses of the society as either the undifferentiated junior generations, or, ranked amongst themselves, as senior and junior siblings. This last representation produces the fine ranking of all groups in the kingdom and implies precedence and mutual respect at the same time as unity. In the circumcision ritual as regulated by Andrianampoinimerina, the image of one large hierarchically organised family was created and acted out according to strict rules of precedence set down by the king. They required everybody to follow the king in performing the ritual and to await their turn according to seniority and rank. As a result, the rituals of circumcision themselves became both a sign of unity in that their performance revealed the whole kingdom as an ordered kinship group and, by use of the hierarchical symbolism, a sign of the subject's submission to the king; again this is made quite clear in the passage from Ellis that I quoted.

The regulation of the ritual by the state in Andrianampoinimerina's speech began a process that continued to develop throughout the early nineteenth century. Overall, this 'nationalisation' of the circumcision ceremony was only one aspect of the general way in which the new state founded by Andrianampoinimerina became established, and then legitimised, as a conceptually organic unit, but it was probably the most spectacular demonstration of this process. All royal actions during this period reflect a concern to achieve this end.

The speech of Andrianampoinimerina is explicit about the new elements that were being introduced: the taxation, the periodisation, the link-up with adoption. In contrast, it only hints at the ritual itself, because, as we are explicitly told, this was not to be changed. Fortunately, however, we possess some indication of what the ritual was like from a source that refers to the period immediately following Andrianampoinimerina's reign.

This is Ellis's *History of Madagascar,* to which I have already referred. Ellis was a famous missionary of the London Missionary Society, with extensive experience in Polynesia. At the time the book was published, in 1838, Ellis had not yet been to Madagascar, and his work was based principally on letters, reports and personal papers sent by London Missionary Society missionaries from 1820 onwards. Ellis's description of the circumcision ceremony is therefore a secondary source and I have not been able to trace the original documents on which it is based. It is clear, however, that these original documents contained eye-witness accounts by missionaries of the circumcision as it was performed in the year 1825, as well as descriptions given by a number of Malagasy informants to missionaries of the London Missionary Society; the style of presentation of some of the accounts and the ordering of events in Ellis's book is typically Malagasy. Because Ellis's account is partly based on descriptions of circumcision given by Merina who must have been acquainted with the ritual throughout their lives, the *History of Madagascar* can be considered as a partially valid source for the way the ritual was practised under Andrianampoinimerina, even though London Missionary Society missionaries only arrived in Imerina shortly after this king's death. One of the difficulties with Ellis's account is that it clearly combines two descriptions of the same ceremony, as though they were one. As a result we find the same events taking place twice in slightly different ways, while by their nature (for example, the breaking open of the gourd) they can occur only once. This, however, is less of a problem than it might appear, because the two original accounts are fairly easily separated. Indeed, the difficulty can even be turned to our advantage if we see Ellis as presenting us with two documents: one account that clearly refers to an earlier period and another that refers to 1825. It is possible to distinguish and date these two sources because in one of the accounts on which the Ellis text is based the king has no role in the ceremony, whereas we have just seen how Andrianampoinimerina instituted a central role for himself and his successors; in the other account the king does have the central role we would expect after these laws, and in any case Ellis tells us that this second account applies to the year 1825.

The account in Ellis that refers to the earlier period extends from the bottom of page 184 to page 186 in volume 1 of the *History*. It only details what happened from the time of the fetching of powerful water to the actual operation.

Basically, the information we are given is sufficient to establish that the following ritual acts occurred:

1. The gourd was prepared by a hole's being struck in it.
2. Silver chains were put into it.
3. It was carried to a running stream.
4. Filled by passing the vessel upstream in a sloping direction.
5. The leader of the party carried a shield and a spear.
6. The party which had gone to fetch the *rano mahery* (powerful water) ran back towards the village.
7. Those left behind went out of the house holding reeds and stones with which they pretended to assault the water-bearers.
8. They sang *Zana-boro-mahery, manan'atody ambato* (song 30).
9. They circumambulated the house three times and entered.
10. A bullock's ear was cut in the courtyard.
11. A drum was placed on the threshold.
12. The child was seated on it, held by several men.
13. The men outside performed the actions of warriors, and shouted, 'Thou art become a man, beloved by the sovereign, may the sovereign continue to reign', and so forth.
14. The *rano mahery* was poured on to the child.
15. While the operation took place, the women crawled about on the floor, throwing dirt on their heads.
16. The child was returned to his mother.
17. Abstinence was enjoined on both of the parents of each child as well as on others connected with him.

Clearly the account is incomplete and Ellis made no attempt to explain the details of what took place, except to suggest parallels with biblical practices. This is done explicitly and implicitly by his choice of vocabulary.

The ritual was in most respects fairly similar to the one analysed in the previous chapters. Thus 1, 3, 4, 5, 6, 7, 8, 9, 12, 14, 15, 16 and 17 could all apply to the modern ritual without modification. Similarly 2, 11, 13 all refer to actions that are very similar, though not identical, to those performed in 1971.

The silver chains put inside the gourd are replaced by an uncut silver coin in the modern ritual, and it is important to note, as is repeatedly done in Merina tradition, that such chains were made out of *ariary* coins. The drum on which the child was seated on the doorstep is today replaced by the mortar, although I am told that the drum is still used in some areas. Finally, the men's invocation during the operation to 'be a man' was, unlike now, accompanied by exhortation to be a loyal subject. This shows most clearly the political character of the ritual already at this early stage. Finally, Ellis also tells us that for slaves the banging of the spear on a shield was replaced by vigorous digging of the earth just outside the threshold of the house, and that this was accompanied by an exhortation to obey one's master. As we shall see later, this practice was still followed in the 1960s in some slave families.

The only totally different part of the ceremony is ritual action 10 – the cutting of the bullock's ear. Ellis describes it in this way:

> A young bullock of a red colour, selected for the occasion being now brought into the courtyard of the house, the person who is to perform the rite advances, cuts a slit in the animal's ear, and dips his knife in the blood which flows therefrom. At the dropping of the blood from the ear of the animal, the children are supposed to be placed under a guarantee from all future hardship. [p. 185]

This practice, like several other aspects of the ritual already noted, prefigures the fate of the child: The cutting of the ear of the bullock on the threshold area of the house is like the later cutting of the prepuce in the same place. This parallel follows the symbolic logic we have discussed in that, like the uncut child, bulls are associated with the vitality of nature. In the songs cattle are associated with the uncircumcised child by substituting, from time to time, the word *zanak mahery* (strong child) for *omby mahery* (strong cattle). In the same vein, we saw how the youth acting the strong bull in the fetching of the powerful water is threatened by a spear; if we take the association bull/child, this can be seen as again presaging the cutting of the child. It follows therefore that the cattle too, like the child, have to be cut before their power can be released.

In fact, the parallel between cattle and the circumcised child may be taken even farther. Cattle are unlike other animals in that they share an element of descent or, in other words, *tsodrano*. This is because they carry a mark on them that identifies them for all their life with the descent group of their owners. Interestingly enough, this mark is the particular way their ears are cut in a pattern that indicates their masters' descent group. In terms of symbolic structure there is therefore a parallel between the cutting of the ears of cattle and the circumcision of the child, in that both place the natural being within descent, through blessing, because the ceremony of cutting the bull's ear always also requires a *tsodrano*. The whole symbolic role of cattle will be discussed elsewhere (Bloch in press a), but this extra element is totally within the structure of the ritual as

121

we have analysed it so far, and indeed serves to remove some obscurities from the present-day practice.

Apart from this addition, the most striking fact that emerges from this, our earliest detailed account, is that, as far as we are able to tell from the admittedly skimpy description supplied in Ellis, there is hardly any difference between the actual ritual practices of circumcision in 1800 or thereabouts and those of 1971.

Circumcision in 1825

We can now turn to the other account given by Ellis, which refers specifically to the year 1825. In that year, he tells us, the ceremony 'occupied the attention of the inhabitants of Ankova' (p. 187). This account differs from the one we have just examined because, in certain respects, the ceremony was different and also because, as a description, it is in nearly all respects much more detailed.

Here is a sequential list of the main features of the ritual as they are described in pages 177–84 of volume 1 of Ellis's *History* and largely in his own words:

Preliminaries

1. The sovereign announced the day when the circumcision was to take place, thus signifying of the opening of the ritual period.
2. Different branches of families gathered together.
3. There was chanting and singing for some days before the actual ritual of circumcision.
4. Women prepared their ornaments and plaited their hair.
5. Oxen were slain and the people feasted in each others' houses.
6. The gourd was selected in each place where the circumcision was to take place.

Binding of the calabash

7. The gourd, *arivolahy*, was carried in procession by a number of men to the sovereign or to his representative.
8. The leader of the procession carried a spear and a shield.
9. The king was, according to Ellis, the high priest on these occasions.
10. The king 'consecrated' the gourd.
11. The king struck off the top of the gourd with his spear.
12. The king bound the gourd with a 'particular kind' of grass and with slender branches of a native shrub.
13. While this binding was taking place, the king, holding a shield in his left hand and a spear in his right, imitated the action of a warrior and exhorted the father of the children to be loyal and devoted to the sovereign.
14. The king lent to the parents of children of high rank silver chains to put in their gourds.
15. The king was given *hasina*, that is, an uncut *Maria Theresa* thaler.
16. Amidst shouting and dancing, people with ornaments, large hats and bands across their shoulders went to fetch the 'sacred' or 'holy' water.
17. The leader of this procession imitated the act of a warrior with his spear and shield as he sang, *'Rano iona itory?' 'Rano masindrano manory'* (What kind of water is this? It is the holy water that heals). (See Chapter 4, song 46.)

18. Those who went to fetch the water camped by the lake so that the water would not be brought inside another house 'as it would interfere with the required sanctity of the ceremony'.
19. A fattened ram was eaten by the waterside together with bananas and sugar-cane.
20. While the party was camping by the water, another group prepared the house where the ceremony was to take place in the following way:
21. All furniture, mats and cooking utensils were removed from the house.
22. Food was distributed to those who had come for the occasion.
23. At dawn the party who were camping outside went to the lake.
24. A 'youth whose father and mother are still living' collected the water.
25. As he did this another similar youth threatened him with a spear.
26. Banana trees, sugar-cane, bamboos, small canes and silver chains used in the ceremony were brought.
27. A party of the men and women left behind went out of the house. The hair of the women was dressed in the *doka* fashion. They sang '*Zana-boro-mahery, manatody ambato*' (Children of the powerful bird who lays his eggs on stone). (Song 30, in Chapter 4.)
28. Those who had gone to the water circumambulated the house three times and entered.
29. There was entertainment until sunset, including bull baiting.
30. The women prepared baskets and hung them on the rafters. The basket for the eldest child was placed first.
31. While this was occurring a sheep was killed outside. This was called *fahazaza*, 'That which makes children be born'. Its head was cut off and thrown away; in the scramble for it everyone seemed to snatch a piece in order to help their fertility.
32. The children were taken across the blood.
33. On the west side of the house they were measured at the level of the head, the waist and the knees.
34. A banana tree was placed in the north-east corner, a torch was made and placed on it.
35. The stem of the banana tree was blessed with water and honey, which was poured inside the hollow trunk.
36. A winnowing tray, rice and a 'match' were introduced.
37. The children were blessed and the silver chains rattled in the winnowing tray.
38. The children were blessed again.
39. The children were encouraged to be good, pious and loyal.
40. Dancing and singing continued the whole night.
41. The bananas in the baskets were placed on the children and then thrown away.
42. The circumcision ceremony itself took place in the same way as in the earlier account, since from this point the two accounts are merged.

This is Ellis's description of the ritual for 1825, based on a letter sent back to the headquarters of the Mission in London. The ceremony, although remaining similar in outline to the earlier account and therefore also to the ceremony of 1971, differed from both in several important ways. Before considering these differences it should also be noted however that this part of the account is much more 'interpreted' by Ellis than the earlier account. These interpretations are strongly influenced by ideas borrowed from Christian theology and may obscure considerably what was going on.

The actions that are the same as, or similar to, those in the 1971 ritual are the following: 2, 3, 4, 5, 6, 8, 16, 17, 20, 21, 22, 23, 24, 25, 26, 27, 28, 29, 33,

34, 38, 39, 40, 42. It is therefore possible to say that, in the main, the ritual was probably close to that practised today.

The differences, on the other hand, should not be underestimated. They are of two kinds. First, there are parts of the ritual that are different and, second, there are differences due to the new role of the king, which affect, if not the main ritual structure, at least the way it was carried out.

The ritual actions which are different are the following: 18, 19, 30, 31, 32, 35, 36, 37, 41. It should be borne in mind, however, that some of these differences may not be real but may be due either to misunderstandings on the part of Ellis, or of his missionary sources. The following differences, however, seem fairly clear and are unlikely to be due to misunderstanding. We shall look at them in turn.

First, we have difference 18, the fact that the youths who had gone to fetch the powerful water camped for a night and a day by the water before returning to the village. This was probably simply a matter of timing, and was due to the longer period necessary for the people back in the village to make the journey to the king or his representative.

Second, there is number 19, the fact that the youths at the waterside participated in a meal which, we are told, included sugar-cane and bananas. If this was so, we may note that this meal involved the symbolic plants that are used at other moments in the modern ritual. In any case, the symbolism affecting these plants, in whatever way it actually happened, corresponds in structure to what is done today. It involves transferring the fertility of the wild plants (*mahery*) to the stream of descent. Because of the potentially dangerous negative power of wild things, however, this requires their preliminary conquest by breaking them up and eating them. The 'meal', as it is described, also uses the inside/outside symbolism discussed above in that the plants are conquered 'outside', as is the child. The parallel is therefore very close. In fact, I would not be surprised if this so-called meal was an attempt on the part of Ellis to describe and understand an account given originally by a Merina of the ritual snatching, taking out and eating of the bananas and sugar-cane that we saw occurring in 1971.

The third major ritual difference between the 1825 account and that given in Chapter 4, nos. 31, 32, concerns the killing of the sheep and the subsequent throwing away of its head, leading to a scramble for a piece that was then consumed in order to increase fertility (no. 31). This practice seems a totally different ritual act to anything we have seen so far. The symbolism involved, however, is once again the same central symbolism of the ritual as a whole. The sheep, a *mahery*, strong, natural entity, is killed, broken up in a struggle, and the torn bits are then ingested to increase the fertility of those who have obtained a piece. The symbolic role of the sheep seems therefore to be identical to that of the sugar-cane and bananas. The taking of the children across the blood of the sheep (no. 32) seems to be a practice associating them with the fertility so produced in the way that they are associated with the conquest of *mahery* things throughout the ritual, a conquest that prefigures their own fate.

The fourth major ritual difference concerns the role of the plaited baskets that were hung up, one for each child, and then thrown away with bananas inside them (nos. 30 and 41). This is such a major departure that it is worth giving Ellis's own words.

> The next morning the fathers of the children who are to be circumcised, fetch the baskets plaited on the preceding day and in which bananas were placed as an offering to avert future evils. These offerings (called *Faditra*) are placed first on the children and are then carried away by the fathers, who prostrate themselves as they leave the house, to a spot at a short distance from the village, where they are cast away. No one dares to touch these bananas as they are deemed accursed, and are devoted to bearing away evil. [Ellis 1838, vol. 1 p. 184]

Faditra, as Ellis rightly states, are those elements that should be thrown away to remove possible harm and are an aspect of many Merina rituals. It is therefore particularly interesting that the bananas that in the modern ritual, and also for the period referred to by Ellis, are deliberately eaten – that is, taken in – should be treated at one stage of this ritual as something to be got rid of and not to be touched again. The puzzle is, however, not a problem of analysis, but the problem concerning *mahery* things, which has been discussed again and again; it emphasises the ambiguous character of the matrilineal force of nature, which has to be thrown out violently, yet also to be recovered violently. The bananas ('of living mother') are therefore thrown out at one stage (significantly by the fathers of the children); at this point they are being represented in their negative aspect and belong to column IV of Figure 5.3; but different bananas must also be reintroduced, in this case bananas that belong to column I, the positive potential of wild things. This double placement reveals yet again the identity of these two columns.

Of course, this whole episode concerning the throwing away of the bananas is not totally absent in the modern rituals. As we saw, the women at the actual time of the operation half-heartedly plait baskets and sing that they are doing so at the same time. It would, however, be very difficult to say much about this remnant if we did not also dispose of the historical accounts. Participants seemed as puzzled by the whole thing as I was. It is, however, within the logic of the overall structure that the baskets, associated as they are with the negative side of *mahery,* should be plaited by women at the moment of their most dramatic humiliation.

Apart from these major differences there are a few minor variants on what is done nowadays. Difference 35 remains obscure to me. Nos. 36 and 37 are also minor variants, the winnowing tray in which silver chains are placed, turns out, as is made clear by Raombana's account (discussed in the next section), simply to have been a large container for water for blessing, and is replaced by a plate

From blessing to violence

in the 1971 ceremony, probably because the old winnowing trays made of wood held water whereas the modern ones are made of reeds.

Overall, therefore, the 1825 ritual, as ritual, differed considerably more from the 1971 ritual than did the earlier ritual also given to us by Ellis. These differences were, however, still relatively minor. The basic structure of the ritual was identical, and those differences that did exist also fell within this overall pattern.

The more important differences concerned not the ritual acts as such but the role of the king. They are to be seen in songs 1, 7, 9, 10, 11, 12, 13, 14 and 15. It is clear that by Radama's time the use of the circumcision ritual as a state ritual, which we saw being first enacted by Andrianampoinimerina, had greatly advanced, and this continued the changing character of the ritual.

Certain aspects of this greater royal role are fairly straightforward. This is the case for the many references to the king in the blessing and invocations.

Other aspects are not clear. For example, there is in this account by Ellis a passing reference (p. 187) to the introduction of the *soratra* dance, but the significance of this is better left to be discussed later in the light of a further account.

There were however two important royal innovations. The first was that the king 'lent' to high-ranking demes the silver chains to be used for the gourd. Silver is associated with the holiness and purity of royalty in a large number of Merina rituals and this has been discussed before. The lent chains can therefore be seen to imply that the king and his holy power were present at the very heart of the ritual, in the gourd *arivolahy*. Although the ritual remained in one way a descent group ritual, it was also a ritual in which the 'blessing' of the king came to participate ever more centrally.

This element is even more clear in the other major difference concerning royalty that Ellis's account reveals. Although that account is not entirely clear, we need have little doubt about what happened when we put his account side by side with the other accounts that we shall also consider. Radama had instituted the practice that the gourd *arivolahy* could no longer be opened by spear by the elders of the local family but had to be brought to the king (or possibly his representative) so that he could strike it open with a spear in his palace. The youths therefore had to go on a journey to the capital or a nearby 'palace'.

This innovation was of the utmost importance in that it meant that without changing the symbolic form of the ritual the monarch had suddenly gained a central role in it. Not only was the circumcision ceremony being 'orchestrated' calendrically by the state; it had also become for every Merina, in part at least, a royal ritual, because, even though most of it took place in individual circumcision houses, one element took place centrally. This was the most important element introduced under Radama; the 'taking over' of the circumcision by the state was well and truly under way. The innovation also explains the long time needed in the performance of the ritual and the delay at the lakeside, due simply, as will be confirmed by further accounts, to the fact that one had to wait one's turn for the rite to be performed by the king. These changes, innovations though

126

they were, were still within the same symbolic constraints, since the whole problem that led to the camping out was that the gourd, the youth and the water could not go *inside* a house until the right moment. This was because of the critical symbolical opposition between the inside and outside of the house, which, as we saw in Chapter 3, 'organises' the whole ritual.

Overall, therefore, in spite of the differences between this account and the earlier one, the similarities remain dominant, especially when we realise that the differences can in nearly all cases be seen to be little more than minor variations on a theme. Indeed the detailed nature of this account ensures that many more identities are highlighted, such as the hair fashion of the women, the 'measuring' of the child, the mention of the youths 'whose mother and father are still living', and so on. Symbolically, therefore, this was much the same ritual, but its political placing within the structure of Merina society had been shifted by the intrusion of the royal element at its very centre.

Apart from the account in Ellis, another short reference to the 1825 circumcision is to be found in a manuscript diary for that year kept by a British traveller, Sir Henry Keating.[6] The main interest of this account is that, unlike the Ellis account, it actually deals with the royal circumcision in the capital. Keating accompanied Radama for the closing part of the ceremony and the king told him that circumcision was 'our ceremony of baptism, which is no doubt different from the European custom' (p. 80). What struck Keating most of all was the great procession, which included many members of the army, and the elaborate costumes of many involved. He noted the ritual giving of the *hasina* to the king and the elaborate hairdo of one woman. 'On her head she had a small tree composed of small red beads like coral and very neatly formed' (p. 81), a description that seems to correspond well to the head-dress of women in the 1971 ritual.

What is particularly revealing in this account, however, is that it shows the royal ritual in the capital had already begun to grow out of all proportion to the domestic ritual, and involved state and army officials. Radama's remark to Keating is also revealing. Bearing in mind the growing political significance of the circumcision ceremony as a mark of allegiance, Radama's equation of baptism and circumcision explains well his total opposition to the missionaries baptising anyone and the violence of the reaction on the part of the Merina government when the missionaries actually dared to start doing so. If circumcision had become a ritual of allegiance to the king, it followed that baptism was, in Radama's terms, a ritual of allegiance to a foreign power.

Circumcision during the reign of Ranavalona I

The circumcision ritual of 1825 was the last one of Radama's reign. The next on which we have significant information is the one that took place in 1844, a time when there were practically no Europeans in Madagascar. The account I shall use is to be found in a manuscript in English by a Malagasy politician, Raom-

127

bana.[7] It is especially interesting because it enables us to see the ritual for the first time directly through Malagasy eyes.

The 1844 circumcision was of particular historical significance because it was the occasion of the circumcision of the future Radama II, who was already seen as a probable heir to the throne. Raombana had special charge of the prince and so was in many ways a privileged observer; however, he describes only the royal circumcision, not the others that presumably took place in the countryside at the same time and after the royal ritual. Of these we know nothing. In any case, it is clear that by that time the circumcision of the members of the royal family had grown into something more than simply the first and most important of this kind of ritual. The royal circumcision had become a different type of event, one of the major state occasions.

Raombana was particularly struck by the scale, the expense and the pomp of this circumcision ceremony. He strongly confirms the impression that the royal ritual was gaining in importance during the whole period from 1810, the beginning of Radama's reign, until 1852, the end of Ranavalona's. Indeed, he very usefully states as much. 'No such grand ceremonies had ever been witnessed in Imerina, for the ceremonies of the circumcisions of former princes were a mere nothing in comparison' (Raombana manuscript, f. 36, cl, line 12). The reason for the escalation of the royal ceremony, which I think can best be described by the term 'inflation' because it involved no structural change but, rather, an increase in every part, was quite clear to Raombana. He tells us:

> By the speeches which Her Majesty pronounced to her subjects on these occasions, and by the distributions of a great number of cattle to them, it was easily perceived that Her Majesty's intention was that they may know that she intends her son to succeed her on the throne and that they must not expect any other power to reign over them, and that they must prove faithful to him. It was also perceived by these great distributions of cattle, and her fair speeches that she wants to hide her usurpation to the throne of Radama, and that she has ascended the throne in the most legitimate manner, and not through fraud and usurpation. These were the ideas which forcibly struck me, as well as some of the people. [ff. 46–8, cl, line 12]

Raombana's rather cynical interpretation is no doubt right and it seems that Ranavalona did indeed turn the circumcision of Radama II into a public demonstration that he was her heir. This, according to Ralaimihoatra, explains the rather odd fact that Radama II was circumcised as old as he was (fifteen). Ranavalona had been waiting for her position to be well established and for an heir definitely to have been chosen.

There is, however, another reason for the 'inflation' of this ceremony, which is less specifically tied to the particularities of the occasion because it applies equally to all 'traditional' rituals under Ranavalona, which were becoming much more large-scale during this period. The reign of Ranavalona was, as we have seen, a period of self-conscious rejection of foreign customs, above all of Christianity. The corollary of this nationalism was the construction of a truly 'Malagasy' state-centred religion to counter the subversive influence of the missionaries. It is clear to any historian, as it was to Raombana and several of his contemporaries, that the wish to build up the legitimacy of the large new bureaucratic state was what consciously lay behind this inflation, which itself was part of creating a state religion. As we shall see, the same trend continued right to the end of the reign.

Many aspects of the growth of the ritual Raombana mentions are simply numerical. Thus he tells us in great detail and with a certain amount of indignation of the scale of exactions, disguised as gifts, obtained by the queen during the preparations. He tells us of the number of shots fired to heighten various stages of the ceremony. He tells us that at the beginning of the ritual, at the time when women prepared their hair, as many as 2,300 head of cattle were distributed to the people and at the end, at the period of thanksgiving, a total of 6,236 head were given away in various localities. He sourly notes, however:

> It is to be told that the expense of all these cattle did not fall on Her Majesty alone, for she did not buy a single cattle out of her own money, for 1,677 were given to her by different people besides the vast sum of money on account of the circumcision of her son, and the greatest number of cattle thus distributed were cattle which had been got or fetched from the grazing country . . . which cattle are reckoned as the cattle of the former sovereign of Imerina. Thus Her Majesty has increased her treasury instead of it being diminished by the expenses of her son's circumcision . . . for Her Majesty was of a too miserly disposition to suffer expenses singly by herself on whatever account. [ff. 42–4, c1, line 12]

Raombana goes on to describe at length the gorgeous costumes used for the rituals by various participants. He stresses the new clothes imported from Paris, brought by de Lastelle, a French trader settled in Tamatave, who acted rather like the queen's commercial agent. These clothes appear unmistakably in the photographs reproduced in the article by Camboué (1902) and reproduced here, proof of the baroque extravagance produced by the ritual inflation of the reign of Ranavalona. The officiants, however, are also wearing the belts of various medicines and charms proper to all high Merina officials. These belts, which are perhaps Sakalava in origin, can already be seen in the early nineteenth-century portrait of the governor of Tamatave that forms the frontispiece of Ellis's history.

In many ways the costumes reveal all the complex political trends in the ritual. The grandiose nature of the occasion and the attempt to emphasise it as a purely Malagasy ritual we have already noted, but the fact remains that this greater traditional state was a product of politico-economic developments originating with the European colonial powers, whence these grand clothes originally came. We can also see, in the incorporation of Sakalava regalia, an attempt to transcend the purely Merina character of the state and to make it in some way pan-Malagasy.

But in spite of the dramatic display, little of the actual ritual was in any way changed, as far as we can tell from Raombana's account. Those differences from

129

An official at the royal circumcision under Ranavalona. This was one of the costumes imported from France.

previous and subsequent circumcisions that do exist are, however, politically significant and are clearly explained by two different aspects of the situation under Ranavalona that were already reflected in the circumcision costumes.

As we noted in the second chapter, by 1844 the Merina kingdom had expanded well beyond Imerina and this was purposefully demonstrated in the ritual. First, we are told that groups of dancers from remote parts of non-Merina Madagascar were brought to Tananarive to entertain and astonish the inhabitants, and simi-larly subject non-Merina princes were made to participate in the general pag-eants. Second, the locations visited in thanksgiving after the ritual had been increased and went well beyond the traditional central Imerina localities. These are of great significance because the monarch, after the end of the circumcisions, reinvolved the whole kingdom by visiting the major high places to give thanks. By enlarging her itinerary Ranavalona symbolically recognised a greater Imer-ina.

The third innovation was however the boldest of all and had more direct ritual significance. Instead of being satisfied with fetching the powerful water from the sacred lakes where the Vazimba Ramasy and Ranoro were buried, water was also fetched from the sea, three hundred miles away, at Tamatave. (The Merina term for the sea is *rano masina*, 'holy water', a term also used, as we have seen, for the water of the circumcision at certain stages.) The sea water was obtained by a large party of 'youths whose mother and father are still living', in reality a military platoon, who crossed the territory of several subject peoples, called upon to do homage on its passage. The political meaning of the innovation was clear for all to see and related to the often repeated claim during the reign of Ranavalona, and also of Radama, that 'the sea was the border of her rice field', in other words, that the whole of Madagascar was her territory.

Another peculiarity of this circumcision ceremony in relation to the previous ones is linked with the fact that the ruler was a woman. This of course posed a particular difficulty as to the role of the queen in a ritual that at one stage in-volved the dramatic humiliation of women.

What happened is well described by Raombana, who was probably intrigued to see how this sovereign, whom he both disliked and admired for her cunning, would get out of the problem. In fact, what Ranavalona did was to take advan-tage of the fact that the representation of women is dual in the ritual. In some part women are represented as essential members of the descent group (in this case the kingdom represented as a descent group) and in other parts as represen-tative of natural filiation, which is anti-descent and has to be driven out in order to obtain blessing. Ranavalona acted as a woman for the parts where women are represented as members of the descent group, and as a man for the parts where women are represented as polluting. The first role she accepted by having her hair done in the way characteristic of the 'mothers of the child'. However, at the critical moment of the circumcision, when the women were crawling about on

131

the floor throwing dirt on their heads, the queen was to be found with the men. In Raombana's words:

> Just as it [the circumcision] was going to take place, and as the circumciser was performing his office, the queen holding a spear and shield in the manner of a man and jumping about in a warlike manner, repeatedly cried out 'May you be brave, and may you be like King Andriamasinavalona, who attained to a great old age, and may you be wise like him, as well as like Kings Andriantsimitoviaminandriana, Andriambelomasina, Andrianpoimerina and Radama.' [ff. 32–3, c1, line 12]

In other words, the queen was at this crucial moment taking the leading 'male' role and at the same time, by reciting the royal genealogy, placing her son firmly at the end of it, making him the legitimate heir of the line.

Apart from these modifications, Raombana's account only serves to verify once again the similarity of the practice at that time to what had gone on before and since, down to the words of several of the songs that were used in 1971 (45, 46), the use of the powerful water and the roles acted by the 'youths whose father and mother are still living' and the 'mothers of the child'.

Our next body of documentation is very much fuller and refers principally to the circumcision ceremony that, as we know from Raombana and others, took place in 1854 and was the last of Ranavalona's reign. This was therefore ten years after the ceremony discussed above.

The problem with this documentation is that for the most part it does not take the form of a narrative account, but rather is presented as 'Malagasy custom'. As such the accounts may incorporate practices from earlier times. None the less, the dating of the accounts is fairly close. They must have been written in or before 1865, the date of the earliest version we possess.[8] We know the account refers to the ritual as it was performed under Ranavalona, because we are told so by Callet in his 1870 letter, which I précis later in this chapter. We also know it can only refer to either the 1844 or the 1854 rituals of that reign, since it involved the use of what were innovations in 1844, for example, the costumes from France. Finally, 1844 is ruled out because the specific practices introduced for the occasion of the circumcision of the future king are not mentioned. For example, in nearly all the versions we are told that the holy water was obtained from lakes in Imerina and not from the sea.[9] It therefore seems to me almost certain that the account is mainly focussed on the 1854 ritual.

The account appears in a bewildering variety of versions, but rather disappointingly it is clear that all these seem to have the same or similar sources, even though we do not know very clearly what that source is. Most probably we are dealing with manuscripts written during Ranavalona's reign (our earliest version dates only two years after her death) originally composed to standardise the custom.

The existence of such a manuscript need not surprise us, because there were many people at the court who were literate. Furthermore, the desire to standardise and organise Malagasy religion into a self-conscious system that could rival

132

The history of the circumcision

Christianity is typical of the situation during Ranavalona's reign. This, as we saw in Chapter 2, was a period when the Merina were trying to organise a distinct and politically legitimate state religion. They set about doing this by trying to value the past by maintaining what they believed were the 'ancestral practices', and at the same time by inflating and systematising them. In the case of circumcision, which in many ways was the prime example of the process, these inflated versions were then transformed into large-scale state rituals when they occurred at the court for the royal family. These royal occasions involved thousands of people and ultimately indirectly the whole kingdom and the army. This transformation of a basically familial ritual into a grand state occasion for political purposes is well understood by our Malagasy sources, sometimes with cynicism, like that of Raombana, and sometimes with more neutral feelings, like those of the author of one of Callet's anonymous manuscripts. He tells us that the customs of circumcision 'have not changed since the time of the ancestors, but that they have continued to grow until our time' (Callet 1908, p. 72). This is the true spirit of the reign of Ranavalona, and of the development of a state religion, a development that we have already glimpsed in Raombana's account of the 1844 ceremony.

The earliest Malagasy version of the account dates probably from 1865. It was collected by Alfred Grandidier and was originally written by an anonymous Malagasy as part of a general compendium of Malagasy 'customs'. It has recently been published in its original form by Rabearimanana in 1976.

The same material next appears in a somewhat different form in a letter from Father Callet addressed to the directors of the Catholic mission in Toulouse. The letter is dated 4 August 1870.[10] Callet is careful to tell us of his sources in this letter, even though he does not do this in his published account. He says that it is based on two manuscripts by two 'high-ups in the kingdom' to which he added his own observations concerning the circumcision of 1869. Callet also tells us in this letter that he obtained further information from J. Laborde, a French entrepreneur who remained in Imerina during most of Ranavalona's reign and who was an eyewitness of the 1854 ceremony. The direct element in Callet's letter, which is absent in the later published account, enables us to get a more vivid picture of what really happened and a somewhat clearer idea of the sequence of events than could be obtained from traditional Merina manuscripts. These, however, remain the basis of the Callet letter.

Callet was subsequently to publish an account of the circumcision ceremony in his compendium of Malagasy history, *Tantaran ny Andriana*. The account was already to be found in the 1873 first edition of the book, but it is more accessible in an unchanged version on pages 72–83 of the 1908 version.

The published account differs from the letter partly in that it is fuller but also because it is clearly much closer, probably identical, to the two Merina manuscripts Callet was using. This is apparent from the typically Malagasy style of the presentation. The principal departures are probably due to the fact that Callet

133

somehow combined the two accounts into one. The mention of *two* manuscripts in Callet's letter is suggestive of the relationship of the Callet version to that collected by Grandidier. In some parts the Grandidier and Callet versions are the same word for word but the Callet version is longer and fuller. The extra parts of the Callet version are probably to be attributed to the second manuscript. None the less it is clear that both manuscripts must have been very similar and they were perhaps two variants of another document.

The Callet version from the *Tantaran* in turn formed the basis of the account given by two later Jesuit missionaries to Madagascar, R. P. Soury-Lavergne and de la Devèze, in an article published in *Anthropos* in 1912 (vol. 8, pp. 336–71), and more recently of the important study by J. Foltz (1965).

Quite apart from what might be called the Callet version of these manuscripts we have another totally independent source, going back to the same original. This is a manuscript collected by the London Missionary Society missionary, J. Sibree. It is found in a box of archives dated 1863 and is in English. It is, he tells us, a translation of a Malagasy original. Clearly this Malagasy original was closely related to the Grandidier and Callet manuscript and was probably identical in most parts. Its interest comes from the fact that if the 1863 date is to be trusted, it would make it our earliest version. Unfortunately, the facts that this version only exists in English and that it is probably incomplete make it rather less valuable, and in any case, it adds nothing to the Callet version. It was probably the basis of the short account Sibree gave in his book *The Great African Island,* published in 1880, although of course by then the Callet version was available in print.[11]

Clearly so many versions of what are probably basically the same or very similar sources present a problem of presentation and evaluation that I will discuss fully elsewhere. Here I shall confine myself to an account of the royal circumcision based on a combination of these different sources, but mainly using Callet's letter and the published account in the *Tantaran,* because together these contain nearly all the information found in the other versions.

Sequence of events for the 1854 royal circumcision

1. The Ordeal of *Tanghena* was administered and the taxes collected in the way mentioned for the previous rituals. Every stage from then on was accompanied by the firing of artillery, especially cannon. The queen was given the *hasina* and gave a blessing.

2. The day of the circumcision was chosen by an astrologer and the queen announced the date for the rituals and said that those who did not participate would not be considered her subjects (in other words they would be considered rebels).

3. The special 'Vazimba' cattle were killed by youths 'whose father and mother are still living' in front of representatives of all the demes, assembled in order of

priority. They had brought the children who were to be circumcised on this occasion. From then on all involved abstained from sexual intercourse. The queen gave the initial blessing asking God, the ancestral kings, the sun and moon and so forth to bless the children and make them men and fill them and everybody with *hasina*. The queen then licked the hump of the cattle that had been killed, as is done on all ritual occasions of royal blessing.

4. The hair of the queen and all the women was dressed as in the previous rituals and in 1971. The men's and the children's hair was also dressed in a special way and looked different from that of the 'mothers of the child'. We are told that the 'youths whose father and mother are still living' had the role of hairdressers.

5. The queen distributed cattle to all her subjects.

6. The queen performed the *soratra* dance usually for several days. This was a very important part of royal circumcision, probably introduced either towards the end of Radama's reign or during Ranavalona's. This description, however, is the first to make clear what happened (see Figure 7.1) The name *soratra*, which normally means writing, probably refered to the complicated pattern of the dancing. The area where the dance took place resembled the board for *fanorana* – a Merina national game rather like draughts. The point of this game is to advance on your opponent along various lines and in the process to take his pieces. In the dance however the process was unimpeded by an opponent.

The area used for the dance was divided into five paths, at the northern end of which were placed on a sacred stone those royal children who were to be circumcised. The dance was a dramatisation of the procession of blessing and of the transmission of *hasina*, since it involved movement towards the holy direction of blessing and the ancestors.

The most expressive aspect of this dance, however, was the difference in the way the participants proceeded along these five paths. The central path was straight and narrow and used by the sovereign and her close relatives. She proceeded straight up to the holy stone. The subjects, on the other hand, took the other four paths and proceeded along an extraordinarily convoluted trajectory towards the sacred north, therefore reaching it long after the queen. As they danced the queen and subjects sang and occasionally whooped, although we do not know the words of the song. When they reached the end, the subjects gave the queen a *hasina* coin by way of subjection and recognition of her greater sanctity. Callet's sources tell us quite explicitly that the point of the dance was to make the king holy (*masina*) (Callet 1908, p. 78).

The differential path of the queen and the subjects illustrated graphically the latter's mystical inadequacy and the former's supremacy. Callet (1870), quoting Laborde, says that 'this gigantic dance has something from antiquity, something from the orient, and something particularly its own which even renders it, in some aspects, grandiose' (p. 4).

7. The house of circumcision was then prepared. Not only did the preparation

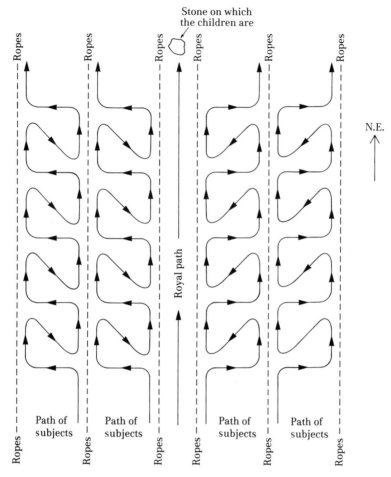

Figure 7.1. The *soratra* dance, which Callet tells us was danced by more than 100,000 people. The diagram indicates the paths of the dancers, which were marked out by ropes. The different paths of subjects and of the monarch symbolically demonstrate the primacy of the latter and the directness of her access to *hasina* as opposed to the indirectness of the access of the subjects. (Adapted from Callet 1869)

involve clearing the house and placing mats, but also the ruler was meant to knock down the southern wall of the house and replace it with mats. The significance of this is clear when we bear in mind the assault on the house, heat, birth and women, which is so important to the symbolism of the ritual. The knocking down of the wall followed, or rather emphasised, the same point. Its exact significance lies in the fact that it was the *southern* wall of the house. This is the wall farthest from the holy corner of the ancestors and is associated with heat

136

because of the hearth, which is placed against it or near it, and above all with women, who always sit to the south of men (see Figure 3.1).

Apart from the preparation itself, the same plants as were brought in 1971 were taken to the north-east corner. To these were added certain other elements not present in the modern ritual. First of all, quartz crystal was added. The significance of this lies in the Malagasy name for quartz: *vato velona,* 'stone of life'. This makes quartz a common element in rituals of blessing. As we shall see, it was also used in one circumcision ritual I witnessed in 1965.

Apart from the quartz a little dry cattle dung was added, a symbol of wealth, and four animals: a water bird, *hango;* a guinea-fowl; an armadillo and an eel. These animals were used only in the royal circumcision and we are not told what happened to them. They are all animals associated with natural fertility and the Vazimba.

Finally, we are also told that an earthenware plate was added to put these various things in.

8. The fetching of the powerful water is well described in all the versions. The gourd was prepared by the queen; it was tied with grass and bark and opened with a spear in a motion divided into seven stages. In contrast to what was done in 1971, the grass and bark was tied in three rings, one at the neck, one at the head and the third to form a ring on which the gourd was placed. It was loaded on to a youth whose 'father and mother are still living', first on his knee, then on his shoulder and then on his head. The youth who carried the gourd, and later the powerful water, was threatened by another with a spear. The youths divided in two groups of seven, then went out in the night to the Lake of Ranoro and three other lakes associated with Vazimba. They took a boat to the centre and scooped up the powerful water. They then returned after having camped out for a night. The youths came back in a military procession but running and singing songs 37 and 38. As they returned the youths were opposed by a hail of stones. They circumambulated the house seven times before being able to place the water in the north-east corner. The children to be circumcised had meanwhile been taken outside to meet the powerful water. Callet tells us especially of the extraordinary costumes of the youths and those who accompanied them, and it is clear that this part of the ritual had turned into a massive spectacle involving 'immense crowds', including the army and many groups of royal singers singing the circumcision songs.

Throughout the accounts we are told of a number of other ritual acts. I do not believe it is possible to reconstruct the order in which they occur because traditional Malagasy narrative technique is not truly sequential. No significance therefore should be given to the order presented here.

9. The children were 'measured' in the same way as was done in 1971.

10. The children were thrown in the air three times.

11. The youths 'whose father and mother are still living' broke into the house with a pestle made of *nato*[12] and used the pestle to pound the plants and animals

137

in the north-east corner. It should be remembered that these plants and animals are all associated with feminine Vazimba fertility.

12. The ritual involving the baskets and bananas, which has already been discussed, seems to have become further elaborated during this period. The main elaboration consisted in two kinds of bananas' being used – one fat and one thin. The women were brought the reed *sandrify,* which they plaited, singing the same song (51) as in 1971; then the thin bananas were thrown out while the fat bananas were fought over.

What seems to have happened is that the two aspects of bananas and the matrilineal Vazimba force they represent were divided by the use of the two species. The ambiguity of this element – that it must be expelled but also reintroduced under control – is to a certain extent further explicated and illustrated by this episode.

13. We are told of several 'separable blessings' taking place at various points in the ritual. However, we are told most about what must have been a blessing that occurred in the middle of the ritual and involved the winnowing tray. The winnowing tray had to be made of a special wood and this might have been an innovation. The significance of the wood lay, as is so often the case for Malagasy ritual objects, in its name. It is called *famelona,* which means 'that which gives life'.

We are told that honey and some young reed shoots were added to the water and silver coins of ordinary blessing. Symbolically honey, like cattle dung, connotes wealth, but as we shall see in the blessing, it was specified that it be honey 'of living mother', that is, taken from live bees. It was thus a substance that participated in the vitality of nature and that, like other Vazimba things, was matrilineal in representation. The young reeds, like the water in which they grew, represented vigorous uncontrolled growth; again they were 'of living mother'; that is, they were sprouts taken from a living plant.

What makes Callet's versions particularly valuable is that he gives us the words of the blessing. A note of caution should, however, be introduced on this point. In my experience informants often give much more elaborate formulae for this type of speech-making when asked about it out of context than the ones they actually use in the rituals.

Here is a translation of the text given by Callet (1908, pp. 78–89), which corresponds closely to that given in the Callet letter and in shortened form in the Sibree manuscript:

> May you be blessed by this holy coin!
> May you be blessed by this honey of living mother!
> May you be blessed by this holy water!
> May you be blessed by this winnowing tray of life-giving wood!
> May you be blessed by this shoot with its leaves full of life!
> May you be powerful, boy!
> May you live a long life!
> May your wound heal!

Then the water was blown on to the child to be circumcised and the blessing began again:

> You are not a child any more, boy!
> You are like a male fish swimming against the current!
> You are not caught in a net
> You are like a banana tree to the north of the house
> Your leaves are not pounded, your fruit is not taken
> You are not a child any more, boy!
> You are like a bird on a stone
> You are not a child any more, boy!
> Your cattle covers the hillsides
> They are so numerous as to make paths all over the mountains
> You are not a child any more, boy!
> You have heaps of money!
> You are not a child any more, boy!
> Your slaves are so numerous as to fill the fortifications!
> You will spurn catching crabs and eels
> But in your fishing basket you will gather silver and cattle.
> You are strong (*mahery*)
> May your wound heal!

All this was sung to the child, and again he was blessed with water. Then unspecified spirits or powers were called to bring the blessings to the child.

This blessing is rather more grandiloquent than the modern one but none the less very much in the same spirit as that given in the middle of the 1971 ceremony by the possessed elder.

14. The description of the actual operation follows well what happened in the modern ritual and at the circumcision of Radama II.

Again the queen seems to have joined the man and shouted blessings as the operation took place, but she seems to have been a little embarrassed by her role and according to Callet, no doubt following Laborde, she stood 'a little aside'. After the operation the child was handed back to its mother through the window.

15. We are told that after the ritual the gourds were thrown away and fought over by those desirous of having children.

16. This was also the case for meat and silver placed on top of a pole, which seems to have replaced the sheep mentioned in the earlier accounts. This was scrambled for in order to obtain fertility. The same symbolism seems to be involved here. The *mahery* fertility of cattle was released safely after the cattle had been cut.

17. Finally, all the accounts go into quite a lot of detail about the thanksgiving that followed the royal circumcision. The queen travelled all over the kingdom having the circumcised children presented to her, occasionally giving cattle and receiving considerable taxes.

This account, combining several versions, is comprehensive, and much of the detail has had to be omitted here where this does not represent a significant

139

departure from the other ceremonies we have so far examined. In many ways it is also the ritual that differs most from the 1971 ritual or for that matter from the earlier ones described by Ellis. The reason is not far to seek. This is a description of the circumcision ritual for the members of the royal family at the time when the royal circumcision ceremony had been made into a military and state ritual of the greatest political importance. Thus this ritual is a long way from the basically familial ritual of 1971 or of 1825. It involved the participation of a whole army, which by then was very large, the continual firing of guns and cannon, the participation of ministers, ambassadors, judges, all in uniform for the occasion. It involved huge crowds and great expense. Above all, it involved the large-scale distribution of cattle by the king and the continual taxation of the subjects.

This state ritual aspect is perhaps clearest in the procession involved in bringing back the powerful water and its accompanying military parade, and in the immense scale of the great dance of *soratra*. All were clearly only relevant to state occasions and it is not surprising that they have completely disappeared. It is also not surprising that these elements should have reached their greatest development in the 1854 circumcision ritual. As we have seen, the development of state rituals and of a state religion went on side by side with the military and administrative growth of the Merina state, a growth that had started under Andrianampoinimerina. After the reign of Ranavalona, however, the growing influence of Christianity meant that Merina religion turned for its state rituals to other symbols. The circumcision of 1854, occurring shortly before the queen's death, therefore marked the peak in the development of a self-conscious Merina religion built up on a basis of familial rituals.

Having said this, however, it is none the less striking how this transformation of the circumcision ritual had not meant much change in its symbolic content. Nearly all the symbols used and their general significance were much the same as in 1800 and 1971, the similarity perhaps most marked in the fact that the songs sung are identical. Furthermore, those changes that did take place were really little more than minor elaborations on already well-established themes. This is true of the animals used by the royal family, the use of the 'life-giving wood' and the division of the bananas into two kinds. The basic *symbolic* stability therefore contrasts all the more clearly with the *political* transformation that the royal circumcision had undergone, and becomes even more apparent when we turn to an examination of non-royal circumcision during this period, which inevitably did not contain the 'state religion' aspects we have just seen in the royal circumcision.

Our sources for non-royal circumcisions during this period are more limited, as might be expected, and it is also more difficult to specify the exact date to which the information relates. Basically, information comes from two main sources. First of all, there is the body of documentation we have just considered, which as we saw, probably goes back to one or two Malagasy manuscripts. In the

140

The history of the circumcision

Tantaran, Grandidier and Sibree versions there is, following the descriptions of royal circumcisions, a section on non-royal circumcision. As for the parts already considered, these are similar in nearly all the versions.

Apart from this body of documentation we have a totally different source: the collection of traditions compiled by W. E. Cousins, one of the first missionaries of the London Missionary Society to return to Madagascar after Ranavalona's reign. It has been published in a number of editions under the titles *Fomba Malagasy* and *Malagasy Customs.* The first edition of the book came out in 1876 and has been repeatedly modified since; I shall use the first edition here, as it is probably the one most relevant to the period under examination. It is clear that the customs were either collected orally from Malagasy informants or based on Malagasy manuscripts, as the style is typically Malagasy. As a result the order of events cannot be trusted and I have reorganised them in terms of what we know from other rituals. The benedictions given in Cousins's text are extremely complex and I believe are best treated as an example of Malagasy belles-lettres rather than as a guide to what was actually said. For reasons of space I shall therefore not give the full text here.

If we combine the Cousins account of non-royal circumcision with that in the *Tantaran,* and exclude certain minor elements from the Cousins description that refer, on the one hand, to the royal circumcision and, on the other, to circumcision ceremonies after the reign of Ranavalona, it is possible to produce, by way of summary, the following list of events for the non-royal circumcision for the latter part of Ranavalona's reign and perhaps for the period immediately following it.

1. Every stage of performing the circumcision was marked by a tax paid differentially according to status. The slaves paid the tax to their masters and those Merina living in the semi-feudal *menakely* of the remote parts of the kingdom paid a part of the taxes to their local lords.
2. The government distributed gunpowder to the people who were preparing for a circumcision ritual, so that the various stages could be accompanied by the firing of guns.
3. The hair of the participants was dressed in the usual way.
4. The participants were to abstain from sexual relations. Only men could obtain water and cook for the children to be circumcised.
5. The house was prepared and the southern wall demolished.
6. Bananas, both fat and thin, sugar-canes, the plant *hasina,* bark and grass, reeds and a liana were collected.
7. The bananas and sugar-cane were fought over, as was a sheep killed for the occasion.
8. The children were 'measured'.
9. A mortar made of *nato* wood was used to break into the house and pound the soil near the banana plant.
10. The torch was made with cattle dung.
11. Reeds were pushed into silver rings.
12. Songs 21, 30, 31, 37, 38, 45, 48 were sung.
13. The thin bananas were thrown away in baskets towards the south after an elaborate ritual.

141

14. 'Youths whose father and mother are still living' went to fetch the gourd. It was prepared as in 1971.
15. The gourd was 'tied' by the elders.
16. The gourd was then taken to the king or a royal representative who 'opened' it with a ritual similar to that used by modern elders when they are engaged in this operation.
17. The gourd was then used to fetch the water, which was scooped up in three scoops.
18. The water was brought back to the house after circumambulation and a mock attack.
19. The 'youths' were threatened by another youth with a spear and a shield.
20. The child was blessed with water from a winnowing tray, the blessing being accompanied by a highly elaborate speech.
21. A dance was performed in honour of the king.
22. A mock circumcision was performed: A child who had already been circumcised was placed on a drum on the doorstep but instead of the child being circumcised a specially strong bull was brought to the threshold and its ear cut instead.
23. The actual circumcision was performed while the women crawled about on the floor inside the house. The child was circumcised on the doorstep sitting on a drum. The men waved spears and shields outside, shouting, 'May you be a man,' and so forth.
24. Banana fibre was placed on the ground so that the blood from the operation fell on it. It was then burned in the fire that had been lit to comfort the child after he had been handed back to his mother after the operation.
25. Further taxes were specified, which had to be paid when the child had healed and the thanksgiving reunion took place.
26. At the thanksgiving the child was again blessed in the normal way but also by having the hump of a bull killed for the occasion held over his head.

This compound description is probably insufficient and the interested reader should refer to the originals, but it gives us a general picture of the ritual of that time for the non-royal circumcision as far as it can be obtained from our sources.

Clearly a large number of differences between this account and the ones we have just considered are directly due to the fact that we are dealing here with a non-royal circumcision. It explains why this ritual is closer to that described in the 1971 account and the early Ellis account for the pre-1825 period, because these are also descriptions of non-royal circumcisions.

The differences between royal and non-royal circumcisions relate to, on the one hand, the scale of the operation and, on the other, specific practices that distinguish the royal from the non-royal circumcision, as the Callet account emphasises. These involve such things as the use of special animals in the northeast corner and the *soratra* dance.

If we forget about the specifically royal practices, we find that this compound account is similar to the description of the royal circumcision for that period and, for that matter, similar also to the non-royal circumcision of 1971, which was the subject matter of Chapters 4 and 5. Some significant differences may, however, be noted in the ritual practices. Number 11 refers to the practice mentioned by Cousins of pushing reeds into silver rings. This is not mentioned elsewhere and seems to be an elaboration on the sexual themes which, as we have already noted, seem at times in the ritual almost to take over.

The mock circumcision (no. 22) is mentioned by Cousins but, as far as I know, by no other scholar. It explains the obscure reference in Ellis to the cutting of the ear of cattle. Here, however, it is much clearer what is happening. The association of the already circumcised child seated at the place of circumcision with the bull whose ear is to be cut is obviously an elaborate acting out in advance of what will happen to the uncircumcised child. It is thus another example of the way various parts of the ceremony anticipate symbolically the central act. There is, however, considerably more to it than this. The practice illuminates the constant equation of the child with the 'wild/strong' cattle in the songs as in the mime by the 'youths whose father and mother are still living', when one acts a *mahery* bull while another threatens him with a spear, thereby once again prefiguring the operation. On the one hand, this is a comment on the child. He is, before circumcision, a *mahery* creature like the bull. This idea must be elaborated in order to make sense of his transition from the world of the Vazimba to the moral world of blessing. On the other hand, it is a comment on the nature of cattle. Cattle are *par excellence* wild strong beings, but they also are 'captured' by blessing, as is the circumcised child, because they are associated with descent by the marks on their ears – cuts that declare the ancestral affiliations of their owners. It is therefore completely understandable that the cutting of the bull's ear should be an appropriate prefigurement of the circumcision of the child. Both operations transform a *mahery* being into a being of descent. There is, however, a difference: The final transition for the bull is being killed and eaten. Cattle therefore are abolished by conquest in order to contribute to something alien to their nature: human descent. The child by contrast is only like cattle to a certain extent. He is only wounded and will recover from his wounds to become a conqueror. The association of the child with the bull is therefore not as straightforward as the ritual acts would suggest. We shall return to the political significance of this in the next chapter.

The other unusual features of this particular ritual are less revealing. The practice of burning the banana fibre with the blood on it (no. 24) seems to me of minor significance and may in fact have also been done in the 1971 ritual without my noticing. Holding the hump of the bull over the head of the child at the thanksgiving is also of minor importance; it is often done on the occasion of a *tsodrano* in certain parts of Imerina. Finally, we may also note that this ritual is the first where the use of *hasina* wood is mentioned; this adds yet one more detail of confirmation of the antiquity of some of the minutest details of the 1971 ceremony.

Apart from these ritual differences there are other features that set this particular account apart from the other. They relate to the political situation. We have seen how the political developments of the Merina kingdom had affected the royal circumcision. In this case we can see how the same difference affected the non-royal circumcision.

The circumcision ritual for subjects in this period stressed submission in a number of important ways. The first was the already discussed obligatory temporal correlation of the circumcision of rulers and subjects. Second, there were endless references to the duties and respect due to the king in the speeches and blessings. Third, Cousins tells us of the occurrence of a dance performed by those who had had a child circumcised. The dance, which was also danced on other occasions, was called *masoandrotsiroa* or 'sun without equal'. This was a reference to the king and the whole dance was an act of respect. Cousins's descriptions suggests quite a little ritual surrounding the dance, involving neighbours, and taking place on the day before the night of the circumcision proper.

Fourth, there was the continual giving of taxes, which quite apart from their not inconsiderable financial significance, were a symbolic expression of submission.

Fifth, there was the receipt by those whose circumcision ritual had been royally approved, and who had no doubt paid their taxes in full, of the gunpowder which was to accompany the ritual.

Sixth, there was the direct participation of the king or his representative in the ritual itself, something that had begun in the reign of Radama I. Apart from a suggestion that the local administrator had something to do with the preparation of the house, the most central and important aspect of the participation was the task of opening the gourd with a spear, which was given over to the king, or a royal administrator or an official royal 'wife', who were also in fact local administrators. The king or his representative opened the gourd in the way in which we have seen it done by the elders in the 1971 ceremony. At the same time he was given money for this task. Only then did the 'youths whose father and mother are still living' go to fetch the powerful water that they would ultimately bring back to the house of circumcision.

This marks the clearest way in which the ritual had become a key ritual marking the political allegiance of the subjects of the kingdom. Indeed one can say that by this time the circumcision ritual had become an important part of the administration of the kingdom. This was not simply because the circumcision ceremony had become a major occasion for tax collection. It also had become a kind of census of the male population. The licensing of the circumcision had by then become the means by which the administration found out who the male children in their areas were, no doubt with an eye to their future military or corvée service. This had already happened during the reign of Radama I but by the end of the reign of Ranavalona the kingdom had taken on a totally different character. It had become highly bureaucratic and registration by circumcision had come to mean, as a result, something quite different.

From the death of Ranavalona to the Christian conversion

The 1854 circumcision ritual was the last one of the reign of Ranavalona, and the dramatic changes that came about with the ascent to the throne of Radama II were also to have great significance for the circumcision ceremony. Ranavalona's death marked the end of the period when the growth of the Merina state was accompanied by the development of a purely 'Malagasy' administration and religion, a system that as we saw, was self-consciously anti-Christian. Ranavalona died in 1861, in other words exactly seven years after the last circumcision held in her reign and at the moment when, in theory at least, another ritual should have taken place. This was to have great significance, because of the innovations by Ranavalona's bizarre successor, Radama II.

Radama II's reign was marked, at first, by an extraordinary liberalisation. Radama somewhat naïvely threw the kingdom open to all and sundry, allowing non-Malagasy full rights, including granting unimpeded trading rights to foreigners.

Similar liberalisation was applied in the cultural and religious field, and the kingdom was thrown open to Catholics, Protestants and even revolutionary atheists. This welcome of other religions was accompanied by a voluntary attitude to Merina religion and a disassociation of the king from royal rituals, specified in a set of laws enacted in 1862 that declared that among other rituals, circumcision could be practised at *any* time *without* the involvement and prior permission of the king. In other words, the elaborate process that had been built up from the time of Andrianampoinimerina whereby the familial rituals had been transformed into an ever more elaborate part of state religion, starting with the insistence on the state periodisation of the ritual, was reversed. As a result of these new laws, it can be said that the royal circumcision as a state occasion was abolished[13] (Raison-Jourde 1977a, p. 298).

The apolitical liberalisation led rapidly to political and economic chaos as Malagasy and foreigners tried to make the most of it. It also led to religious and cultural chaos. The manifestation of the cultural chaos was the growth in 1863 of a millenarian movement called the *Ramemenjana,* which has often been discussed in the literature but especially well in an article by Raison-Jourde (1976).

The *Ramemenjana* seems to have been a popular reaction to the apparent disintegration of traditional culture. The participants were strongly anti-European and anti-Christian and seem to have wanted to force on the king the maintenance of the royal rituals, especially those of the bath and the circumcision. The manifestation of this 'mass hysteria', as it has been described, was as follows. People in several parts of the kingdom became possessed and acted as the messenger of the supposedly returning Queen Ranavalona. Their possession took many forms, but the one that concerns us most here is the one that relates to circumcision. It manifested itself in a series of acts by the possessed that seem to indicate they were trying to force the monarch to carry out the performance of the royal circumcision that should have been held at the beginning of the reign.

The actions of the possessed relating to circumcision are the following. The possessed dancers insisted, with great violence, that all around them should take their hats off (Ellis 1867, p. 266); as we saw, this is a sign that a circumcision ritual is about to begin. The possessed dancers stole sugar-canes, bananas and *hasina* plants, which they brought to the capital with them, thereby acting the part of the 'youths whose father and mother are still living' as if they had taken over the task of preparing the circumcision house. Even more clearly, the dancers went to the sacred lakes, where the powerful water was traditionally collected for the circumcision, and they brought it up to the capital in *arivolahy* gourds (Raison-Jourde 1976, p. 275). We can therefore conclude that the *Ramemenjana* was, among other things, an attempt to force the king to perform the royal circumcision, but this was part of a more general move to restore the 'old' order (which ironically, as we saw, was in fact a relatively recent creation) associated in the minds of the possessed dancers with Queen Ranavalona, whom they were 'bringing' back to reign over them.

In the end the *Ramemenjana* was one of the contributory factors that led to the downfall of Radama II and his murder by palace officers, who took control in order to restore some sort of order and at the same time feather their own nests. The rebels who murdered Radama II were led by the future 'prime minister' Rainilairivony, who put Radama's widow on the throne as a puppet. He married her at the same time and he subsequently did the same for the following two queens. This meant that from 1863 to 1896 Rainilairivony was for all practical purposes the ruler of Madagascar.

In spite of the trouble that had been caused by the abolition of the royal circumcision and the privatisation of the familial circumcision under Radama II no royal ritual was performed following the accession of the queen who succeeded him. This was no doubt because of the serious internal and external political situation. Sibree, in a book published in 1870, tells us that 'no general circumcision has taken place since the death of Ranavalona in 1861 and probably not for some few years previous to that time' (Sibree 1870, p. 238).[14]

As a result the circumcision ceremony remained a matter organised independently by various families at various times as it had been under Radama II. Naturally, an effect of the privatisation of circumcision was that we have far fewer accounts of the ceremony, but at least one account seems certainly to refer to the period 1862–8. It is to be found in an article published by Father Paul Camboué in the 1902 volume of *Anthropos* (volume 4), entitled 'Les dix premiers ans de l'enfance chez les Malgaches: Circoncision, non, éducation'. Most of this article deals with the circumcision ceremony. The first part of Camboué's study refers to the pre-1861 period and adds nothing to the accounts we have considered, but the article also contains a section dealing with the circumcision after the abolition of the royal ritual but before 1869. This account is based on notes by two Jesuit missionaries: Fathers Abinal and de la Vaissière, who were in Imerina for the period in question.[15]

Camboué first confirms that people were able to circumcise whenever they wanted, although they actually did it only in the cold season. At the same time Camboué suggests that the normal age for the circumcision was some time after the first birthday; in other words at much the same age as now. In contrast, the enforcement of the seven-yearly circumcisions had led to rather old children, sometimes up to the age of ten, being circumcised.

Here is an approximate list of ritual acts as recorded by Camboué for this period:

1. The 'mothers' and 'father' of the child were chosen.
2. Sexual abstinence was enjoined.
3. No hats were to be worn.
4. Ordinary greetings were forbidden.
5. A banana tree was used.
6. Songs 38 and 43 were sung.
7. The child was measured.
8. A *fototra* (giant match) was made.
9. The child was blessed with water from a winnowing tray containing silver and young reed shoots.
10. The gourd was tied.
11. The powerful water (*rano mahery*) was fetched.
12. Song 31 was sung (the music is given and is clearly the same as that for the 1971 ritual).
13. On return of the *rano mahery* mock fighting took place.
14. The child was sat on a drum or a mortar and was circumcised.
15. The men shouted the same words as in 1971.
16. The father of the child swallowed the prepuce in a small piece of banana.[16]

Although this description is somewhat perfunctory, we are dealing with a ritual that is very like the 1971 circumcision. The only exception is the mention of the fact that it was the father who swallowed the prepuce. This is a relatively minor point, which Camboué may well have got wrong. Furthermore, not only does this ritual closely correspond to the 1971 ritual, it also inevitably greatly resembles our earliest description. In other words by that time, probably around 1865, the ritual in terms of its symbolic forms had by and large returned to its earliest forms and has since then changed little. This of course is not very surprising, because, as we saw, the main transformations that did occur were the result of the ritual's being first orchestrated with the royal circumcision and then developed into the state ritual, which reached its greatest elaboration in 1844 and 1854. It is precisely these elements that have been abandoned.

It might well be thought that the type of circumcision just described on the basis of Camboué's article as resembling so closely the modern ritual would indicate that there had been little variation in the last hundred years. This, however, is not entirely true. There was in 1869 a rather half-hearted attempt to restore the main royal form of the circumcision with all the accompanying modifications such a move implied.

This is strange because earlier in 1869 the queen – and, what is more important, Rainilairivony, her prime minister husband – had converted to Protestant Christianity. Their decision was as much political as religious, and in particular it involved making Christianity the state church. This use of Christianity was rather similar to the way familial Merina religion had been made into a state religion; it involved taking over beliefs and rituals but using them for a different political purpose.

The decision to hold a royal circumcision the same year as the conversion can probably best be understood as an attempt to ensure that the monarch did not cut herself off completely from the more deeply rooted practices of her subjects and to soften the blow of the queen's Christianity for the large number of non-Christians. The memory of what had happened to Radama II was still fresh.

We are fortunate in having some notes on the 1869 royal circumcision from the Callet letter written in 1870. As we saw, Callet was most concerned with the 1854 circumcision, but he added at the end of his letter a summary of the differences he noticed between his main account and what he had witnessed in 1869. Here are the basic differences he observed:

1. There was no obligation on subjects to have their children circumcised at the same time as the royals. However Callet tells us that all did so.
2. The queen herself did not take the leading role but was replaced by someone whom Callet calls her 'secretaire d'Etat'. This probably meant Rainilairivony.
3. All the preliminaries involving the administration of the ordeal did not take place.
4. No *soratra* dance.
5. No firing of cannons, only guns.
6. The queen did not distribute cattle.
7. The tying and opening of the gourd was done by the queen only for members of her immediate family and entourage. The gourds of the subjects were not tied by the queen or her representative. Only those living in 'the semi-independent' fiefs called *menakely* took them to their local lords; for the others the gourd was prepared by the elders.
8. As a direct result of the queen not tying the gourd the associated taxes were not collected.
9. Callet notes that the whole performance was on a much smaller scale and that the ceremony was probably in the process of dying out.

The overall changes of the 1869 ritual were therefore mainly negative and involved the abandonment of the elaboration in the royal ritual that had accumulated from the reign of Radama I onwards.

From 1869 to 1971

That of 1869 was probably the last state-wide circumcision ritual, although a French book written by A. Durand, *Les derniers jours de la cour Hova,* gives a different impression. This book was published in 1933 but was based on notes written by Dinard, a French official, which were not for publication. Durand was in Tananarive from 1892, on and off, until 1898, after the French invasion. He was the person responsible for escorting Queen Ranavalona III, the last queen of Madagascar, out of Madagascar. He writes on page 134 that the ceremony was held every seven years under Ranavalona III, although he states that it later became a private ceremony so curious that it could not be described in the French language (p. 135).

The history of the circumcision

If Durand is right, we can presume that the seven-yearly ritual continued until the French conquest but must have been even more attenuated than in 1869. In any case, it is clear from both Camboué and Sibree that private circumcisions ceased having necessarily to follow the royal ones during the period between 1869 and the French invasion.

We have no further detailed account of the circumcision ritual for the period up to the French conquest in 1895 except that all the writers who do mention the circumcision ritual state, as Sibree, Callet and Camboué do, that the ritual was in the process of disappearing, if it had not disappeared already.

The French conquest, of course, ended all possibility of royal circumcisions because it ended Merina royalty. The colonial period is as a result the period for which we have the poorest record of the ceremony. One thing is clear from what many people, both Malagasy and European missionaries in Imerina, say of the circumcision during this period: It had become a mere vestige, only to be found in the remotest parts of the countryside. Most writers referring to the colonial period seem to believe that the ritual had disappeared altogether. This opinion was still current in the mid-1960s. Most of the missionaries I talked to then actually believed that the ceremony had died out completely.

This view was probably always an exaggeration, and probably the ritual practices continued nearly everywhere, though on a very small scale, and partly hidden because of the disapproval of the church and the urban intelligentsia it represented. This group dominated Merina society during the colonial period. Its prestige in the countryside came not only from its high social status but also because it came to be identified with the growing independence movement throughout the first part of this century. Thus practice that was unacceptable to the church and the bourgeoisie of Tananarive was also tainted with collaboration, in that it seemed to betray the claim to be civilised and Christian, which at that time seemed an essential element in the demand for independence.

The colonial period is therefore not only a period on which information is limited but also a period when the ritual only existed on a small scale and took place, if at all, in secret. What evidence we have for what the ritual was like during this period comes from a lone account of a ritual, observed in 1910, which is to be found in the second part of the article by Fathers Soury-Lavergne and de la Devèze published in *Anthropos*.

The two authors stress that the circumcision ritual took place in a 'very remote' part of Imerina and this is why the ritual took place with any degree of elaboration at all. In other parts of Imerina, they tell us, almost nothing of the traditional ritual was left and indeed in many families circumcision was nothing more than a surgical operation (Soury-Lavergne and de la Devèze, p. 632). Consequently, like nearly all the authors from 1860 on who refer to the circumcision ritual, the two Jesuit fathers announce its imminent and total demise.

The particular ritual described by the authors was not observed by them but, they tell us, by a "trustworthy" eyewitness who, it is clear from the text, re-
149

mained outside the house for the period of the ritual. As a result the description lacks details of much of what was going on.

Here, however, is a list of the main ritual acts mentioned in the article.

1. Throughout the account it is stressed how small-scale the ritual was and how carelessly it was carried out.
2. The house was cleaned and new mats placed on the ground. Sexual abstinence was enforced.
3. The women's hair was dressed, and an attempt made at the men's.[17]
4. Sugar-cane was obtained.
5. Dancing and singing took place throughout the preceding day and night.
6. A bull was killed and a *tsodrano* made. The meat was distributed.
7. Young reed shoots, a banana tree and the grass for the gourd were obtained. (We are told that the gourd was filled at this stage, but that must be wrong because we are also told that it was filled later on.)
8. The 'youths whose father and mother are still living' went down to the water threatening one another. They then returned, were attacked and circumambulated the house seven times. Songs 24, 31 and 39 were sung.
9. A blessing using the winnowing tray was carried out.
10. Cattle fat was burnt on a plate in the north-east corner.
11. The operation took place at dawn with the men outside, the women inside, and the child on the doorstep.
12. The men dug the ground with a spade instead of a spear, shouting the usual exclamations.

This ritual, or rather what we know of it, therefore followed very closely the 1971 ritual, although it is clear that it was a very small-scale affair, quite unlike that occasion.

Only two differences need be noted. The first is the burning of the cattle fat. This is paralleled by the lighting of the giant match in earlier rituals and seems not to be done any more. The reason is probably that for the rituals I attended either a paraffin storm lantern or a smaller paraffin lamp was used and hung in the north-east corner.

The other difference lies in the fact that during the operation the men, instead of brandishing spears and shields, used spades to dig the ground. This, as we saw, was done for the circumcision ritual of slaves in the past, and is still done, as we shall see, in some slave families to the present. This probably means that the ritual witnessed in 1910 was performed for members of a slave family.

I have not been able to find any full description of the circumcision ceremony for the period 1910 until the time of my first field-work in 1965. There are numerous references to the circumcision ceremony in books published in this period but they either talk of the circumcision as it is described in the *Tantaran ny Andriana* or simply say that the ritual has disappeared.

The only really important exception is a short article published in the Bulletin of the Malagasy Academy for 1959 by a psychoanalyst, Dr. L. Marx (Marx 1961). It is difficult to obtain clear information about what the circumcision ritual

150

was like at that time since the doctor tells us that the ritual was 'well known'. I very much doubt that she in fact witnessed the ceremony, she gives no evidence to suggest this; rather it is clear that she based her account on information obtained from schoolchildren and other informants.

Apart from the usual banal and unsubstantiated statements about the effects of circumcision on children that characterise psychoanalytic writing, she gives us a few hints as to some aspects of the ritual as it presumably was practised in the period, roughly 1940–59: (1) The children were circumcised between the ages of three to seven years; (2) the child was taken out of the house to be circumcised, while the mother and other women remained inside; (3) he was welcomed by a group of men shouting 'he has become a man' with a lot of noise; (4) the child was kept awake all night before the operation (therefore that it took place at dawn). These meagre facts seem to confirm that indeed the ritual was taking place during this period and in roughly the same way as in 1910 and in 1965. The only difference seems to be the age of the child; it is later than for the other two periods and may be due either to a mistake or to the fact that Marx seems to assume that she can use classical accounts of the ritual, referring to the nineteenth century, as a guide to what was happening in the period she is discussing.

My only other information comes from what people have told me about their memories of the circumcision ritual for the period between 1910 and 1965. I asked a number of Malagasy and also several European missionaries who had been in Madagascar during that time. On the whole I obtained very little information in that way. The missionaries clearly knew very little and would not have attended the ritual. The Malagasy I discussed the matter with seemed to be very uninformative, partly because the subject was and remains somewhat embarrassing, and partly because they were unable to remember differences between what they did and what they had done previously. Some general facts did, however, emerge. First, all the rural Merina I asked did confirm that in their family at least circumcision was not abandoned but continued as a small private ceremony rather like that described for 1910 or as it took place in 1965–6 during my first fieldwork. I was told that in middle-class families in Tananarive the ritual had been entirely abandoned and that the operation was simply done at the hospital, though sometimes accompanied by a certain amount of dancing and singing of the traditional songs. This may have indeed been the case, but in my experience informants in the 1960s always tended to exaggerate the extent to which they had abandoned traditional Merina customs, in much the same way as later they tended to exaggerate how much they had retained them.

Without further detail I assume that in the countryside at least, the ritual continued on the small scale witnessed in 1910 and 1965. What, however, is quite clear is that the possibility of not circumcising male children was never considered, and that all Merina boys were circumcised in one way or another. This is all the more significant in that the French, the colonial power for this whole

151

period, do not usually circumcise at all and that nearly all other French customs have been adopted to some degree by some sector of the population at some time.

I have from my first field-work in Imerina detailed notes on four circumcision ceremonies that all took place in 1965. Three of them involved people closely related to those who carried out the 1971 ritual, the description of which formed the main subject matter of Chapters 3 and 4. All these ceremonies took place near the village of Ambatomanoina in the north of Imerina. I also attended the gathering of neighbours, which usually precedes the ritual itself, at a certain number of other circumcision ceremonies involving a wider range of people. I was, however, unable to stay for the full ritual itself on those other occasions, since only people closely associated with the family (usually only very close relatives) were present.

The first circumcision ritual I observed fully was an almost totally secret affair, as were the other three. The reason for this secrecy was, I was told, partly the fear of witches, or poisoners, who might take advantage of the occasion. It was also quite clear that there was a double embarrassment involved in the ritual. First, it was thought to be non- and perhaps anti-Christian. I was told especially not to reveal to any English missionaries that these particular people practised the ritual. There was also a feeling, no doubt heightened by my presence, that the ritual was *barbare,* 'barbarous', and showed lack of sophistication (see Bloch 1971a, p. 14).

The ritual itself was relatively small-scale, involving approximately thirty-five persons. Although the ritual followed the general pattern of the 1971 circumcision, several practices were left out. The hair of the 'mothers of the child' was not done in the traditional manner. There was no measuring of the child. Only a few of the songs were sung, but they included all the main circumcision-specific songs of the 1971 ceremony. Instead of using bark and grass for tying the gourd, leaves of sugar-cane were substituted. There was only one blessing at the beginning. Apart from these omissions, the most striking inclusion was the fact that around ten o'clock a short religious service was held including a homily from an elder, a couple of hymns and a prayer.

Overall, this was a very small-scale affair, carried out almost surreptitiously, and I was surprised at the time by the apparent anomaly of the combination of the richness and complexity of the symbolism and the small scale and near secrecy of the practice. I was then unaware that the ritual I was seeing was a reduced version of what had once been very much more important.

The second circumcision ritual I witnessed was an even smaller affair, involving only fifteen persons. Furthermore, I did not see this ritual from the very beginning, as I arrived with some relatives at only nine o'clock at night. What, however, made this ritual particularly interesting was that it was carried out in a family of ex-slaves. For the part of the ritual I saw, and of the preliminary ritual acts, only the fetching of the powerful water, the throwing of the child in the air and the 'measuring' was done. In particular the gourd, although opened ritually, was not tied. Many of the songs and dances, however, although not repeated so often, were identical to those in the 1971 ritual.

The main difference, however, concerned the fact that at the time of the actual ceremony the men, instead of brandishing spears, picked up spades and began to dig the ground vigorously. This action was, as we saw, that specified for families of slaves by Andrianampoinimerina, but it is very interesting and curious that long after the abolition of slavery, and under no obligation of any kind, these people chose to continue what was a mark of their inferior status.

The third circumcision ceremony was unusual in that as in 1971, two boys were circumcised simultaneously. This was a much fuller ritual than the two preceding ones, entailing all the ritual acts performed in 1971. It was none the less still a relatively small-scale affair, involving only approximately forty persons and, like all the rituals witnessed in 1965, lasted only one afternoon and one night.

This was, however, the first time I saw the women's hair dressed in the traditional manner. The principal elder present told me then that this was also the first time since he was a young man (approximately forty years previously) that the practice had been observed, and that he had insisted on it because he knew I was interested in 'Malagasy' custom. But the next circumcision ritual I witnessed, which involved many of the same people, again included the dressing of the women's hair, and in 1971, as we saw, this practice, which had been an important part of the nineteenth-century ritual, was again carried out. Indeed in 1971 I was told that this family had *always* done it since the 'time of the ancestors'.

Otherwise there were only minor variations. Several songs not sung in 1971 were included, although they were not specially significant; only one seemed directly linked to the circumcision ceremony. The words of this song were *'Faly Arlette fa n'tera'dahy'* ('Arlette is happy because she has had a male child'). Also, for a reason I did not discover, I was told that the grandmothers of the child could not sit down from the time when the water had been fetched to the moment of the actual circumcision.

Another variation that I was told of on this occasion by someone who was present but came from a little farther away was that in his area the prepuce was not swallowed but buried near a source of powerful water. What is particularly interesting about this alternative is that it reveals particularly well the circular nature of the notion of *mahery*. On the one hand it is driven out in its negative prepuce form. But it is placed where it will return in its positive form with the powerful water.

The fourth circumcision I witnessed was again very similar, except for two rather strange events. Half-way through the proceedings it was discovered that the gourd *arivolahy* had been stolen. It was assumed that it had been stolen by someone who wanted to keep it in order to have children. After a short conference, the senior elder announced that whoever had stolen the gourd would bear

153

a child without a mouth; the reason for this was that the gourd had not yet been opened by the spear. After a while the gourd was returned as mysteriously as it had disappeared. The reasoning behind the elder's statement was ad hoc and clearly had the desired effect, but it shows yet again the power of the whole ritual to pass on fertility to all present.

The other episode that marked this occasion was that early in the evening the real father of the child went out of the house and refused to continue to take part. He sat by himself, signalling that something of importance was troubling him. The elders went out to comfort him and to find out what was the matter. He told them that he was troubled because he knew that a brother-in-law of his was sitting alone in his house sorrowfully because although he too had a son of circumcision age, he had not enough money to contribute to the expenses that would enable him to have the ritual performed for his child. The father of the child who was to be circumcised said he was afraid that because of this the ancestors would be angry at their lack of solidarity in not helping the poor father and that as a result some misfortune would occur, perhaps to the circumcised child. Indeed the father of the child really gave me the impression that he was going 'on strike' and refusing to let the ritual continue unless something was done about the other child. As a result a collection was organised, with the elders giving most. After that the other child was brought in and he and his family participated in the ritual.

Of course there was much background to this story that need not concern us here, and the action of the father was motivated by the great kindness that always characterised him, but it is significant as revealing yet again some of the general ideas behind the ritual. Above all, it shows how the blessing of the circumcision *should* be a group blessing and any suggestion of division makes it not only ineffective but dangerous.

Apart from these somewhat extraneous events there were a certain number of differences between this ritual and the 1971 ritual. First of all, five elders gave the original blessing, only one of whom was a woman, and she was not ridiculed. Second, new supplies of sugar-cane were brought by the 'youths' during the night as the supply ran out. Third, the tying of the gourd was done by the 'youths whose father and mother are still living', although they did it under the instructions of an elder, who led the repetition of the formula. Fourth, on their return with the powerful water, the youths were not just pelted with cattle dung but also with bits of banana. Fifth, a little quartz was placed at the north-east corner. Sixth, great play was made of the fact that the 'father of the child', the circumciser, had come on foot from the *tanin-drazana*, 'ancestral land', of that particular village (see Bloch 1971a, pp. 105–11), which was almost thirty miles away.

By and large, however, this ritual was very close indeed to the 1971 ritual in everything but scale. This of course was the striking difference between the ritual of 1971 and all the ones I had seen before. The number of people involved, the expense of money, rice and cattle and the length of time of the whole proceeding were dramatically greater.

The reason for this new inflation is not easily attributed to a single cause. The first and most obvious explanation was simply that the people who organised the 1971 ritual were richer than those who organised the rituals I witnessed in 1965. This was true to a certain extent. In particular the uncle (F.B.) of one of the children in question had a profitable business selling petrol.

However, I do not believe that this was the only or the most significant factor. All concerned, including the principals, agreed that this was an unusually large-scale ritual and that a few years back their circumcision rituals were small-scale affairs like the ones that I had witnessed. They also agreed that large-scale circumcision rituals had recently become much more common.

The other possible explanation for the size of this ritual was that the family in question was particularly traditionalist and proud of Merina traditions. Again, there is no doubt that this was so, especially since they were members of the Andriamamilazabe deme, which had a tradition of nationalism and traditionalism (see S. Ellis 1985, pp. 150–4). In this, however, they were not significantly different from other members of that same deme, who had performed three of the circumcisions I had witnessed in 1965. Indeed I would say, purely impressionistically, that the people involved in these earlier ceremonies were probably more 'traditionalist' than those involved in the 1971 ritual.

Overall, therefore, I have no doubt that the increased scale of the 1971 ritual represented a significant historical change. My opinion was confirmed by the general view of all the people I knew in the villages where I had worked during my first field-work, who were aware of, and by then often wanted, a revival of 'Malagasy' things. They saw the elaborate circumcision ritual as a sign of this revival. Parallel to it was a clear turning away from Christianity, especially Protestantism, marked by the fact that 1971 ritual contained only very few Christian elements. All this was taking place in the context of much greater economic penetration by the national and even international economy.

It is therefore justifiable to conclude that by 1971, a short time before the series of uprisings that led to the removal of the pro-French government of Tsiranana, the circumcision ceremony had once again begun to inflate, although in a rather different way than it had done under Ranavalona. The reason seems to me to be because by this time the rural Merina were turning not only against colonialism, which they associated with the government, but also against the urban élite, which had in the past been the spearhead of nationalism but was, by then, felt to be compromised by its close association with government. This élite had, as we saw, been closely linked with Protestantism, and to a certain extent with the Catholic Church. It was this association that had made the rural Merina embarrassed about a ritual such as the circumcision ceremony. They felt that it made them appear in the eyes of their rich urban relatives as primitives and pagans, and by extension traitors to the nationalist cause. By 1971, however, the rural population felt considerably alienated from the Tananarive urban élite and this manifested itself in anti-church feeling. One manifestation was renewed enthusiasm for the ritual that had always been considered the least Christian: circumcision.

This chapter has given a detailed account of the history of the circumcision ritual in Merina for the period 1780–1971 and has begun to relate the change that occurred to the general social context. The full implications of these historical changes must, however, be considered separately and these will form the basis of the next chapter.

8

The circumcision ritual in history: towards a theory of the transformation of ideology

The historical paradox

Despite a patchy and incomplete record, the history of the circumcision ceremony for the period from 1800 to 1970 examined in Chapter 7 is sufficiently clear for there to be little doubt about what happened in the main. The overall pattern that emerges is apparently paradoxical, for we can find in it at once an image of stability and an image of change.

From the formal point of view, the ritual seems to have altered surprisingly little in its symbolic aspects: the ritual acts, the songs, the objects used. On the other hand, if we take a functionalist theoretical perspective, which stresses transformations in the ritual's role in the organisation of the social and economic system, the ritual seems to have changed fundamentally – passing, for example, from a descent-group ritual to a royal ritual and back again. Accompanying this change in the social function of the ritual have been changes that can be called logistic; these follow directly from the functional aspect and concern such matters as the number of people involved, the expense and the length of time given over to the ritual.

Both the formal and the functionalist points of view are reasonable approaches, and both would further our understanding. This makes the fact that each produces such a different image all the more puzzling. In this chapter the two approaches will be brought together in order to explain how the stability of the one and the plasticity of the other can be understood in relation to each other. The first step, however, is to take each approach separately.

If we are to understand the functional history of the circumcision ritual, we must look at it against the background of the political and religious history of Imerina outlined in Chapter 2. (See Figure 8.1.)

The reigns of Andrianampoinimerina and Radama I were marked by the setting up of a large and fairly efficient expansionist military state. This involved not only territorial expansion but also ever greater internal regulation in Imerina itself, which is reflected in the circumcision ritual. First of all, we have the regulation of the ritual at fixed intervals, marked by the gathering of taxes. Then

From blessing to violence

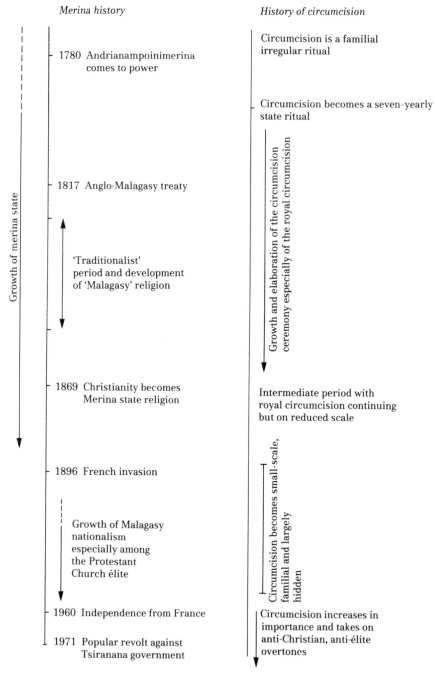

Figure 8.1.

we have the development of the ritual as a kind of primitive census, mainly for the purpose of recruiting for military and corvée service, but also to mark adoption.

The regulation seems to have led to two automatic results, one being a rise in the maximum age of the children circumcised, due to the fact that some children had to wait a long time before another state occasion for circumcision occurred. The other result was more important. One of the effects of regulating the time for circumcision was that the ritual became an opportunity for demonstrating rank order. In the folk conceptualisation of Merina social organisation, any social unit is represented as internally divided by differential rank. This is manifested in the emphasis on seniority among siblings and the respect due to different generations and is an aspect of nearly all the South-east Asian societies to which the Malagasy are related. These societies are usually represented in the idiom of kinship and in a kingdom the social order is also represented as one consisting of graded differential rank (Bloch 1977a). The ranking expresses organic solidarity and not division, but it also legitimates authority. Given this representation of the kingdom, it was inevitable that the fixing of a period within which all the circumcision ceremonies had to take place meant that the different groups of the kingdom were expected to wait their turn in order of precedence. Not only was the unity of the kingdom thus expressed but also its cohesiveness as one large united family.

This temporal precedence itself implied a fact that was to become of major importance. The circumcision ritual for the royal family became a focus for the whole kingdom. The royal ritual was of course the first carried out, but as time passed it became something more than merely the first ritual: It became something of a different order, an important state ritual.

The development of the royal circumcision into something quite different from the subjects' marks the whole period from the reign of Andrianampoinimerina to the death of Ranavalona I. Under Andrianampoinimerina and Radama I it was largely a matter of having ever more people concerned in the royal circumcision, so that the whole capital became involved, and even the whole kingdom, as when the initial cleaning of the circumcision house, which would precede any circumcision ritual, was extended to include the 'cleaning' of the entire kingdom.

Particularly significant in this expansion is the fact that the growing number of royal administrators and servants were given some of the roles in the circumcision ritual of royals that in the circumcision of lesser people were taken by kinsmen. Particularly, the army's growing role in the ritual reflected the changing character of the army itself, which during this period grew in size and organisation at an extraordinary rate, thanks in part to technical assistance from European powers. Because of the involvement of the army in the ritual, the circumcision ceremony for the royal family became, under Radama I, a military parade involving thousands of soldiers and many subsidiary participants.

The characteristics of the functional changes that marked the circumcision

159

ceremony under Andrianampoinimerina and Radama continued to an increasing degree during the reign of Ranavalona. This is particularly clear for the scale of the royal circumcision: Under Ranavalona the number of persons involved, the time taken and, above all, the expense never stopped increasing. The whole occasion became grandiose, chaotic and extravagant, as is well shown by the bizarre costumes introduced from Paris. None the less certain trends that had existed before become clearer during the queen's reign, and they are linked to the changed political circumstances of this period.

Perhaps the most important aspect of these new political conditions is the ambiguous relation of Madagascar to Britain and France. Overall, as we saw, it was a relation of hostility, although how thorough it was and how much the reign really differed from earlier ones can be exaggerated. More significant is the fact that even though the Merina were hostile to the imperialist powers, they were nevertheless highly conscious of their presence. This consciousness manifested itself partly in the attempt to create 'Malagasy religion' as an alternative to the 'Christian religion', which was being fought off.

The circumcision ritual naturally had a role in this construction and some of the changes it underwent are best seen against this background. The changes, however, began before the reign of Ranavalona.

The first point to note is the attempt to involve the ruler ever more deeply in non-royal rituals. This went well beyond simply making the royal ritual the signal for the permission to carry out non-royal circumcisions. The development of the ruler's involvement was marked by the monarch's giving ever more objects to be used in the rituals of the subjects. Perhaps the most important of these things was gunpowder, which was used at various stages of the ritual to mark high points. Gunpowder was, most appropriately, a royal symbol. Its use meant that the ritual of subjects was seen to be heightened and formed by royalty.

Most important of all was the major innovation whereby the ruler, or his representative, replaced the elders at the moment of the opening of the gourd 'a thousand men'. We shall return to this later in the chapter. Clearly this change implied a direct involvement of the monarch in an act that was at the very centre of the ritual of subjects. Apart from its political significance, the innovation led, as we saw, to a number of logistic changes that greatly lengthened the time taken by the non-royal ritual.

These innovations and the increased pomp of the ritual presented the image of a state ritual that was much more organised than any that had existed before. The changes resulted in a blurring of the distinction between the royal and the non-royal ritual, a distinction that had been brought about by the same forces but that now seemed about to disappear. This was because by Ranavalona's reign the circumcision ritual of non-royals and royals had become so closely linked that it could be seen as one unitary ritual that went on for a long period.

Not only did the circumcision ritual gain internal consistency as a result of the attempt to create Merina religion; it also became a major constituent part of an entity that was no longer just an aspect of the political but was an alternative to Christianity. Thus the circumcision ritual became more closely linked to other rituals such as that of the royal bath, and the totality they formed was that new entity.

The change from the kind of religion with which we are familiar in early states, where any distinction between the secular and the religious aspect of royal power can only be analytical, to a situation where religion becomes a social institution, as such, can be seen only as a possibility during Ranavalona's reign. The process never developed to such an extent that one can be totally sure that there was a conscious attempt to bring about Merina religion, but it is worth noting that nearly all recent historians of Madagascar have argued along these lines, although in somewhat different words (for example, Raison-Jourde 1983). This shadowy appearance of a Merina religion was of course to take on much solidity later on, as a result of very different circumstances.

The development of Merina religion did not mean that the political and royal importance of religion were in any way diminishing during this period, in fact quite the contrary. The political significance of the ritual could not be shown more clearly than by the use of the circumcision ceremony for the public demonstration that the infant Radama II was the legitimate heir to Ranavalona. This particular ritual had all the appearance of a stage-managed performance for short-term political ends; it was even true of innovations in the symbolism, such as the fetching of the 'powerful water' from the sea, which made the limits of the kingdom quite different from what they had been previously.

This clear manipulation of the ritual raises the question of intentionality. The political function of the changes in the ritual that took place during the period 1800 to the death of Ranavalona I have been obvious to all commentators, whether contemporary or later. Were they also obvious to those who brought about these changes, and as a result can we consider these functions as the intentional causes of the changes? Of course evidence for this is very difficult to obtain, but there is a little that points this way.

We do not possess any direct comments from Radama concerning the circumcision ritual except those reported by Keating, which show that he viewed the whole proceedings with a good deal of detachment from the perspective of comparative sociology. We do, however, have a record of highly cynical remarks made by Radama to his European portrait painter, André Copalle, whom he got to know well. Talking of traditional religion in general Copalle tells us that Radama 'sometimes laughs when referring to this type of religious activity and he told me that it was a matter of politics,' and more generally he is reported to have told Copalle that religion was nothing but 'political institutions, fit for governing children of all ages' (Copalle 1970, pp. 31, 32, my translation). We need to treat such remarks with care; Radama was perhaps trying to impress the free-thinking Copalle, who is often sarcastic about religion, but at least it shows that the political function of ritual had occurred to the king.

Then we have the much better documented and often repeated statements of Ranavalona herself. They are not at all cynical, but they show perfectly clearly that she saw the possibility of her subjects turning to Christianity and abandoning the religion of her forefathers as *political* treason.

Clearest of all, however, is Raombana. We must again be careful here; Raombana, with his international education, was no ordinary Merina. His cynical evaluation of the uses of circumcision to back up the position of the queen and to legitimise her heir are very plain. He does tell us, however, that his opinion was widely shared, and even more importantly we know that he was himself one of the organisers of the ritual. In other words, in his case we have one of the innovators telling us that he was consciously aware of the use of the ritual for political ends.

On the basis of this admittedly slender evidence, I feel confident in believing that many of the originators of the changes in the ritual were conscious of the political implications of what they were doing, and that this motivated what they did. The theoretical implications of this are not, however, as simple as they might seem, and we shall return to them later.

The transformations that took place after Ranavalona's death during the reign of Radama II cannot, in contrast, be explained by the conscious intentions of the participants. Radama II's abolition of the great state rituals did not lead, as we might have expected, to a return to the pre-Andrianampoinimerina situation, which is roughly what happened after the French invasion. We do not know anything about non-royal circumcision during this short period; nor in a sense do we know anything about the royal circumcision, because it did not take place. What we do know, however, is the popular reaction to its absence, which emerges from the circumcision aspects of the *Ramanenjana*. Clearly the denial of Merina religion by the king was opposed, probably for political reasons, but also for reasons of the type that we normally understand as religious. In other words Merina religion had finally become an entity in itself at the same time as its direct connection with the political system ended. What had happened was that the political institutions, of which the religious manifestations had been a part, collapsed under them, leaving the religion existing on its own. It is probably this that finally fixed 'Merina religion' as an entity separate from other institutions, a situation that was to continue in the Christian and the colonial period, even though in those times it was largely a half-hidden object of thought, largely a thing of the past were it not for the occurrence of such rituals as circumcision.

Of course, the end of 'Merina religion' as an integral part of the political process did not mean the end of its political significance altogether. From the time of Radama on, however, one can say that 'Merina religion' had a life of its own rather like the life of a world religion. As a result its relation to politico-economic events became dialectic and not direct. This is the situation that has continued to the present day, and it seems to have also characterised the Christian period from 1868 to 1896.

The circumcision ritual in history

To what extent the royal circumcision rituals disappeared during this period is not clear. They definitely lost the prominence they once had. The idea of 'Merina religion', however, remained probably as something to be partly hidden but also to be valued in opposition to Christianity.

This continuing valuation of Merina religion is to be seen most clearly during the *mena lamba* revolt that followed the French invasion. This was a complicated matter and we cannot be certain how it linked up with the circumcision ritual. It is clear, however, that the symbolism used was borrowed from the ritual of the royal bath, the other main royal ritual of pre-colonial times.

The Protestants identified 'Merina religion' with the *sampy,* and as a result the anti-Christian elements among the *mena lamba* identified their movement with these very same *sampy.* But the nature of the repression against the *mena lamba* meant that the antagonism between Protestantism and traditional Merina religion largely disappeared as the French insisted on lumping both systems together in opposition to Catholicism and French rule.

Thus although symbolism associated with circumcision had come to the fore during the *mena lamba* rebellion as part of the general valuation of non-Christian Merina religion, it could not constitute a continuing tradition of anti-colonial resistance that involved pride in non-Christian practices such as the circumcision. This was because the aftermath of the revolt led to Protestantism's taking on this role of an anticolonial religion, and non-Christian practices became a kind of betrayal of the nationalist cause.

Largely as a result of French colonial policy, nationalism and Protestantism had become merged and such practices as the circumcision ritual were neither approved by the colonial powers nor a suitable symbol of opposition. The effect of this on the ritual seems to have been twofold. On the one hand, the ritual became ever more hidden and small-scale in terms of the number of people concerned and the expense involved. The attempt to hide the ritual led to the situation I found in field-work during 1965–6, when I was baffled by the contrast between the small scale of the proceedings and the richness and complexity of the symbolism. On the other hand, this situation explains the various attempts in Protestant families to harmonise the ritual with some elements of Christian worship, such as the interludes for a prayer and a hymn that we saw in several of the rituals of the mid-1960s. This period following the official end of colonial rule was still characterised by the same political atmosphere as had dominated French rule.

During this period another element manifested itself. It is clear from many of the events which took place, for example during the 1947 revolt, that the acceptance of Protestantism, or even Christianity in general, as the standard-bearer of nationalism and anti-colonial resistance was far from total, at least in rural areas. The reason for these doubts sprang from the class situation that developed during, and immediately after, the colonial period. During these years a group of largely urban Merina began to gain dramatically in wealth, and later in power.

163

This class was in part the heir of the old ruling groups from the Christian period of the Merina kingdom, who had been able to amass considerable wealth, not all of which they lost as a result of the French invasion. Perhaps even more significant was the educational advantage that they had gained from their close connection with the missionaries. After the dust of the conquest had settled, they were able to deal with the French Government and to a certain extent recover their social position and transform it to suit the new conditions. In particular, educated Merina took great advantage of educational opportunities and very soon began to qualify for jobs in the colonial administration as well as in the professions. They were particularly successful in law, medicine, pharmacy and education. Their achievements brought them rewards of income and prestige, and the achievements of a few were often the basis for similar success by their relatives. Overall, therefore, a fairly comfortable urban bourgeoisie grew up during the period 1920–70.

This group's relation to the colonial power was ambiguous. On the one hand they depended on the institutions of the colonial state, on the other they produced the most vocal of the nationalists. In this latter role they could expect the support of the majority of the rural population, but as a dominant class, in league with the colonial power, they also aroused growing antagonism. In the religious field, because the urban bourgeoisie was closely identified with Protestantism, Protestantism was both accepted and resented. The resentment did not often surface, but by the end of the 1960s and early 1970 it began to emerge more openly.

The reasons for this were complex. The power and exactions of the urban bourgeoisie increased considerably during the post-colonial period. Even more importantly the nationalist role of the bourgeoisie became less and less clear (Archer 1976). Even if they were not the most obvious supporters of the government put into power under Tsiranana by the French, they were certainly the most obvious beneficiaries. At least this was how things were seen in the countryside. As a result the peasants, who had once viewed the urban bourgeoisie as their vanguard, now saw it as their dominators. The religious manifestation of this reversal was that Merina religion, by then a very hazy notion not really distinct from Christianity, became redefined and revalued in opposition to Christianity with its urban bourgeois associations. What remained of Merina religion were bits and pieces, but particularly prominent was the circumcision ritual. This had been one of the elements that had been largely left alone by the missionaries but that unlike other rituals, such as those associated with tombs, had never become much syncretised with Christian elements. As a result the circumcision ritual became an obvious focus for the attempt to revive Merina religion over and against Protestantism.

This is the setting for the renewed growth of the ritual in terms of length of time involved, expense and number of persons, which marked the situation in 1971. By that time, as we saw in Chapter 4, the ritual had again grown dramatically.

164

The circumcision ritual in history

This brief survey of the 'functional' history of the circumcision ritual during the whole period 1800 to 1971 reveals the ritual as closely affected by politico-economic changes during this time. It appears almost as a barometer of the political situation, and no doubt, if we knew the history in even more detail, this rapid reaction to events would be even more marked. It is therefore surprising that if we look at another aspect of the ritual, its symbolic content, we get a totally different picture.

The image we obtain is one of surprising stability, as though the functional changes in the ritual had no significance for its content. This stability takes two forms. On the one hand we find that all the most important ritual acts, symbols and songs remain virtually unchanged in all our accounts. On the other, if we were to carry out the kind of symbolic analysis of the overall pattern of the ritual that formed the substance of Chapter 5, we would obtain exactly the same result for *any* of the rituals in question.

Despite this overall lack of change, there were of course some modifications in the symbolic content of the ritual, and these must be examined. They seem to fall into three categories:

1. Ritual acts that are added to the ritual but remain external to its basic structure
2. A greater or lesser repetition of the same themes, using different symbols (The significance of these different symbols, however, seems to be the same as that of the more permanent symbols.)
3. The appearance and disappearance of certain elaborations

The ritual acts that are added to the ritual but seem external to it are, on the one hand, bits of ritual imported from other, similar Merina practices and, on the other, chunks of ritual belonging to other traditions. Of the first we have the example of types of blessing reminiscent of part of the royal bath ritual, which appeared under Ranavalona I. Of the second the most obvious is the *soratra* dance, of whose origin we cannot be sure, and more obviously the same Christian services that are introduced at various moments. These introductions never seem to become integrated with the rest of the ritual, and their symbolism remains unconnected with the symbolism of the ritual as a whole. Another of their features is that they seem to disappear as easily as they came, leaving no trace.

The second element of change is that we find a greater or lesser degree of elaboration in the symbolism. As we saw in Chapter 4, the symbolism behind many of the songs and actions is identical; we are dealing with continuous repetition. It is of two kinds: Either different symbols with the same significance are used, for example, the many symbols that can be said to be 'of a living mother', or there may be simple repetition of exactly the same acts or songs. This is clearest for the songs, which may be repeated many hundreds of times. It is not surprising, therefore, that when the ritual is compressed for functional reasons the repetition becomes less and when it is expanded it increases. It is notable, however, that in no case was the compression such that any part of the central symbolic structure was left out.

From blessing to violence

The third element of change does involve the appearance and disappearance of different symbols. These changes are of various kinds. Sometimes we are dealing with substitutions of specific things that have the same symbolic value. Examples of this are the substitution of silver chains for silver coins, the substitution of the winnowing tray for the plate, the substitution of the drum for the mortar; or the alternative of disposing of the prepuce by swallowing it or by placing it at a confluence of two streams. In this latter case both alternatives enter within the same logic, but the second makes the logic more explicit. Such substitution even took place within the one year in 1965 when because one family did not possess a spear it substituted a knife. Substitutions that are symbolically neutral may, however, not always be without significance. For example, the substitution of sea water for water from the holy lakes at the circumcision of Radama II was, as we saw, highly revealing politically although symbolically insignificant. This is also true of the fact that slaves in the past, and descendants of slaves this century, used spades instead of spears at the time of the actual operation. The alternative expresses well the difference in status between two types of people but its symbolic reference to the work of men is the same for both groups.

Another type of change in the symbolism seems to be linked with the problem of compression. For example, the dropping of the elaborate ritual involving two types of bananas and the throwing away of the 'thin' bananas in plaited baskets seems to have been due to the simplification that the whole ritual underwent between 1868 and 1965. There was simply no time for all these actions in the compressed ritual of later years. It is interesting to note that some remains of these actions still existed in 1965 and 1971, in the form of the women's songs about plaiting baskets, but by then they had become meaningless to the participants and no amount of symbolic analysis would have recovered the original meaning. Why such survivals can continue is problematic. Perhaps they strike some chord, however obscure, in the participants; perhaps, as will be discussed in the next section, the nature of the ritual is so fixed that it can 'carry' dead elements for a long time. In this connection it must be remembered that the history of the circumcision ritual also shows that we must be very careful not to assume that elimination or omission is necessarily permanent. The dropping of the elaborate hair-styles for 'mothers of the child', for example, was only temporary, and they had reappeared by 1971.

Such reappearances are, I believe, more common than can be seen from the particular case given here. The reasons are also less mysterious than might be thought. First of all, the lifetime of individuals, when they actively participate in the ritual, may be as long as seventy years. Thus, in periods when a ritual such as this is undergoing a period of growth, the old will be questioned about what they can remember from the past. I actually saw this occurring on a number of occasions, and although memory may be faulty, and some old people may imagine things that never happened, I was repeatedly struck by the detailed nature of recall of many old people when they were asked in this way.[1] Another factor of importance is that in this account the poverty of the historical record has not enabled us to see the contemporary variations that must have existed at any one time. Only for 1965 was it possible to catch a glimpse of such variation. But since such variation must have always existed, it must have always been possible for groups that had lost certain elements to reintroduce them again by borrowing from contemporaries who had retained these elements.

Finally, there are differences involving ritual sequences that have totally disappeared. Two in particular are notable: the cutting of the bull's ear on the threshold and the scrambling for the sheep on the maypole. As we saw, the significance of these acts is identical with that of acts performed now that closely resemble them. They can therefore be seen as reiterating much the same ideas as those expressed elsewhere. The ideas, in any case, are repeated again and again in the ritual even when these elements are missing.

Overall, therefore, although there are differences and variations between the rituals relating to the symbolic construction involved in the basic ideas and emotions in the ritual, it can be said quite categorically that no ideas have been added and none taken away as a result of these modifications. If we add this fact to the recognition of the large parts of the ritual that have remained totally symbolically unchanged through this period of nearly two hundred years, we are faced with an extraordinary stability, not to say lack of innovative change.

This stability is all the more puzzling when we bear in mind that it has occurred in a ritual that seen from the functional perspective, has reacted with extreme plasticity to politico-economic events. Furthermore these politico-economic events for Madagascar in this period have been extreme by any standard, involving the development of a large-scale pre-industrial state, colonisation by a foreign capitalist power, de-colonisation and the effects of neo-colonialism. How then can we resolve this apparent paradox of adaptation from one point of view and non-adaptation from another?

The historical potential of the symbolism

The first step in solving this problem requires that we look again at the nature of the symbolic 'argument' itself, as given in Chapter 5, bearing in mind that such an argument is, to a certain extent, a misrepresentation because it ignores the 'ritual' nature of the ritual. For the moment, however, this problem will be ignored.

The central point of Chapters 4 and 5 was that the circumcision must be seen from the actor's point of view as transmitting the blessing of the ancestors to the newest generation. The form of the circumcision ritual as a whole is that of a greatly expanded ritual of blessing and that is the first thing the Merina say about it.

From the actors' point of view blessing is the transmission of the power of the

167

ancestors to the living, or, better still, merging the living with the ancestors into a permanent mystical unity. From the observer's point of view the image is reversed; it is a case not of the living becoming like the ancestors but, rather, of the ritual creating the image of the descent group that appears to the participants as creating them. It is through the rituals of blessing and circumcision that the image of the past as unchanging and conquering the present is created. In other words, while the actors see the ritual within a mystical framework, we must see the ritual as creating that mystical framework, which in this case is the notion of descent.

Descent is primarily denial of time through denial of the relevance of death and, by implication, birth. This is because descent is an image of the true social unit, which endures for ever. The living are mere representatives of a force that they have received from the dead and that only truly belongs to the dead. The purpose of the ritual is first of all to *clarify* that element of time-defying descent in the living, so that it can emerge shining and cleaned from ultimately unworthy incarnation. This makes the living identical to the previous and succeeding generation. It merges successive generations as they are merged in the tomb. As a true descent-being a person is like the dead and the process of becoming like the dead is the receiving of blessing, first of all, at circumcision.

In descent the difference between generations is irrelevant. All generations are in the end the same, and so the passage of time that separates the generations is ignored. This has one indirect and two direct implications. The first direct implication is that the identity of different generations makes the negation of the acts of birth and death essential. The second direct implication is that what differentiates the living from the dead, that is, life itself, must be represented as being in opposition to descent. The indirect result of the notion of descent is the irrelevance of individuality. For the Merina, individuality results from life, whereas the descent element is identical for all descent-group members. As a result individuality, too, is opposed to descent, and this is demonstrated by the fact that it leads to division within the descent unit. As the living go through life, they receive more and more the blessing of the ancestors, which makes them more and more 'descent beings'. However, it is only when they are dead, when their bodies have finally been placed in the tomb from which they will not move any more, that this potential for total depersonalisation is fully realised. (For a fuller discussion of this point see Bloch 1971a, pp. 161–71.)

Descent furthermore is an absolute denial of time because it is based on the denial of movement. Only when the dead are *placed* in the tomb of their final repose are they truly descent beings. Once there, they do not decay because after the process of decomposition, which the Merina represent as a process of drying, their remains are believed to stay unchanged for ever, and it is the first duty of the living to ensure this preservation. However, the Merina shift the focus of emphasis from the actual remains to the tomb itself, which declares permanence triumphantly. This is expressed in the hardness and massiveness of the tomb and

168

the stones used in its construction, which demonstrate in material form the victory over time and also over movement. Tombs are emphatically placed in a particular highly significant place and they are there for ever. Descent for the Merina merges the idea of being the children of particular people and being the children of a particular place. Indeed, the Merina often say that they are the children of the 'land of their ancestors', *tanin drazana*. Descent means, therefore, not only to remain still amidst the vicissitudes of time but also to remain still in space. The image created by descent is a fundamental negation of the experience of life, of movement, and of human creativity, which has no place in a world where everything is and nothing becomes.

This is how the concept of descent deals its most fundamental blow against 'this world': Descent makes the action of creating valueless. Any change is represented in Merina rituals as loss. What human beings should do is avoid all action, since this implies the dispersal of descent. Furthermore, since it is recognised that in fact dispersal will occur (after all, humans are alive) rituals should attempt to restore what has been dispersed – to atone for having been alive. The Merina political leader and Protestant theologian R. Andriamanjato long ago saw this idea as the central one in Merina religion and discussed it in a very different type of book from this, only to reach identical conclusions on this point (Andriamanjato 1957).

Thus its construction is such that descent emerges out of the ritual as the true reality, while this life and its activities appear to be mere shadows on the wall of the cave. Furthermore, as it was for Plato, such a declaration is the first step toward defining legitimate authority, because descent also implies obedience. It implies honouring the ancestors in the tomb and the elders in this life, indeed following the dictates of anybody closer to the ancestors than oneself. This usually means someone closer in age, but not always. Obedience is the corollary of the permanence and immobility of the tomb and of descent. If one is to become through life a descent being or, in other words, more like an ancestor, any deviation in one's actions from the intentions of elders and ancestors is wilful nondescent; it is dispersal. The ancestors are pure authority, the elders should be as close to this ideal as possible and they should therefore be obeyed, but the representation of descent means that this authority is not experienced merely as an external constraint from an alien force. Any member of a descent unit, that is, anybody who receives blessings, is becoming an ancestor. As a result obeying the elders, the representatives of the ancestors, is also obeying the better part of oneself – the part that will become dominant as one passes from the warm house of birth to the cold and permanent tomb.

This seems to me the true secret of the extraordinary power of traditional authority, and why it is only challenged with such difficulty. Traditional authority implies a total order of which both superior and inferior are a part though in different degree.

In obeying the person in the role of 'elder' (even though he may be a gross

169

local politician), one is aligning oneself with a virtue that is believed to be, in the end, the source of one's own true self. Obeying is a matter of doing what one should want, and which one will want, when one has fully received the blessing of the ancestors, that is, when one is in the tomb finally.

The fact that the authority-legitimating aspect of the notion of descent does not involve the experience of submission of self to another, but of submission of self *and* other to a transcendental authority, explains the continuing strength of the concept. A revolt against descent would appear to be a revolt against oneself. The image of timelessness and immobility in space is therefore the counterpart of obedience. When one is timeless and still one's desires will be dissolved in the eternal will of descent, one will be dissolved in the ancestors.

The image of descent is not just constructed positively in the ritual, as we saw, it is created even more clearly out of opposition with its antithesis. Even in the few preceding paragraphs, which attempted to specify the very core of descent, it was impossible to avoid reference to what descent is not: 'this life', birth, death, decomposition, movement, change and durational time. The reason is of course evident. The only way that an image of the transcendental can be created is by manipulation of the apparent. The ritual, therefore, is largely concerned with acting out an image of this life that is the opposite of descent. The image evoked is, however, far from an innocent one. 'This life' is, above all, seen as one of dirt, chaotic disorder, unpredictability and immorality. The ritual puts much more effort into presenting this chaos on earth than into specifying the order and peace of the tomb. The two are linked as in a mirror, where the image reverses the orientation of the object it reflects. 'This life' is one wherein birth, in the hands of women only, leads to death and the pollution of decomposition. 'This life' is one wherein time is historical and leads to disorderly acts of dispersal, wherein men are like animals and plants. In 'this life', were it not for the cooling stream of descent, men would be without culture, like the Vazimba, who as will be remembered, knew no crafts, were ruled by women and had no descendants.

The image of 'this life' is therefore a construction that pretends to represent the here and now in contrast to the tomb, but in fact misrepresents it to vilify it, to make it appear as something that must be escaped. The significance of this negative creation is crucial and complex. The antithetical image is indeed linked to daily experience of interaction between people and between people and the environment, and therefore it has credibility. It is, however, also a selection from experience that represents it as purely negative, the opposite of the desirable. As a result the tendentious representation of 'this life' by acted out chaos is an attack on the value of human creativity, especially an attack on durational time and movement, which are the first requirements for human action to be perceived as creative. It is an attack on the distinction between plants and animals, on the one hand, and humans, on the other. It is an attack on the value of the processes of procreation, especially sex and birth. Above all, it is an attack on life itself so

170

that death can appear desirable, in the hazy image created by antithesis of a deathless and birthless life, that is, descent.

There is, however, another element in the ritual, other than the creation of descent by antithesis, which results from the inevitable problem of a symbolic construction that absolutely devalues life. The problem manifests itself in the ritual in the fact that the 'cleaning' of the child or the 'cooling' of the child, or the 'making' of the child like an ancestor, that is, dead and dry, can be achieved only *to a certain extent*. The child is, for the moment at least, of this world, so the ritual faces the problem that this life, which it first denied, is necessary, especially if production and reproduction are to continue. This modification leads to the apparently lame and contradictory recognition that reproduction only by blessing and descent, even though it has been set up as an ethical ideal, will simply not work for the living.

The original antithesis set up the problem. Descent was constructed on the denial of the value of 'this life', but it was also given as an ideal for the behaviour of the living. The ritual, however, also proposes a solution to the problem: Vitality is reintroduced for the living but *only* under the violent control of descent. This explains the puzzle that was discussed in Chapter 5: that the matrilineal element which is denied and driven out, to create descent, is in the end reintroduced. For the reintroduction not to be totally contradictory it is qualified. This qualification is acted dramatically, the Vazimba matrilineal wild world is brought back, but *under violent control*. Vitality is brought back but *tamed;* only then can it be used by descent in this life.

If the source of the problem can be seen in the logic of transcendence – where transcendence is by definition not of this life but nevertheless has its relevance in the world of the living – then the solution through violence transforms the problem into a key positive element of central political significance. In a certain light the whole ritual can be seen as a ritual of conquest. It is a conquest of this life by the ancestors, it is a conquest of the junior generations by the senior, and it is a conquest of the wild, feminine 'this earthly' by all the participants. This conquest is achieved by successful violence, which has an ever more central role in the ritual actions. The wild, strong *mahery* plants and animals are threatened and killed or broken up. The house of circumcision, and the femininity it represents, is conquered by being broken into by the 'youths whose father and mother are still living'. The gourd is threatened by the elders and then speared and broken into. The *mahery* water is threatened with the spear. The various make-believe *mahery* 'bulls' are threatened by spears. The real bull is killed and cut up with great brutality. Above all, of course, the child, when he is still associated with the world of wetness, women and *mahery* things, is wounded by the representative of the ancestors. This wounding has been charged with meaning via the parallel with the bull, which is stressed throughout the ritual and increases the significance of the violence inflicted on the child. It will be remembered that he is continuously associated with *mahery* bulls, animals that in the ritual are either

171

being threatened or killed. As a result the wound inflicted on the child symbolically almost kills him. This theme becomes even more explicit when we remember that while the operation is taking place the women are acting in a way that is reminiscent of mourning for the dead.

It might be thought that with the circumcision of the child the final violent conquest has taken place, but in fact this is not so. Once the child has been conquered in his *mahery,* feminine aspect he himself then becomes the violent conqueror of the same entity. He re-enters the female house through the window, an act full of violence and sexuality because, as we saw, this is seen as violent sexual penetration.

There is also another side of this sequence of violence that is dramatised throughout. Violence is a preliminary to consumption. The banana and sugarcane are fought over and broken – but then they are eaten, an act that increases the fertility of the eaters. Much the same happens to the powerful water, which is a focal symbol in the whole performance. The powerful water 'gives strength' in the words of the song, but this is only after it has been threatened continuously with a spear, scooped up violently, again under the threat of spears, and finally *used* in the blessing, an act that goes diametrically against its *mahery* nature. The bull that is killed at the beginning of the ritual provides meat to be eaten and gives strength to the descent beings who participate in the ritual. (For a discussion of the symbolism of meat eating see Bloch in press a.) Finally, as the parallel with the bull would lead us to expect, the child is also 'consumed' to give strength to descent. But in contrast to the other *mahery* entities such as the plants and animals this consumption is only partial and becomes for him a preliminary to himself conquering, conquering femininity, which will lead to the continuation of the group. This is what marks the difference between him and the bull. The bull is only one substance; the bull is fully *mahery.* In the ritual he is therefore consumed by descent beings and abolished for the sake of their reproduction. The child, however, as he is the recipient of blessing, consists of two elements, the *mahery* element, and the descent element. In so far as he is a *mahery* being he is threatened, killed and consumed, in fact, his prepuce, the most feminine part, is literally eaten by an elder. In so far as he is a descent being he threatens, kills and consumes exactly that same *mahery* element.

The contradiction of the return to 'this life', which has been shown to exist in the ritual, is a contradiction only from the point of view of the absolute standard of the ancestors. From the point of view of the living the contradiction becomes a cause for rejoicing, the explanation of the need for continuing violent conquest of this world by those close to the transcendental so that they can be strong.

From this perspective it becomes clear how apposite to the whole ritual is the myth of origin discussed in Chapter 6. The creation of the ritual is attributed to Andriamanelo, the violent conqueror of the Vazimba by means of spears of iron. Andriamanelo is not just the conqueror of the Vazimba, he is also the person who sets in motion the practices that ensure that once conquered the power of these very Vazimba, that of natural fertility, can be *used* by the conquering Merina. That is what the circumcision ritual in the myth is said to do. It is a set of precautions so that the power of the lake where the Vazimba queens have been buried is given to Andriamanelo's children. But this is a dangerous enterprise. There is the danger that the power of the Vazimba will totally take over the child, in other words that the contradiction of the reintroduction of the wild element will indeed be a contradiction. Only when careful and violent devices have been found for handling the conquered Vazimba is this reintroduction successful.

The myth therefore parallels well the whole ritual action; it repeats its meaning in another way. Moreover, it does something of great political significance: It equates military conquest with the conquest of what is 'this earthly' by the ancestral even though it is the military conquest of mythical beings, the Vazimba.[2] There is, however, yet another element in the myth that is highly suggestive. Andriamanelo, the Merina conqueror of the Vazimba, is himself half Vazimba through his mother. In other words the violent conqueror is himself the product of a violent conquest. This is, of course, the case with the child in the ritual. The child is violently conquered by the circumcision, but as a result of this conquest he becomes, in the words of the men waiting for him outside, a man, that is, a future conqueror, a destiny that he marks by his violent entry into the house he has left. Life becomes a continual series of conquests and a continual series of consumptions of what has been conquered so that it will give strength and fertility.

This explains more clearly the apparent puzzle of the women's willing participation in the ritual. There is a paradox about women in this ritual. Merina women have a very high social status in everyday life – that is, by the standards of comparative ethnography. When they reach a certain age Merina women can be, and often are, the heads of households. They often dominate men because of their wealth or because their marriage is uxorilocal and their husbands are in a weak position. Women are shown great respect and have a surprising degree of freedom of action. Their behaviour is not in the least subservient to men and yet they are willing to participate in a ritual that appears to give them a humiliating role. In fact they are not just willing to participate; they are eager and enthusiastic participants (Bloch in press c).

The answer to the puzzle of why this should be lies in the very nature of the ritual. As we saw it represents two sides of life – the ancestral and the 'this worldly', the latter being represented in a strongly negative way and given to women to act out. They only *act* a negative role, however; it is not women, as such, who are represented. This distinction is made possible by the notion emphasised throughout the entire ritual: that human beings, whether male or female, are a mixture of both the transcendental ancestral element and the 'this worldly', mainly female, element. This was so of Andriamanelo with his Vazimba mother. It is so of all living human beings in that they are both 'wet' and 'dry'. Yet all are in the process of becoming 'dry' and all partake in the conquest of the 'wet' and its consumption. Women, therefore, are also partly 'dry' because women too are part of the general order of descent. It is worth stressing here that the descent concepts of the Merina are bilateral, that women are both members of their descent group and potential transmitters of this membership, especially when they live uxorilocally (see Bloch 1971a, pp. 193–5).

We saw earlier that the implied obedience at the heart of the Merina concept of descent is experienced not as external but, rather, as obedience to the 'better' part of oneself. This is so for women too, in so far as they are descent beings; as a result the victory that is being acted through their role taking is also their victory. This is not very different from what happens to the boy in the ritual; he too is both conquered and conqueror as was Andriamanelo in so far as he was both Merina and Vazimba. It is not simply that when they are dead and dry in the tomb both women and men will become timeless ancestral stuff, it is also that in so far as they are both already partly ancestral in this life, they are also conquerors and users of *mahery* substance and so they, too, rejoice in circumcision. But this construction explains also the puzzling fact that women are particularly eager to participate, even more than men. The reason is that by participation they are demonstrating that they too want to be on the side of the ancestors and that they do want to master and conquer femininity and the world symbolised by the Vazimba. They are showing the enthusiasm of converts, eager to show their sincerity by emphatic vilification of what they have left behind. In any case, when you are in a family where the ritual is taking place, taking part or not taking part is never a real question. None the less, all recognise that the ritual is their duty, and all feel it satisfactory. This is because in a way all, both men and women, are honoured by it, and all demonstrate their strength by it. Of course, the reason why they feel it is so right is not just because of the immediate pleasure it gives but because they *recognise* it as right – a feeling that has been constructed by a lifetime of participation in related rituals of which the circumcision ritual is only one type.

When all is said and done, however, it remains clear that the ritual does imply that men are 'more ancestral' than women. Not only are women more *mahery* in themselves, but also there is no equivalent for women to the circumcision ceremony. Women only begin to receive ancestral blessings later, and they receive them in normal circumstances less often. The occasions when women are most clearly in receipt of ancestral blessing are when they participate in *famadihana* (secondary funerals) or in circumcision rituals held for their male relatives, and these are both occasions where they are humiliated as representative of the non-ancestral. Women only become descent beings to any significant degree when they become old and even then their status often remains somewhat ambiguous. We have seen an example of this in the mixture of irony and respect with which the blessing of the female elder was received in the ceremony described in Chapter 4. For women, as for junior people, the ritual is in the end humiliating, but this humiliation is transformed into enthusiastic participation by the encompassing nature of the overall message.

The general image created by the ritual is, within the ritual, perfectly clear and unchallengeable. It is the creation of a transcendental order in which all will have a place, and it is the creation of the legitimacy of conquest of 'this world', which is both external (the plants, the animals, the water, the Vazimba) and internal (the wet in oneself, sexuality, enjoyment, strength, creativity) so that the order in which one will have a place might be maintained.[3]

Not only does this general pattern fit nearly all Malagasy rituals but also others throughout the world. For example, Scott Guggenheim and I showed how this pattern is found in many other parts of the world, for example, for Christian baptism (Bloch and Guggenheim 1981), and Jonathan Parry and I showed how it fitted funerary rituals from all over the world (Bloch and Parry 1982). The central point of this structure is the creation of the ordered transcendental by devaluation of the value of human experience and action. The problem of the reintroduction of vitality is a consequence of the first opposition. But it makes the violence of conquest of 'this world' appear as necessary and justified. The particular form of different rituals varies but the basic point is the same: the cultivation of the hatred of life for the sake of authority. Actually the similarities go even further than this overall identity and it is no accident that we find, again and again, the same symbols, the devaluation of femininity and birth, the revelling in putrefaction, ritual wounding of the genitalia, the killing of animals, and so forth, put to the same or similar uses. There are only a limited number of tools to be employed that lend themselves to the establishment of the transcendental.

The symbolism of circumcision and the theory of ideology

The similarities in the empirical phenomena from all over the world make it necessary to turn for explanation to social theory not tied to any particular instance. As a starting point I shall consider therefore how far the data corresponds to the Marxist notion of ideology.

What ideology is, in the Marxist sense, has proved difficult to define. It can be defined functionally as misrepresentations of the world that legitimate exploitation; thus Althusser in a brilliant essay defines it as a 'representation of the imaginary relationship of individuals to their real conditions of existence'. The function of ideology for him is to ensure the reproduction of the relations of production and it is given its 'reality' by what he calls the 'rituals' of 'Ideological State Apparatuses'. These, in capitalist society, are such institutions as education, the church, the family, the mass media. When going on to consider feudal society Althusser notes that the principal ideological apparatuses are the church and the family; especially the church, which has the functions of education and

175

the mass media. Continuing the same line, without accepting the classification he uses fully, it would be possible to say that in certain other types of societies such as the one under consideration, kinship and religion are merged and we are dealing with a single ideological apparatus, which is manifested in rituals such as the circumcision ritual. It would therefore be possible to say that when we look at the circumcision ritual we are looking at the main ideological apparatus at work in nineteenth- and twentieth-century Madagascar, and we are getting some idea of how ideology is manifested in history. This is because, for a society such as the Merina, ritual has the main burden of carrying ideology. Furthermore, it has recently been suggested by a number of writers that this might be true to a greater extent than we imagine in nearly all society.

It is surprising how few anthropological studies of ritual consider the Marxist theory of ideology.[4] Yet it is striking how well the theory fits a case such as this. The first step in such a study might well be to look in *The German Ideology* at the notion of alienation, which Marx, in this early work, regarded as a precondition for the construction of the ideological. Marx argued that if the expropriation by capitalists of the product of the worker's labour is to appear legitimate, the labourer must consider his work as insufficient for production. In other words, his work must be devalued by the representation of creativity as being principally the product of a supernatural force, which in the case of capitalism is capital. Once this mysterious fetishised force has been constructed, the worker must 'rightly' subject himself to the power-holders, in this case the capitalists, as they appear to have supplied the necessary conditions of his existence – capital. Now, if we take this perspective and apply it to non-capitalist systems, we must look for an equivalent to capital that is none the less different. In this case this equivalent must be the ancestors and the tomb because they are similarly seen as the *true* source of creativity, a construction that also depends on a negation of the creativity of ordinary human beings.

Once the image of the ancestors has been established in this way as the true source of creativity, the parallel with Marx's theory continues on the political level. It becomes 'only right' that the representative of the ancestors, the elders (a role that as we saw can be stretched to include almost any power-holder), should be obeyed, and that a part at least of the product of ordinary people should be handed over to them. Thus as the ideology of capitalism explains why the control of the workers by the capitalists is legitimate, so the ideology of circumcision legitimates the control by the elders, whoever they might be. But it does something else, as well: It legitimates conquest by the elders of the non-transcendental world. The ultimate significance of this for capitalism is clear in nineteenth-century representations of imperialism and, as we shall see, is similarly significant for the wider political uses of ritual in Imerina. Thus many aspects of the Marxist theory prove highly illuminating once modified in this way, but there is one difference between capitalist ideology and the circumcision ritual: The creativity that is devalued and then fetishised in capitalism is only the creativity of labour, whereas among the Merina labour *and* human reproduction are merged. This is a difference between the ideology of capitalist and non-capitalist systems.[5]

There is, however, a problem in this theoretical formulation, a problem partly avoided by Althusser, as has been pointed out by Goran Therborn (1980), but which comes to the fore in the work of other Marxist writers. This is the problem of the historical construction of ideology. Marxists, such as Althusser, stress the role of ideology as making the reproduction of exploitative systems possible by hiding their true nature so that the exploited consents to his exploitation. That ideology does this is well illustrated by the circumcision ritual; for example, we have just seen how its construction makes women accept their humiliation. The recognition of this function, however, is not the same as saying that the ritual is as it is because of this function, but this is precisely the implication of some Marxist literature on ideology. The problems with such a leap in the argument are familiar, they are the old difficulties raised by functionalist theories discussed in Chapter 1. Two objections were noted. The theory of ideology as a plot on the part of power-holders is ridiculous. The scenario it implies is totally unlikely. One cannot understand how the power-holders could decide on such subtlety. It is clear that, if we are to see ideology as mystification, we have to face the fact that in most cases the power-holders are as mystified as anybody else. Second, the theory of ideology as a falsehood fails to explain the compulsive power of the ideas it contains. This point was made long ago by Emile Durkheim in *The Elementary Forms of the Religious Life* (1912).

On top of these objections, the data examined in this book bring to the fore a third difficulty: Ideology does not change when the politico-economic circumstances do. If ideology were merely the product of these circumstances it would logically follow that it would be moulded by them and change when they do. In other words the determination of ideology by the politico-economic world implied in the theory is too specific. Therborn again puts the point in a nutshell: 'For example no theory of the feudal mode of production can explain why Feudalism was accompanied in Europe by Catholic Christianity and by Shintoism in Japan' (Therborn 1980, p. 48). Are we then to abandon any idea of social determination, and as a result give up the attempt to see ideology as a device for legitimating power by making it into authority? This opposite position is not supported either by the history of the Merina circumcision ritual. Not only does the legitimating function of this ritual emerge at every stage of the analysis, but furthermore it seems probable that this function was and also is evident to the participants, although they see themselves as using something which is. there rather than creating it *ab initio*. The latter part of this chapter is an attempt to modify the theory of ideology so that it can cope with the historical problem without losing the elements in it that have been shown to be of value.

Ideological knowledge and ritual

It is necessary to leave for a moment the general theoretical discussion of ideology and go back to its actual manifestation in our particular example. One aspect of theories of ideology is that they assume that ideology represents an ordered consciousness, a complete system of knowledge, which directly organises the action of individuals.[6] This, however, would be to forget that the construction of ideology takes place in very specific and limited kinds of activities. In this example it takes place almost entirely in ritual. The significance of this can be perceived in a preliminary way by reminding ourselves of the case of the image of women who in everyday life are not at all what they appear to be in the ritual. It is therefore necessary, before proceeding further, to examine what is the significance of the fact that Merina ideology is formulated in a ritual and to ask what type of knowledge is created in this way. It is no longer possible to ignore any more, as has been done for the sake of argument up to this point, that ideology is produced in this case in a very special type of activity.

In Chapters 4 and 5 an attempt was made at interpreting the meaning of the ritual and at unravelling its message. In a sense, however, this is totally misleading – there is no way in which it can usefully be said that the ritual expresses the structure summarised in the figures of Chapter 5, because this distillation is not the equivalent of the ritual. The participants would not tell the anthropologist, even with a little pushing, that this was what the ritual stood for. The interpretation is an analytical construction not a deciphering of an obscure code. On the other hand, it would also not be true to say that the construction comes from the preconception of the analyst, that it does not reveal something fundamental about the ritual and that it does not explain, to the reader of this book at least, much of what the ritual means to the participants. The very possibility of carrying out such an analysis with a degree of plausibility shows the contrary to be the case.

When dealing with what the ritual communicates, we must therefore use a theory of communications that sees ritual and symbolism not merely as a code for the transmission of knowledge that is to be elucidated, or as something that simply does not signify anything, a symbolic act rather than a symbolic statement. Finding a middle way between these extremes has been the concern of much recent theoretical discussion in anthropology. It is therefore worth retracing briefly the history of controversies that have attempted to deal with this question in order to be clear about what the difficulties are, and how they relate to this case.

The theoretical perspective in which ritual is seen as stating a view of the world has a long history. It is implied in most Western theology and in the antireligious traditions that originated in the Enlightenment. In anthropology it has been associated with the name of the nineteenth-century anthropologist E. B. Tylor, who elaborated a theory of the origins of religion as arising out of misunderstanding the phenomenon of dreaming (Tylor 1871). Other theories of

178

this kind saw religion as an attempt to explain the forces of nature. Still others saw religion as an attempt to explain misfortune, disease and death. Such approaches, which Evans-Pritchard called 'intellectualist' because they saw the concerns of religion as scientific or pseudo-scientific, are far from dead. R. Horton, in a relatively recent publication, proudly described himself as a 'neo-Tylorian' and argued that religion was a type of scientific knowledge unfortunately lacking in Popper's principle of falsification, without which it was not entirely satisfactory (Horton 1967). Lévi-Strauss, in a book that did not concern itself with religion as such because it followed an earlier prologue (Lévi-Strauss 1962a) that by implication dismissed the distinction between religious and non-religious knowledge, also argued that what we normally call religious phenomena are a type of knowledge and a form of intellectual activity. Again, this was not quite science, but close. Lévi-Strauss baptised it 'savage thought'; for him it characterises all human knowledge except for the peculiarity of true scientific thought, which is found in only a few cultures where, even there, it concerns only a minor part of knowledge (Lévi-Strauss 1962b). A less explicit view of religion as a kind of explanation or template of knowledge is also implied by writers who see the task of the anthropologist as a matter of demonstrating the 'cosmology' of various peoples by means of their ritual, for example, Alfred Gell (1975), Stephen Hugh-Jones (1979), and R. H. Barnes (1974). By 'cosmology' they mean the most general principles organising knowledge and cognition. Inevitably, therefore, rituals and other religious activities are seen by these writers as presenting complex explanations of the place of man in the world, if not in a scientific way, as would be the case for Lévi-Strauss, at least as a meta-science. In fact these views are not very dissimilar to those of the Marxist writers we have discussed, who see ideology as a system for giving meaning to the world. Such approaches in anthropology naturally lead to the kind of analysis carried out in Chapters 4 and 5, which stressed the symbolism of circumcision and ignored its socio-political aspects.

The earlier 'intellectualists' had originally been criticised by Durkheim in *The Elementary Forms of the Religious Life* (1912). His main point was that religion could not be considered as a pseudo-science because, if that was all it was, it would continually be open to debate, whereas religion is seen as compulsory, external, beyond question, in Kant's term categorical. Durkheim's view was that religion produced social classification and solidarity, but it was itself the product of social interaction. Religion, brought about by society as an empirical phenomenon, organised knowledge and society as a moral phenomenon. This meant that, in the end, his position also closely linked knowledge and religion. Indeed, religion was for Durkheim the basis of the principles of the most fundamental aspects of knowledge, such as the conceptualisation of time, space and person.

Durkheim therefore merely reversed the epistemological basis of the intellectualists. It was not that the problems set by the empirical nature of the world led to religion but, rather, that religion made us see the world in a particular way.

179

From blessing to violence

Durkheim's theoretical position is also found in the work of M. Douglas (Douglas 1966 and 1970). Again a similar, if less systematic, position has also been re-echoed by Clifford Geertz in an essay entitled 'Religion as a Cultural System' (Geertz 1966), where he argues that religion 'is a system of symbols which acts to establish powerful persuasive and long lasting moods and motivations in men by formulating conceptions of a general order of existence and clothing these conceptions with such an aura of factuality that the moods and motivations seem uniquely realistic'. In other words, religion organises cognition and gives meaning to culture. Geertz qualifies this later on in the essay by saying that there is also a commonsense perspective, among perhaps still others, with which the religious perspective interacts. In this he differs significantly from Durkheim. The relation between these different 'perspectives' is not, however, discussed further, except that for Geertz religion seems to be a superior, dominant, organising perspective. Religion is basically a system of knowledge used by man to deal with such imponderables in the human situation as the problem of evil, why things happen, and the problem of the presence of suffering.

There is, however, a major difference between writers such as Durkheim, Douglas and Geertz, who see religion as a mechanism for establishing 'powerful and persuasive moods', and those already referred to as intellectualist and cosmologist. The former stress ritual as a special kind of activity that gives an extraordinary validity to its messages. For both Geertz and Durkheim the stress is on the power, especially the emotional power, of the schemas of ritual, something almost absent from the theories of the intellectualists or of Lévi-Strauss, a point made by M. Fortes (1967). The other aspect of Geertz's and Durkheim's formulation is that they raise directly or indirectly the connection between the religious and the politico-social. In looking at the power of ritual these writers are therefore forced to look not only at what kind of statement rituals make but also at what kind of acts they are. The connection between the two aspects, however, remains unconvincingly unanalysed in their work but is seen as a mystery described by such terms as 'effervescence' (Durkheim 1912) or 'transporting' (Geertz 1966).

Finally, there is the functionalist perspective discussed in the first chapter, which as we saw is in some respects like some of the Marxist theories. Here ritual is seen as the exact opposite of a statement; it is merely an action. Rituals are what rituals do. For these writers (for example, Radcliffe-Brown 1952) religion is a device for maintaining the unity of groups, and the emotional power of religion is simply a matter of explaining why religion does this job so well. Similarly, E. R. Leach, in a book published in 1954, expressed himself as follows: 'Ritual acts are ways of "saying things" about social status' (p. 279).

I have already discussed the objections to this position: the false theory of action it implies and its reductionism. The fact that the circumcision ritual fits well with the political configuration at any one point should not, as we have seen, lead us to think that this configuration causes it to be as it is. This is shown

180

by the fact that when political circumstances were very different the ritual was much the same. The problem of reductionism is well demonstrated also in that it was possible to carry on the 'functionalist' analysis in the earlier part of this chapter with almost no reference to the detailed content of the ritual itself. It is this very possibility that enabled functionalists to argue that social circumstances determined rituals by almost completely ignoring them.

Neither the intellectualist nor the functionalist approach is wrong yet neither is right, and for the same reason some Marxist theories fail. The problem lies in the fact that rituals are neither an exposition of the knowledge of the people studied: a statement; nor are they actions whose meaning lies simply in their performance. Rituals are events that *combine the properties of statements and actions*. It is because of this combination that their analysis has proved endlessly elusive.

Some recent work on ritual as an intermediate between statement and action has, however, gone a long way towards enabling us to deal with the problem. One of the first contributions in this line was D. Sperber's influential book entitled in English *Rethinking Symbolism* (1974), which initiated an attack on those approaches that saw symbolism as a semiological code, a statement of knowledge. His general contention is simple and surely right: If symbols, like signs, simply stood for some signified concept, we would have had little problem in carrying out the transcription. Rather, Sperber argues, we must consider symbolism as a form of knowledge that is different, not in content but in its very nature, from other types of knowledge, and that therefore cannot be expressed as though it were like these different types of knowledge. What symbolic knowledge is, Sperber has further elaborated in a more recent article (1979) where he argues that symbolic thought operates 'when the rational device is overloaded'. This idea is full of problems as has been shown by C. Toren (1983), but the implied idea that symbolism must be understood in terms of a theory of the nature of symbolism, not as though it was ordinary knowledge, is valid (Sperber 1982). Sperber criticises a number of writers for adopting a semiological approach, among them V. Turner, whose work will be considered later in this chapter.

But neither Sperber nor Turner, who defines symbols as the 'smallest unit of ritual' (Turner 1967, p. 19), links the problems of the way of meaning of symbols with the problem of understanding the ritual communication in which they are embedded. This is what I attempted to do in an article, 'Symbol, Song and Dance and Features of Articulation: Is Religion an Extreme Form of Traditional Authority?' (Bloch 1974). The article concerned almost exclusively the various uses of language in ritual, ranging from homilies to spells to singing, which were seen as a continuum along a line of increasing formalisation. I argued that as formalisation of the uses of language increases, the nature of semantics changes because ordinary linguistic semantics depend on the possibility of choice, and as a result the ability of language to signify by expressing propositions is diminished. As this ability is diminished the fact of using language becomes what matters, rather than what is said. The analysis was extended to material symbols also, because they are somewhat like highly formalised language and singing, in that they are not governed by rules of syntax that make recombination meaningful. Ritual language and material symbols can never express propositions similar to the propositions expressed in other language uses. Rituals cannot form a true argument, because they imply no alternative. Attempts to represent the messages of ritual as though they are propositions are bound to fail because as we move towards the more formalised or ritualised pole in communication, in the end we drift out of meaning altogether. This, however, can never occur completely; most ritual communication, by contrast with other language uses, is on the way towards losing propositional force but it cannot do this entirely. Similarly, E. Ahern has argued that rituals are partly expressive but at the same time internally defining, constitutive, as though they do not address any phenomenon outside themselves (Ahern 1981). It is thus the *changed balance* between the propositional and performative aspects of language that makes ritual so difficult, and makes ritual knowledge contrast with other types of knowledge. If ritual had totally abandoned the ability to express propositions it would not be ritual any more, but similarly this would also be the case if it had totally retained it.

The difference between ritual communication and non-ritual communication, therefore, implies a shift away from propositional force towards the prominence of the illocutionary act itself. However, this is only partial. For example, rituals use language developed from ordinary language but modified in a certain way to a certain extent and material symbols a little like signs in a natural language, also in a different way. In other words, although the first task of the analyst of ritual is to stress how little propositional force is left in ritual, his next task is to remind us that there is *some* left.

This balance explains why it is possible at the same time to produce from a ritual such as the circumcision an analysis of the 'meaning' of the ritual that is revealing (as was done in Chapters 4 and 5), as well as an explanation why such an analysis is also always misleading. The anthropologist is inevitably faced by a dilemma, stemming from the fact that he is trying to express in analytical language something that is in another medium and is different in nature because of the way it is communicated. On the other hand, this medium is also sufficiently close to language to make it inevitable and fruitful that the attempt should be made.

The fact that rituals are on the boundary between statements and actions explains why both the intellectualist approach and the functionalist one are so unsatisfactory. The intellectualist approach considers the ritual as a statement, the functionalist one as an action. In great part the difficulty comes from our narrative style, which has means of dealing with statements and means of dealing with actions but has no means of dealing with the in-between. As a result, when anthropologists write about ritual they find themselves pushed either in one direction or the other.

The difficulty of describing a kind of knowledge that differs from the kind of knowledge dealt with in analytical work is well illustrated in the numerous works of V. Turner. For Turner symbols, especially dominant symbols, condense a whole host of notions, some of them contradictory, and join them together. These conjoined notions range from explicit ethical principles to, at the other end, a sensory pole arousing semi-physiological responses. It is this combination of the many aspects of symbols that explains for Turner their power of transforming the obligatory into the desirable, presumably by associating satisfying responses with authority. But in the end, for Turner, symbolism and ritual must remain enigmatic and the literary attempts to get at what they might mean for the participants a battle lost before it has been fought. Indeed the value of Turner's work may ultimately prove simply to have shown how complex the whole matter is.

Somewhat more rigorously, this also seems to have been the conclusion reached by G. Lewis (1980) and E. Ahern (1981). G. Lewis has rightly shown how an overly intellectual interpretation of ritual makes way for totally unwarranted suggestions. He feels, for very similar reasons to those already discussed, that rituals are not ways of communicating but rather of expressing. But the difficulty with Lewis's approach is similar to the difficulty with Turner's. Although pointing to the complex semantic implications of the nature of ritual and symbolism he ultimately defines the task of the anthropologist as catching what rituals mean for the participants. To a certain extent this is valuable, and the empathy that comes from participant observation makes it partly possible. However, the result must always be finally uncertain and vague, leading to an infinite regress of problems of interpretation. The value of these various studies of ritual and symbolism has been that they have shown how ritual knowledge is a special kind of knowledge, different from other types of knowledge, but by doing this they seem to have reached conclusions that imply that ritual knowledge is beyond analysis.

There is, however, a way of coming to grips with the nature of statement-actions that avoids the uncertainties of seeing what they do for participants and bypasses the literary difficulties of expression. It is to look at ritual in the same way as this chapter began, and in the way this whole book has been organised – that is, historically. In such a perspective it is not any more a question of trying to grasp the nature of the phenomenon by searching for what it means for the participants, but by analysing how the ritual is manifested in history. It is rather as if instead of understanding the nature of particles by looking at their apparent structure one analyses them by looking at their trajectory and dispersal in an accelerator: a procedure typical of modern physics.

Within such a perspective we can look again at the theories of ritual discussed above and see what their historical implications are. The basic agreement on this matter that emerges from the various studies of ritual communication mentioned is striking. The common elements particularly relevant for understanding the historical potential of ritual are (1) repetition, (2) formalisation and (3) the construction of a particular image of time.

All the writers discussed stress the repetitious nature of ritual. This takes a number of forms, which are well illustrated in the circumcision ritual. First, different ritual sequences seem to carry much the same message, illustrated in this case, for example, by the way the ritual of the *mahery* bull is easily equated to the treatment of the sugar-canes and bananas. Second, there is identical repetition; if we look at such things as the songs in the ritual or the formula accompanying the opening of the gourd the repetition becomes extraordinary; the same two lines are, in some cases, repeated several hundred times. Third, if we look at smaller units, such as the occurrence of the word *mahery,* the repetition becomes such that it is reasonable to ask if this type of activity does not cause an automatic physiological response (Gell 1980). This repetition of every kind is indicative that we are not dealing with a statement with a clear proposition but, rather, with something that shares attributes with a semi-hypnotic spell.

A spell is not something that is modified to fit the circumstances; rather, it is turned on itself; in Ahern's terms, it is constitutive. This point is therefore the corollary of the previous one. Ritual communication lacks plasticity; indeed, several authors attribute the redundancy of repetition to the fixity of the ritual message. As far as the linguistic side of ritual is concerned this fixity both explains, and is due to, the prominence of special uses of language such as singing or intoning. (This is argued more fully in Bloch 1974.) Fixity means a lack of adaptability, of matching the particular ritual expression to a particular event. This implies a special relation between the specificity of the events, in this case the particular circumcision of a particular child at a particular place and time in specific politico-economic circumstances, and the identically repetitive and non-adaptive character of the ritual. As a result rituals represent events as though they were general occurrences. The circumcision of each particular boy becomes that of any and every boy. The same ritual procedures, the same gestures, the same songs and so forth are used. Rituals reduce the unique occurrence so that they become a part of a greater fixed and ordered unchanging whole; this whole is constructed identically by every ritual performed in a hazy, weakly propositional manner; it appears to have always existed, and will always exist. Because of this, ritual makes the passage of time, the change in personnel, and the change in situation, inexpressible and therefore irrelevant.

The image of the irrelevance of the passage of time, of cyclicity, created by ritual has often been noted in the anthropological literature, notably by Leach (1961) and Lévi-Strauss (1962b). In the circumcision ritual it has been seen that the fundamental idea that underlies it, the idea of descent, does by its very nature constitute a denial of time because it implies the ultimate irrelevance of the difference between different generations. It is thus a typical product of ritual. It would, I believe, be wrong to attribute such a construct merely to the nature of ritual communication, but it is only possible because of ritual, because ritual can create a world of hazy timelessness in antithesis to another world, which it caricatures the better to deny it. The creation of timelessness by the ritual is therefore not simply the result of the effect of the fixity of the communication used but also the result of the denial of the validity of this world. This theme is central to the ritual and takes many forms, such as the assaults on the 'living mother' entities, on the individuating features of the child, on his matrilateral connections, on his 'wet' mother, because all these distinguish him from others in the descent unit. The ritual implies that only when he is in the tomb with his dried substance mixed with that of his ancestors will he be a truly moral being. This of course will also be when time will have become irrelevant.

These assaults, however, seem to contradict the typification of ritual communication given as involving highly fixed and predictable sequences. These sequences are characterised by the very opposite: chaotic behaviour, fights, chases, stealing. The role of such parts is, however, understandable when we see them as preliminaries to the ordered parts of the ritual concerned with descent. They are there to act out the opposite of what the ritual constructs so as to define it by antithesis. This point is made by Leach in an article that discusses the significance of such chaotic behaviour in ritual (Leach 1961). Leach goes on to stress the significance of such chaotic activity for our representation of time. The role of these chaotic sequences seems like part of the demonstration of the lack of validity of the world without the order of timelessness created by ritual. In a sense what is acted out in these sequences is Vazimba matrilineal chaos, which the ritual promises will be overcome and conquered by descent. This is expressed in fixed ritual sequences. As such, the chaotic parts of the ritual, although they seem to manifest the very opposite of the features of ritual first discussed, are there as preliminaries to the presentation of timeless order.

It would, however, be a large theoretical step to say that because rituals create the image of timelessness they are also really time-defying as historical phenomena. It is simply that ritual transforms and reduces events so that they lose their specificity and re-represents these events vaguely as part of a timeless order. The image produced in the ritual can accommodate by this means a great variety of different specific events and make them appear the same. The ritual can thereby be repeated unchanged even if the specific events it re-presents are significantly different.

Of course, it would be ridiculous to argue that rituals never change and never disappear. We have simply noted a characteristic that explains their ability not to change in changing politico-economic circumstances. Such an observation would need to be complemented by a study of the forces that do lead to change. Tambiah, at the end of the essay already referred to in this chapter, makes the same point:

From blessing to violence

> One of our tasks, then, is to specify the conditions under which rituals – which ordinarily convey both symbolic and indexical, referential and pragmatic meanings – take opposite turnings: to the right when they begin to lose their semantic component and come to serve mainly the pragmatic interests of authority, privilege, and sheer conservatism; and to the left when committed believers, faced with a decline of referential meaning but with a surfeit of manipulated 'implicatures', strive to infuse purified meaning into traditional forms, as often happens during the effervescence of religious revival and reform. [Tambiah, 1979]

Tambiah himself makes no attempt to specify the conditions he asks for, but the evidence presented in Chapter 7 does go some way in this direction. We have seen that in dramatically changing circumstances the symbolic content of the ritual of circumcision has remained remarkably static. The changes that we have seen are hardly changes at all; they are either repetitions of certain themes already there, or the dropping of themes expressed elsewhere. Ritual is revealed as an area of human activity very low indeed in creativity.

This stability offers some kind of answer to Tambiah's question. It tells us, first of all, that the ritual has amazingly managed to maintain a middle path, turning neither to the right nor the left. How has this 'middle path' been maintained?

There are at certain points in the history we have examined some suggestions of possible turnings. For example, in periods of revolt such as during the *Ramamenjana* or during the *mena lamba,* the kind of millenarian activity that Tambiah seems to have in mind when he talks of a turn to the left does make an appearance. These movements seem to attempt to reshuffle everything, rather like cargo cults have been reported so to do. Particularly significant for this book, these millenarian tendencies have, in the process, used symbols borrowed from circumcision. These innovations, however, led to something completely different from the original ritual. It led to an efflorescence that did not settle down and that therefore in the end did not permit the tree to bear fruit. It seems that the political failure of the revolts doomed any possibility of real ritual innovation. We may, however, suspect that if these revolts had been successful, they would have only implied the reassertion of the old rituals because this is what happened in other instances when results were successful, as after the overthrow of Radama II.

The possibility of a turn to the right is also present in the historical record discussed. This would involve a reduction of the ritual to a mere expression of a political value, a situation where its symbolical content had become irrelevant. Lévi-Strauss in an early paper discusses under what conditions this occurs with myth (Lévi-Strauss 1973); as for Tambiah for rituals, it is when myths become mere political charters that they lose their nature. The use of the circumcision ritual as a symbol of opposition to the urban Christian bourgeoisie that occurred in 1971 could have led to such a situation. In fact this did not occur because the use of the ritual in this way was not explicit and it retained its internal subtlety.

186

The circumcision ritual in history

Again, it is as if the social change was not sufficient to cause fundamental change in the ritual symbolism. There was something in the ritual itself that resisted reductionism.

Overall the ritual maintained stability and avoided turns either towards the right or towards the left. The political changes, however great, were not enough; we did not get the kind of adaptation suggested by Tambiah. In other words, we are thrown back on the fact of an amazing stability, where the balance between total meaninglessness and clear statement was maintained, and this is what must be explained.

The circumcision ritual as ideology in history

The possibility for this historical stability is to be found in the nature of ritual. There is, however, an obvious difficulty in recognising the historical lack of flexibility in ritual, and the lack of response to events, and attributing it merely to the nature of ritual communication. The difficulty is that if this were all there was to it, we still could not understand how it was that the ritual could remain relevant to the participants in changed circumstances. The fact that the ritual form does not adapt easily does not explain why it continues to be useful. In this case the question can be put very specifically. If the circumcision ritual has stayed by and large the same symbolically, how is it that it has been able to do so many different things functionally?

This, of course, was the difficulty raised by considering the circumcision ritual in terms of the theory of ideology. Now, however, we have the tools for dealing with the problem. The difficulty arose because the theory bound ideology *too closely* to the politico-economic conjuncture, and it did this by suggesting that ideology was what organised the reproduction of the socio-economic formation. Althusser's definition implies a contrast between the 'real conditions of existence' and the 'imaginary relationships' established by ideology. Althusser thinks that the 'imaginary' must obliterate the 'real' to organise reproduction within a particular social formation. If that were so, ideology would obviously have to change when the socio-economic formation changed. In this case the ritual would have had to vary in its content as the political situation changed and we know this was not so.

Now, however, we can see that the ideological image is not directly the source of knowledge in the ordinary sense. Practical knowledge would have to adapt to the immediate tasks to be performed in changing circumstances. This kind of knowledge must exist, but it is not ritual knowledge. Ritual implies a type of knowledge, isolated by the medium of ritual communication, that does not replace practical knowledge by the 'imaginary'; rather, it has an indirect relation to practical knowledge.

The Merina do not simply think that, as a result of the ritual, it is the ancestors who create people, while sex and nurturing do not. They do not believe that the

187

ancestors are simply the source of the fertility of their rich fields and that labour is irrelevant. They hold both views in different contexts and they do not see them as contradictory because the image of the ritual is isolated in a heavy world between actions and statements. For the ritual to conflict with other types of knowledge it would have to be removed from the communication that characterises ritual. The two images of the world – the ritual and the everyday – cannot in ordinary, non-revolutionary circumstances, compete with each other.

This fact has been noted in a variety of ways by a number of writers. Althusser himself notes the 'generality' and vagueness of ideology. Leach (1967) in his discussion of the ideas concerning procreation in the Trobriands and among Australian aborigines stresses how it is both possible to believe that men have no part in procreation and also to know, on another level, that they do. More generally, R. Firth in a seminal work, *Social Change in Tikopia* (1959), similarly argues that culture is dual and then goes on to show how this implies that the two types of culture change in different ways and at different rates. This 'disconnection' is expressed in a particularly challenging way by E. Gellner in an article on ideology where he notes the challenge or the 'offensiveness' of ideologies towards other types of explanation, which they thereby acknowledge (Gellner 1980).[7] This was a point I made in two articles that also stressed the difference between ritual and non-ritual knowledge (Bloch, 1977, 1977b), and it has been made yet again by Turton and Tanabe (1984) to explain the possibility of peasant revolt. Ideology is partly, as it were, in a world of its own and therefore it does not have a direct relationship with the political.

It is, however, going too far in this direction to argue for *total* 'disconnection' of the political from the ideological. This is basically the position of Geertz in a recent book entitled *Negara,* where he argues that the world created by the great royal rituals of Bali was totally apart from the day-to-day political world and therefore had no reason to change at all in response to political circumstances (Geertz 1980). Such an approach is the very opposite of the functionalist one, in which one sees ideology and the reproduction of the social formation as two sides of the same coin. The problem that this position raises can also be dealt with by the acid test of history. The Merina ritual *did* change, directly in its functional aspects and indirectly in its symbolic aspects, although this change was not in harmony with the politico-economic changes.

What we therefore need in order to understand what happened to the circumcision ritual in history is a theory about the indirect *interrelationship* of two types of phenomena, the ideological and the politico-economic, which we must first recognise are of different kinds and which occur in different types of communication.

In fact the main elements that link ritual and non-ritual knowledge have already been reviewed. The ritual is a matter of transforming knowledge of the world obtained outside the framework of the ritual. This must be implied by the negative aspect of what is acted out. The ritual is saying that the world one

188

knows outside ritual, where sex and birth lead to life, where labour leads to production, where time is irreversible and potentially productive, will not ultimately be the basis of transcendental existence. In order to express such ideas it is necessary that the reality of non-transcendental processes be recognised. The ritual does not replace the knowledge of this world by the transcendental one; it merely suggests the transcendental world, just over the horizon, after death.

This explains the emotional power of the ritual. It re-presents everything, the sensations of hot and cold, sexuality and decay, and establishes from these images an idea of authority that can appear as everybody's authority, as everybody's victory over this life and death. The willing participation of women in such an anti-feminine ritual has already been commented on and is illustrative of ritual as a whole. It comes from the fact that the ritual appears to establish the authority of everybody, in so far as it brings blessing to everybody, and by this means transforms everybody, men and women, into descent beings. Of course in the process the ritual also establishes differential degrees of authority, and, indeed, these distinctions are the only politically relevant ones, but it presents these as part of an authority and transcendence which all share, or rather will share. Indeed one cannot imagine a person so devoid of all status that he or she would not derive some satisfaction from having a place in an ordered whole that stands against immorality, unpredictability and death.

It is this general promise and this emotional rightness that explain the continuing individual relevance of the ritual in changing politico-economic circumstances. Althusser, in the article already referred to, makes the point that all actors have already been moulded ideologically by the very ideologies they will be presented with and will create in such a ritual. As a result they will 'recognise' its rightness. But there is more to it than that; the content of the ritual itself is of central significance. It contains two key propositions which, as we noted, are found in all such rituals: (1) Creativity is not the product of human action but is due to a transcendental force that is mediated by authority, and (2) this fact legitimates, even demands, the violent conquest of inferiors by superiors who are closer to the transcendental ancestors. Now such a message is of value for the legitimation of any power-holders so long as they can be identified with the key role of mediators between this life and the transcendental order. This is precisely what happened. The ritual continued to be of political relevance because those who had power were able to place themselves in the position of 'elders'; who was an elder changed according to political circumstances. Sometimes the elders were powerful members of descent groups, sometimes they were rich local bigwigs, sometimes they were the representative of the king or the king himself, sometimes they were leaders of social disaffection. All, however, were able to take over a role created by the ritual in a process which we have examined, and thereby demonstrate the rightness of their dominance.

This point brings us back to the question of intentionality. Perhaps the problem is clearest in the way the circumcision ritual was used to legitimate the growing

189

power of Merina rulers. I have no doubt that this was done consciously, but this intention was not seen as the creation of a new ritual; it was seen as the natural use of something that was there already and defined legitimate authority in a way that was so fundamental that it was beyond question. The kings did not see themselves as creators, but users, of something which was packaged by the communicative nature of ritual. This shows how misleading the functionalist history of the ritual would be as an explanation of its symbolic nature. The uses to which the ritual was put only indirectly caused its content, bringing about a few minor transformations that remained within the general logic of the symbolism as it had existed before. In other words, the intentional political uses to which the ritual was put explain little of its content since it was used largely ready-made.

The recoverability of this ritual and the relation of function and content it implies is well illustrated by the only significant change undergone by the ritual, which has not so far been discussed. This is the change in the person who opened the gourd. The crucial symbolic importance of this act will be recalled. The opening of the gourd is what enables it to contain the water that will bless the child. It is the most prominent act of the elders in the transmission of the blessing. The gourd is also a mediating symbol, and its recovery by male ancestral violence from the side of matriliny, where it had been bound by grasses 'of living mother', to the side of descent, sets in motion the central part of the ritual. The opening of the gourd is the moment when the elders substitute themselves for the real parents of the child, and declare that it is they, in so far as they are the ancestors' representatives, who create him by beginning the process of spearing that will culminate in the actual operation. This therefore is a key moment, when the devaluation of 'this life' and its manner of production and reproduction is declared unworthy, and is then replaced by transcendental mystical descent reproduction, which in turn has the right to conquer 'this life' by violence.

The substitution of the king for the elders in the ritual is a demonstration of the adaptability of the ritual from one system of domination to another. It was, however, a change only in who precisely was the agent of mystical reproduction and violence, not a change in that fundamental notion itself, and because the image of descent productivity is created on the denial of 'this worldly' productivity in general, the king could be legitimated by the same devaluation. This is as close as the functional changes in the ritual came to bringing about major symbolic change. However, the change was small and, most significantly, reversible. As we saw, after the collapse of the Merina kingdom it was once again the elders who opened the gourd. Alienation, the first step in the establishment of any authority, can be used again and again and serve as the basis for more elaborate developments irrespective of which domination is involved.

But of course this point also serves to illustrate the insufficiency of an analysis of ideology to understand power. Because the ritual can legitimate any authority, it actually legitimates the authority of those who have the coercive potential to insist on being considered as elders or kings. It is not the ritual itself that determines who will be legitimated. Legitimation of violence and domination is only possible for those who already dominate by violence. The historical chapters of this book have shown the mechanisms that explain who was able to legitimate their authority through the ritual.

We are now in a position to understand the changes undergone by such a ritual in the course of history. Basically, in spite of the politico-economic changes, the circumcision ritual itself changed very little. This does not mean that the ritual was somehow isolated from the politico-economic world. What it does mean is that because of its symbolic nature and because of the communicative medium that typifies ritual, it could be recovered from moment to moment with minimal change. This is because the ritual is a vague, weakly propositional, construction of timelessness built on an antithesis that will do for any domination. It strikes at the very roots of experience to act out an alternative that vilifies human creativity in a way apparently satisfying to the participants. But of course this order is phantasmagoric in that it is constructed on the originally biased representation of 'human action' as chaotic, as Vazimba-like. It offers them order in exchange for submission.

This last point shows again the significance of the communicative nature of ritual for understanding the history of rituals. The circumcision ritual is in the end an attack on non-ritual experience, an attack on the visible in order to create the invisible. The invisible, however, can only appear as valid by negation, however hazily it appears; unlike the visible it cannot be validated or invalidated by experience. Validation by experience is ruled out both by the attack on this life and by the nature of a type of communication that itself cuts the connections between events and representations. In so far as the ritual remains a ritual, that is, in so far as it turns neither to the left nor the right, it is largely immune from history.

The link between the two ways of looking at history examined here, the history of the symbolism of the ritual and the politico-economic history of the Merina, occurs in the role of the elder/king. Because the definition of who is to take this role is so loose, because it can accommodate traditional elders, government administrators, influential relatives from the city, local political leaders of revolt against the bourgeoisie, it is possible for the ritual to adapt to changing personnel and also to changing types of politico-economic situation. But because the ritual has fixed the symbolic context into a different type of communication, which reacts differently to events, this context does not change in harmony with the politico-economic. Political dominators put on a mantle that has been worn by different types of dominators before them, they do not make this mantle anew (Fortes, 1962).

There is, however, one aspect of the process that is missed in this formulation. At the very heart of the ritual is an ambiguity that enables it to express not just

191

the reproduction of legitimate authority but also the expansion of the authority of the person who takes on the role of the elder, and this element is the violence that plays such a crucial role in the whole proceeding.

One representation of the ritual is that of stable continuity. This can be expressed in the following way. Descent goes on forever because the ancestors are able to conquer the living, who are then able to conquer 'this life', which enables them to reproduce a new generation, which will then be conquered by the ancestors; the new generation will then conquer 'this life'; and so on. This is a homeostatic model where all will in the end be equal as ancestors. In such a model the child to be circumcised and even the women will, like the elders, in the end become ancestors, which explains why the ritual is so satisfactory to all participants. The image, however, is actually false; not everybody, by a long way, becomes an elder and this is especially true of women. When we bear this in mind we can see that even though the ritual may represent an order where all are equally conquerors and conquered, in fact some are more conquerors and some are more conquered. For them the violence of the ritual represents acquiescence in permanent domination and coercion.

The misleading character of the homeostatic model becomes much more evident when we move from the family ritual to the royal ritual, where the king acts as an elder. In that case it would have been ridiculous to suggest that the ritual was welcomed because all subjects know that in the end they would become kings. But the adoption of such a ritual as a state ritual obscures this point, as does the royal rhetoric, which involves talking of subjects as though they were children. The hidden implication of absolute domination, which was already present in the familial ritual, becomes central in the royal ritual.

In fact the royal ritual pushes the ritual even further in this direction. It is important at this point to remember that under Ranavalona the Merina army took a central role in the ritual, replacing the 'youths whose father and mother are still living'. This is particularly significant when we bear in mind that the power of the army and the violence it represented was not merely a matter of ritual symbolism. During this period the Merina army, with the help of European technology, was killing, pillaging and enslaving on a terrifying scale and with horrible brutality. What had happened in the transformation of the circumcision ritual into a state ritual was that the mythical conquest and consumption of the Vazimba in the myth of origin of the ritual, and the symbolic conquest of the 'this earthly', mainly represented by femininity, in the ritual itself, had become identified with the very real conquests of the Merina state, directed sometimes towards its subjects and sometimes towards its neighbours.

Now we can understand the significance of representing actual domination in the idiom of circumcision. As we saw, the ritual quite misleadingly represents power and conquest, not as phenomena where there are two classes, one of dominators and the other of dominated or one of conquerors and one of conquered, but as one where all have in the end both roles. This explained the

192

willing participation of the women. The linking up of political and state power with this familial ritual achieved the same result for the relation between rulers and ruled. Merina subjects became able to see themselves in the ritual not only as conquered but also as conquerors; they made their humiliation their pride. This explains the popular revolts that followed the abolition of the rituals under Radama II. Then the Merina had been deprived of the illusion of participating in their own oppression and had been left with the much more stark alternative of pure exploitation. Nothing could show better the ideological power of the ritual. In a sense, therefore, the ritual of circumcision when used as a royal ritual is the very opposite of what the theory of ideology would lead us to expect: that it was a mystification carried out by superiors on inferiors. Rather it was a case of collusion between inferiors and superiors, with the inferiors accepting the implications of their own submission because their submission as Merina implied their ultimate domination and conquest of others, who might like themselves be in turn conquerors if they too were Merina – these would be their 'children' – or would be seen merely as prey if they were non-Merina. For nearly everyone, however, this promise of conquest was equally illusory in both versions.

It is in this complex collusion that the power of the ritual and of the ideology it conveys is to be found, especially its ability to survive in times of politico-economic change. It could, however, be said that such a conclusion fails to answer the basic question about how the symbolic content of the ritual has come about. This is true; at the time of my historical starting date, 1800, the ritual was already formed. This, however, is, in itself, quite as relevant and significant for the study of social change as if the ritual had undergone continual and rapid transformations. At the very least, a negative point has been made that the ritual has resisted direct modification in response to politico-economic change that many theories in the social sciences would have led us to expect. It is possible to say categorically that the symbolic aspects of this ritual, and probably others like it, are not products of the politico-economic conjuncture of a particular time. A demonstration of how the ritual fits in a politico-economic context would at any particular point in our historical sequence be quite convincing and indeed probably valid, but it would *not* be an explanation of the symbolic content of the ritual.

There are also, however, two more positive points that emerge concerning the origin of the symbolic form. First, we have seen some change occur in the ritual, however slow it might be. This is change brought about by the functional changes the ritual has undergone. These are not to be understood as direct responses to circumstances; they often appear as ad hoc abbreviations or expansions. These changes are, moreover, not as insignificant as they might appear at first sight. They do alter what is done in a way that in the long run, must lead cumulatively to major changes. This, however, would be over a long time, a longer time than the two hundred years of this study. What is probably happening is that the actors see themselves as merely manipulating a ritual that they do not have any idea of creating, but only of using; but they are in fact creating on a time-scale quite different from that governing their intentions.

The social sciences seem to oscillate continuously between theories such as functionalism and transactionalism, which describe intentionality as the source of social change, and theories that deny any historical relevance to purposeful human action. It is, possible, however, in the light of this example, that these positions are not opposed. First, our example shows that we should not assume that all aspects of culture react similarly to events and intentions. It has been shown why reaction is manifested in rituals in a special way, which is explained both by their content and their communicative nature. Second, it shows that in ritual purposeful human action does affect history both in the way intended and unintentionally on a much longer time-scale.

Also, another comment must be made to answer the criticism that a historical study that fails to account for all the cultural phenomena it observes is somehow failing in the task of giving a social origin to cultural facts. Such a criticism is based on one of the most common theoretical misapprehensions in anthropology. History has no beginning: People always act in a world constructed by previous generations. What we are seeking, therefore, when we try to understand how events construct culture are not rules of formation from a zero point but rules of transformation of an already existing system. In this light this study has suggested a telling hypothesis: that different cultural phenomena react to events differently. Rituals, such as the Merina circumcision ritual, and the images they activate have, because of their nature, a much greater fixity than other aspects of culture. The reason for this has been suggested above. If we accept this fact, however, its effects can be used to formulate further hypotheses.

If these rituals remain largely unchanged in different politico-economic circumstances, they must in turn partially affect how these circumstances are seen and therefore to a certain extent mould them. We have to imagine culture in history as consisting of different elements that are made to react more or less directly to circumstances and that, because of this difference, set up further interactions that themselves lead to historical events. The political significance of the relative stability of a ritual such as the circumcision ritual has been shown to affect the direction and specificity of many events in the history of Madagascar. At the very least, the persistence of such rituals may explain the long-term cultural continuities on which anthropologists are continually commenting. They may, for example, explain why it is possible to say that there are 'typically Austronesian' cultures in spite of the extraordinarily varied history of the people who are bearers of such cultures. We might ask questions about the relation in history of culture that is carried by such ritual to culture that is more directly created by practical considerations, and thereby imagine articulations that would yet again bring together the traditional concerns of the historian and the anthropologist within a manageable theoretical framework.

The circumcision ritual in history

Most generally of all, however, the stability of the ritual tells us something of the nature of ideology. The reason the ritual does its ideological job is that it carries at its core a simple and general message, which can be recovered and used for almost any type of domination. It is that this life is of little value, that it must be rejected, as far as is possible, and exchanged for the still transcendence where time has been vanquished by order and where therefore the relevance of birth, death and action has disappeared. It is only by this argument that power and violence can be made to appear necessary and desirable, and this applies to any power and violence that become indissolubly linked.

The message of ideology cannot be maintained simply as a statement, however, because it is by its very nature in contradiction with human experience in this world. This contradiction is, as we have seen, half recognised in the ritual itself, which must contradict and modify its central theme in an endless regression. In practice the full force of the contradiction can largely be ignored because the ideas expressed in the circumcision ritual are isolated from normal discourse by the very nature of ritual communication, which places what it communicates in a hazy, non-discursive world, isolated from events and argument. The central contradiction of the ritual, that death is the best sort of life, can largely be forgotten because it is expressed in something that is not fully a statement and not fully an action: a ritual.

Notes

Chapter 1. The social determination of ritual

1 This would obviously be an impossible task, as there might be other types of rituals, but even within Tsembaga there is the possibility of slaughtering as many animals as one wants at funerals.

Chapter 2. Background politico-religious history of the Merina, 1770–1970

1 See also Delval (1972), *Radama II*.
2 *Vato, Vy, Sakelica:* Stone, Iron and Spears.
3 Many of the social administrators in Madagascar were freemasons, in particular the then governor, de Coppet.
4 The best-known *sampy* of Andrianampoinimerina and Ranavalona I.

Chapter 4. Description and preliminary analysis of a circumcision ritual

1 A description of these practices and a possible explanation are given in C. Ranaivo's medical thesis, *Pratiques et croyances Malgaches relatives aux accouchements,* Paris 1902. Razafimino also discusses the symbol of heat in Malagasy thought, but he conjoins it with the symbol of fire in a way that I do not think is valuable, because the notion of fire seems to be associated with the notion of purification. Razafimino was, I believe, influenced in this by the theories of Frazer. Lévi-Strauss, in *Le cru et le cuit* (1964), discusses the custom of 'cooking' the women who had children as a way of restoring them to the world of culture (pp. 340–4). Although I feel that his analysis may be relevant here, it cannot be applied straightforwardly because, as we shall see, the heat in this case is rather a symbol of nature.
2 In this case no element of the killing of the bull could be seen as suggesting any notion of sacrifice. In other cases I witnessed I would be less categorical. I consider this question in a future publication (Bloch in press a).
3 Single inverted commas indicate proverbial sayings, which are marked out in Merina speeches by intonation and pauses.
4 This is again a reference to the supposed forest origin of the Andriamamilazabe deme.
5 This is a somewhat free and shortened translation.
6 There is, however, another possible interpretation of the white smock, which was not confirmed by informants because I did not think to ask them. At secondary funerals in particularly traditional families, the men who actually enter the tomb should be

196

dressed in white, and I was informed that this was done in the past. There is perhaps a connection between the white smock of the child and this tomb garment.

7 An attempt was also made to use a battery-powered gramophone brought by the Tananarive youths so that they could dance European dances, but this got drowned by the noise, and in any case the batteries gave out and I meanly refused to supply replacements for the sake of my recording of the traditional music.

8 Like many other plants, the *seva* is subdivided into a species defined as male, *sevalahy,* and a species defined as female, *sevavavy.*

9 The Malagasy word *omby* literally means 'cattle' in the singular. Since there is no equivalent word in English, I have used the word 'bull'. This is only misleading to a certain extent, as the *omby* of the ritual are sometimes qualified by the word *lahy,* meaning male.

10 This ceremony was to a large extent enacted twice in this case, as there were two boys to be circumcised. Two gourds were prepared, and the water was fetched by two parties of youths, although they went and came back together. There were also obviously two operations. For the sake of clarity, I shall, however, write of only one sequence.

11 A knife was in fact substituted on this occasion because spears are illegal and the political tension in the country at the time was such that the risk was not worth taking. In other ceremonies I attended a spear was used.

12 The numbers three and seven are considered auspicious. In this case there were seven elders.

13 To give uncooked, as opposed to cooked, food is a sign of respect. Normally children would only be given cooked food.

Chapter 5. The symbolism of circumcision

1 In fact this power goes beyond living things to include such things as stones and localities. Above all, it includes running water, but this is classified as living.

2 The gourd 'a thousand men' can also be used for the same purpose for different types of blessings, which will be discussed in another publication.

3 It is interesting to note that there is a parallel but opposed proverb to the one that gives the gourd its name. *Arivo vavy iray tanavra toy mifandrandrana, toy ny zozoro,* which means 'A thousand women in one village do not unite, they are like papyrus reeds.' This shows how women are associated with division, hence antidescent.

Chapter 6. The myth of the origin of circumcision

1 I saw the youths wearing torn shrouds among the Zafimaniry.

Chapter 7. The history of the circumcision

1 One-quarter of an *ariary. Ariary* were silver coins in use in Madagascar. They were Maria Theresa thalers and were cut to produce smaller units such as *kirobo.*

2 An *ariary.*

3 One-eighth of an *ariary.*

4 One-sixteenth of an *ariary.*

5 This probably includes the high demes called Andriana, who were related to the king.

6 There are two copies of this manuscript. One in the library of Trinity College, Cambridge, and the other in the Bodleian Library, Oxford (English Miscellaneous c. 29). My attention was drawn to this document by S. Ellis.

7 Raombana was one of the group of Malagasy sent in 1820 to England, where he remained for nine years. He became the adviser of the future Radama II. His journal was written in English and has been the object of a study by S. Ayache, *Raombana l'historien* (Fianarantsoa, 1980). This manuscript is being gradually published both in the original and in a French translation by Professor Ayache. The first volume is already available, *Raombana Histoire,* vol. I, Librairie Ambozontany, Fianarantsoa. Professor Ayache has kindly made available to me a copy of the description of the 1844 ceremony. It comes from the Fond Prive – Docteur Raoely James, c1, line 12. the description was, however, published separately in a French translation in an article by E. Ralaiminoatra in the 1952 issue of the *Revue de Madagascar*. This contains a translation of Raombana into French.

8 The oldest Malagasy version is the version of the 'Manuscript Hova' reproduced in the article by Rabearimanana in *Omaly sy Anio* nos. 3–4, 1976. The date 1865 is that written on the notebook from which the text was taken (Musée de l'Homme version).

9 The exception to this is the Grandidier manuscript, an account of which will be given later.

10 This eight-page letter is in the Provincial Archive of Toulouse. It was photocopied for me by G. Berg.

11 The Sibree manuscript is in the archives of the London Missionary Society deposited at the School of Oriental and African Studies in London (Sibree Personal Box No. 1).

12 This is a hard, mahoganylike wood of which are made the best pestles, but the wood itself is associated with holiness and royalty.

13 Callet in the circumcision letter talks in several places of a royal circumcision taking place during Radama II's reign. I believe this was a mistake and probably a misunderstanding on his part on being told of the ritual of Radama II's own circumcision. This is suggested by the fact that he mentions that the circumcision water was fetched from the sea, which as we saw, occurred at that event. Ellis's detailed description of the reign of Radama II (Ellis 1867) makes no mention of a royal circumcision's being held, and it seems to me unthinkable that if one had been held it would not have been mentioned. In any case there was hardly time for the circumcision to take place, because Radama was murdered in May 1863, at the beginning of the circumcision season.

14 Sibree does note in a footnote, however, that a royal circumcision took place in 1869 (Sibree 1870, p. 238n.).

15 Abinal arrived in 1860 and de la Vaissière in 1863.

16 I have ignored Camboué's often erroneous interpretations of these actions.

17 The authors describe the problem of putting the men's hair in the proper fashion with short hair and how it fell out of place within minutes. This shows that the change in men's hair fashion to short hair, initiated by Radama I, is no doubt the explanation of the disappearance of the distinctive circumcision hair fashion for men.

Chapter 8. The circumcision ritual in history: towards a theory of the transformation of ideology

1 It was especially infuriating that my culturally inappropriate questions about the past usually failed to elicit this type of information but that questions asked by young participants of old people as part of the preparations for, and performance of, the ritual often proved very fruitful.

2 Girard, in a book entitled *La Violence et le sacré,* makes points that have a superficial similarity to the ones here. I believe, however, that the conclusions he draws are unwarranted and clearly at odds with the critical position of this book.

3 A theoretical discussion of this process referred to as 'interpellation' is to be found in Althusser (1971).
4 I know of only two: S. Feuchtwang (1974), M. Godelier (1982).
5 Althusser would not accept the linking of alienation and ideology as I have done in this passage.
6 This view is clear in the work of the Marxist writers mentioned so far – Althusser, Godelier and Therborn – and is also found in the work of non-Marxists who have used the term 'ideology' – for example, Dumont (1966 and 1977) and Augé (1975 and 1977).
7 Gellner argues unconvincingly in the same article that tribal religions are not ideological because they are 'the heightening of ordinary social life'. I hope that this book will make it clear that such a view is untenable.

References

Abinal, R. P., and R. P. Malzac. 1963. *Dictionnaire malgache–français* (first edition 1888). Paris: Editions Maritimes et d'Outre-mer.

Ahern, E. M. 1981. *Chinese Ritual and Politics,* Cambridge Studies in Social Anthropology No. 34. Cambridge: Cambridge University Press.

Althusser, L. 1971. *Lenin and Philosophy.* New York: Monthly Review Press.

Andriamanjato, R. 1957. *Le Tsiny et le Tody dans la pensée malagache.* Paris: Présence africaine.

Archer, R. 1976. *Madagascar depuis 1972, la marche d'une révolution.* Paris: L'Harmattan.

Augé, M. 1975. *Théories des pouvoirs et idéologie.* Paris: Hermann.

1977. *Pouvoirs de vie, Pouvoirs de mort: Introduction a une anthropologie de la répression.* Paris: Flammarion.

Ayache, S. 1976. *Raombana l'historien 1809–1855. Introduction a l'édition critique de son œuvre.* Fianarantsoa; Ambozontany.

Barnes, R. H. 1974. *Kadang: A Study of the Collective Thoughts of an Eastern Indonesian People.* Oxford: Clarendon Press.

Bateson, G. 1958. *Naven: A Survey of the Problems Suggested by a Composite Picture of the Culture of a New Guinea Tribe Drawn from Three Points of View.* Second edition. Stanford: Stanford University Press.

Berg, G. 1979. 'Royal Authority and the Protector System in Nineteenth Century Imerina', in *Madagascar in History: Essays from the 1970s,* R. Kent (ed.). Albany: The Foundation for Malagasy Studies.

1981. 'Riziculture and the Founding of the Monarchy in Imerina'. *Journal of African History,* 22, 289–308.

Biedelman, T. O. 1966. 'Swazi Royal Rituals'. *Africa,* 36, 373–405.

Bloch, M. 1968a. 'Astrology and Writing', in *Literacy in Traditional Society,* J. Goody (ed.). Cambridge: Cambridge University Press.

1968b. 'Tombs and Conservatism among the Merina of Madagascar'. *Man: The Journal of the Royal Anthropological Institute,* 3, 1, 94–104.

1971a. *Placing the Dead: Tombs, Ancestral Villages, and Kinship Organisation in Madagascar.* London: Seminar Press.

1971b. 'Decision making in Councils among the Merina of Madagascar', in *Councils in Action,* A. I. Richard and A. Kuper (eds.), Cambridge Papers in Social Anthropology No. 6. Cambridge: Cambridge University Press.

1974. 'Symbols, Song, Dance and Features of Articulation: or Is Religion an Extreme Form of Traditional Authority?'. *Archives Européenes de Sociologie,* 15, 55–81.

1977a. 'The Disconnection between Rank and Power as a Process: An Outline of the

References

Development of Kingdoms in Central Madagascar', in *The Evolution of Social Systems*, J. Friedman and M. Rowlands (eds.). London: Duckworth.

1977b. 'The Past and the Present in the Present'. *Man: The Journal of the Royal Anthropological Institute*, n.s. 18, 178–292.

1978. 'Marriage amongst Equals: An Analysis of Merina Marriage Rituals', *Man: The Journal of the Royal Anthropological Institute*, n.s. 13, 21–33.

1980. 'Modes of Production and Slavery in Madagascar: Two Case Studies', in *Asian and African Systems of Slavery*, J. Watson (ed.). Oxford: Blackwell.

1981. 'Hierarchy and Equality in Merina Kinship'. *Ethnos*, 5–18.

1982. 'Death, Women and Power', in *Death and the Regeneration of Life*, M. Bloch and J. Parry (eds.). Cambridge: Cambridge University Press.

1983. 'The Changing Relationship between Rural Communities and the State in Central Madagascar during the Nineteenth and Twentieth Century'. *Rural Communities*, 233–47, Recueil de la Société Jean Bodin, 11.

In press (a). 'Almost Eating the Dead'. *Man: The journal of the Royal Anthropological Institute*.

In press (b). 'The Ritual of the Royal Bath in Madagascar: the Dissolution of Death, Birth and Fertility into Authority', in *Rituals of Royalty: Power and Ceremonial in Traditional Societies*, D. Cannadine and S. R. F. Price (eds.). Cambridge: Cambridge University Press (Past and Present Series).

In press (c). 'Sources of Contradiction in the Representation of Women of the Kinship', in *Gender and Kinship*, S. Yanagasico and J. Collier (eds.). Stanford: Stanford University Press.

Bloch, M., and S. Guggenheim. 1981. 'Campadrazgo Baptism and the Symbolism of a Second Birth'. *Man: The Journal of the Royal Anthropological Institute*, 16, 376–86.

Bloch, M., and J. Parry (eds.). 1982. *Death and the Regeneration of Life*. Cambridge: Cambridge University Press.

Boiteau, P. 1958. *Contribution à l'histoire de la nation malgache*. Paris: Editions Sociales.

Callet, R. P. 1870. Manuscript letter of 4 August 1870 in the Provincial Archives of the Society of Jesus in Toulouse.

1873. *Tantaran ny Andriana eto Madagascar* (first edition). Tananarive.

1908. *Tantaran ny Andriana eto Madagascar* (second edition). Tananarive: Académie malgache.

Camboué, R. P. 1902. 'Les dix premiers ans de l'enfance chez les malgaches: Circoncision, non, éducation'. *Anthropos*, 4, 375–86.

Copalle, A. 1970. *Voyage à la capitale du roi Radama 1825–1826*, reprinted from the edited version from vols. 7 and 8 of the *Mémoire de l'Académie malgache* in *Documents anciens sur Madagascar* No. 1. Association malgache d'archéologie.

Cousins, W. E. 1876. *Malagasy Customs* (later published under the title *Fomba Malagasy*). Tananarive: London Missionary Society.

Délivré, A. 1974. *L'Histoire des rois d'Imerina: Interprétation d'une tradition orale*. Paris: Klinsieck.

Delval, R. 1972. *Radama II, Prince de la Renaissance malgache 1861–1863*. Paris: L'Ecole.

Deschamps, H. 1972. *Histoire de Madagascar*. Mondes d'Outre-mer. Paris: Berger Levrault.

Domenichini, J. P. 1971. 'Tantaran ny Sampin-Panjakana teto Madagascar/Histoire des palladiums d'Emyrne. Introduction, edition et traduction'. Thèse de doctorat de 3ième cycle, Paris.

References

Douglas, M. 1966. *Purity and Danger: An Analysis of Concepts of Pollution and Taboo.* London: Routledge & Kegan Paul.

1970. *Natural Symbols: Explorations in Cosmology.* London: Gresset Press.

Dumont, L. 1956. *Homo hierarchicus: le systéme des castes et ses implications.* Paris: Gallimard.

1977. *Homo aequalis: Genèse et épanouissement de l'idéologie économique.* Paris: Gallimard.

Durand, A. 1933. *Les Derniers Jours de la cour Hova.* Paris.

Durkheim, E. 1912. *Les Formes élémentaires de la vie religieuse.* Paris: Alcan.

Ellis, S. 1985. *The Rising of the Red Shawls: A Revolt in Madagascar 1895–1899.* Cambridge: Cambridge University Press.

Ellis, W. 1838. *History of Madagascar* (2 vols.). London: Fisher.

1858. *Three Visits to Madagascar during 1853–1854–1856.* London: Murray.

1867. *Madagascar Revisited: The Events of a New Reign and the Revolution Which Followed.* London: Murray.

Endicott, K. 1979. *Batek Negrito Religion: The World View and Rituals of a Hunting Gathering People of Peninsular Malaysia.* Oxford: Clarendon Press.

Esoavelomandroso, F. 1981. Introduction to I. Pfeiffer, *Voyage à Madagascar.* Paris: Karthala.

Estrade, J.-M. 1977. *Un Culte de possession à Madagascar: Le Tromba.* Paris: Anthropos.

Evans-Pritchard, E. D. 1965. *Nuer Religion.* Oxford: Clarendon Press.

Feuchtwang, S. 1974. 'Investigating Religion', in M. Bloch (ed.), *Marxist Analyses and Social Anthropology,* ASA Studies 2. London: Malaby Press.

Filliot, J. M. 1974. *La Traite des esclaves vers les Mascareignes au XVIIIe Siècle.* Mémoire 72 of ORSTOM, Paris.

Firth, R. 1959. *Social Change in Tikopia.* London: George Allen & Unwin.

Flacourt, E. de. 1661. *Histoire de la grande isle de Madagascar.* Paris.

Foltz, J. 1965. 'Contribution à l'analyse de l'ancienne cérémonie de la circoncision en Imerina (centre de Madagascar)'. Thèse de 3ième cycle, Strasbourg.

Fortes, M. 1962. 'Ritual and Office in Tribal Society', in M. Gluckman (ed.), *Essays on the Ritual of Social Relations.* Manchester: University Press.

1967. 'Totem and Taboo'. *Proceedings of the Royal Anthropological Institute for 1966,* pp. 5–22.

Freeman, J. J. and D. Johns. 1840. *A Narrative of the Persecutions of the Christians in Madagascar.* London: Snow.

Friedman, J. 1974. 'Marxism, Structuralism, and Vulgar Materialism'. *Man: The Journal of the Royal Anthropological Institute,* n.s. 9, 444–69.

Fustel de Coulange, N. D. 1864. *La Cité antique.* Paris: Durand.

Geertz, C. 1966. 'Religion as a Cultural System', in M. Banton (ed.), *Anthropological Approaches to the Study of Religion,* ASA Monograph No. 3. London: Tavistock.

1980. *Negara: The Theatre State in Nineteenth Century Bali.* Princeton: Princeton University Press.

Gell, A. 1975. *Metamorphosis of the Cassowaries: Umeda Society, Language and Ritual.* London School of Economics Monographs in Social Anthropology No. 51. London: Athlone Press.

1980. 'The Gods at Play: Vertigo and Possession in Muria Religion'. *Man: The Journal of the Royal Anthropological Institute,* n.s. 15, 219–48.

Gellner, E. 1980. 'Notes towards a Theory of Ideology', in *Spectacles and Predicaments: Essays in Social Theory.* Cambridge: Cambridge University Press.

202

References

Girard, R. 1972. *La Violence et le sacré*. Paris: Grasset.

Godelier, M. 1973. *Horizon, trajets, marxistes en anthropologie*, Paris: Maspero.

1982. *La Production des grands hommes*. Paris: Fayard.

Gow, B. A. 1979. *Madagascar and the Protestant Impact: The Work of the British Missions, 1818–95*. London: Longman.

Horton, R. 1967. 'African Traditional Thought and Western Science'. *Africa*, 37, 50–71 and 155–87.

Houlder, J. A. (ed.). 1960. *Ohabolana ou proverbes malgaches*. Tananarive: Lutheran Press.

Hugh-Jones, S. 1979. *The Palm and the Pleiades*, Cambridge Studies in Social Anthropology No. 24. Cambridge: Cambridge University Press.

Huntingdon, W. R. 1973. 'Death and the Social Order: Bara Funeral Customs (Madagascar)', *African Studies*, 32, 65–84.

Jarvie, I. C. 1965. 'Limits to Functionalism and Alternatives to it in Anthropology', in D. Martindale (ed.), *Functionalism in the Social Sciences*, Monograph of the American Academy of Political and Social Science No. 5.

Keating, Sir H. 1825. Manuscript journal in the Bodleian Library, Oxford, English Miscellaneous c. 29.

Leach, E. R. 1959. *Political Systems of Highland Burma*. London: Bell.

1961. 'Two Essays Concerning the Symbolic Representation of Time', in *Rethinking Anthropology*, LSE Monograph on Social Anthropology No. 22. London: Athlone.

1967. 'Virgin Birth'. *Proceedings of the Royal Anthropological Institute of Great Britain and Northern Ireland for 1966*, 39–50.

Lévi-Strauss, C. 1962a. *Le Totémisme aujourd'hui*. Paris: Presses Universitaires de France.

1962b. *La Pensée sauvage*. Paris: Plon.

1964. *Le Cru et le cuit. Mythologiques I*. Paris: Plon.

1966. *Du Miel aux cendres. Mythologiques II*. Paris: Plon.

1968. *L'Origine des manières de table. Mythologiques III*. Paris: Plon.

1971. *L'Homme nu. Mythologiques IV*. Paris: Plon.

1973. 'Comment meurent les mythes', in *Anthropologie structurale 2*. Paris: Plon.

Lewis, G. 1980. *Day of Shining Red*, Cambridge Studies in Social Anthropology No. 27. Cambridge: Cambridge University Press.

Marx, K. and F. Engels. 1963. *The German Ideology*. London: Lawrence & Wishart.

Marx, L. 1961. 'Quelques Réflexions inspirées par certaines pratiques se ratachant à la circoncision en Imerina'. *Bulletin de l'Académie malgache pour 1959*, 55–62.

Maybury-Lewis, D. 1967. *Akwe Shavante Society*. Oxford: Clarendon Press.

Mayeur, N. 1913. 'Voyage dans le sud et dans l'interieur des terres et particulièrement au pays d'Hancove'. Reprinted in *Bulletin de l'Académie malgache*, vol. 12 for 1913, 139–76.

Molet, L. 1979. *La Conception malgache du monde, du surnaturel et de l'homme en Imerina* (2 vols.). Paris: L'Harmattan.

Munthe, L. 1982. *La Tradition arabico–malgache vue à travers le manuscrit A–6 d'Oslo et d'autres manuscrits disponibles*. Tananarive: Lutheran Press.

Needham, R. 1962. *Structure and Sentiment: A Test Case in Social Anthropology*. Chicago: University of Chicago Press.

Ottino, P. 1965. 'Le Tromba à Madagascar'. *L'Homme*, 5, 85–93.

Rabearimanana, L. 1976. 'Mystique et sorcellerie dans le manuscrit de l'Ombiasy II – la circoncision'. *Omaly sy Anio*, 3–4, 303–21.

Radcliffe-Brown, A. R. 1952. *Structure and Function in Primitive Society*. London: Cohen & West.

References

Raison-Jourde, F. 1976. 'Les Ramanenjana: Une Mise en cause populaire du christianisme en Imerina', in *Iles occidentales, littératures et traditions orales. Asemi*, 7, 271–93.

1977a. 'Radama II ou le conflit du Réel et de l'Imaginaire dans la royauté Merina', in *Les Africains*, 8, 271–91. Paris: Jeune Afrique.

1977b. 'L'Echange inégal de la langue: L'Introduction des techniques linguistiques dans une civilisation de l'oral (Imerina au XIX siècle)'. *Annales ESC*, 639–69.

Raison-Jourde, F. (ed.). 1983. *Les Souverains à Madagascar. L'Histoire royale et ses resurgences contemporaires*. Paris: Karthala.

Ralaiminoatra, E. 1952. 'La Circoncision du Prince Rokoseheno (extraits du manuscrit de Roanbana)'. *Revue de Madagascar*, 20–9.

Ramilisaonina, 1974. 'Ny omby mahery teo amin'ny mponina Ankay'. *Taloha*, Revue du Musée d'Art et d'Archéoloqie, 6.

Ramilison, E. 1951, 1952. *Ny Lohrana ny Andriana Nanjaka teto Imerina Etc. Andriantomara – Andriamamilaza* (2 vols.). Tananarive: Ankehitriny.

Ranaivo, C. 1902. 'Pratiques et croyances malgaches relatives aux accouchements'. Medical thesis, Paris.

Raombana. 1980. *Histoire. Edition et traduction française par Simon Ayache* (see also Chapter 7, note 7). Fianarantsoa: Ambozontany.

manuscript. Fond Privé, Docteur Raoely James.

Rappaport, R. A. 1967. *Pigs for the Ancestors*. New Haven: Yale University Press.

1977. 'Maladaptation in Social Systems', in S. Friedman and M. Rowlands, *The Evolution of Social Systems*. London: Duckworth.

1979. *Ecology, Meaning and Religion*. Richmond: North Atlantic Books.

Razafimino, C. 1924. *La Signification religieuse du Fandroana ou de la fête du nouvel an en Imerina*. Tananarive: FFMA.

Razafindratavo, J. 1971. 'Hiérarchie et tradition chez les Tsimahafotsy (Imerina)'. Thèse de 3iéme cycle, Paris.

Razafinsalama, A. 1982. *Les Tsimahafotsy d'Ambohimanga*. Langues et civilisations de l'Asie du Sud-Est et du monde insulindien, No. 6.

Richardson, J. 1885. *A new Malagasy–English Dictionary*. Antanarivo: London Missionary Society.

Robertson-Smith, W. R. 1889. *Lectures on the Religion of the Semites*. London: Black.

Sibree, J. 1863. 'The Customs of Circumcision Observed by the Sovereigns and his Relations who are circumcised together with his Children'. Manuscript in Personal Box No. 1, London Missionary Society Archives, School of Oriental and African Studies, London.

1870. *Madagascar and Its People. Notes on Four Years Residence*. London: The Religious Tract Society.

1880. *The Great African Island: Chapters on Madagascar*. London: Trubner.

Sibree, J. (ed.). 1900. 'The Fandroana, or New Year's Festival of the Malagasy'. *Antananarivo Annual*, 24, 489–96.

Soury-Lavergne, R. P., and R. P. de la Devèze. 1912. 'La Fête de la circoncision en Imerina (Madagascar): autrefois et aujourd'hui'. *Anthropos*, 7, 336–71.

Sperber, D. 1974. *Le Symbolisme en général*. Paris: Hermann.

1979. 'La Pensée symbolique est-elle pré-rationelle?', in M. Izard and P. Smith, *La Fonction symbolique*. Paris: Gallimard.

1982. 'Les croyances apparemment irrationelles', in *Le Savoir des anthropologues*. Paris: Hermann.

Spiro, M. E. 1965. 'Causes, Functions and Cross Cousin Marriage: An Essay in Anthropological Explanation'. *Journal of the Royal Anthropological Institute*, 96, 30–43.

References

Tambiah, S. J. 1979. 'A Performative Approach to Ritual'. *Proceedings of the British Academy*, 65, 113–66.

Therborn, G. 1980. *The Ideology of Power and the Politics of Ideology*. London: Verso.

Toren, C. 1983. 'Thinking Symbols: A Critique of Sperber 1979'. *Man: The Journal of the Royal Anthropological Institute*, 8, 260–8.

Tronchon, J. 1974. *L'Insurrection malgache de 1947*. Paris: Maspero.

Turner, V. 1962. 'Chichamba the White Spirit: A Ritual Drama of the Ndembu'. Rhodes Livingstone Paper No. 33.

1967. *The Forest of Symbols: Aspects of Ndembu Ritual*. Ithaca: Cornell University Press.

Turton, A., and S. Tanabe. 1984. *History and Peasant Consciousness in South East Asia*, Semi-Ethnological Studies No. 13. Osaka: National Museum of Ethnology.

Tylor, E. B. 1871. *Primitive Culture: Researches into the Development of Mythology, Philosophy, Religion, Language, Art and Custom* (2 vols.). London: Murray.

Vig, L. 1969. *Charmes: Spécimens de magie malgache*. Oslo: University Press.

Vogel, C. 1982. *Les Quatres Mères d'Ambohiboa: Etude d'une population régionale d'Imerina*. Langues et civilisations de l'Asie du Sud-Est et du monde insulindien, No. 13.

Willis, R. (ed.). 1973. *The Interpretation of Symbolism*, ASA Studies No. 3. London: Malaby Press.

Index

207

Index

208

Index

CAMBRIDGE STUDIES IN SOCIAL ANTHROPOLOGY

General Editor: Jack Goody

211

212

* Also available as a paperback